The Ouroboros Code

Reality's Digital Alchemy Self-Simulation
Bridging Science and Spirituality

Antonin Tuynman Ph.D.

Foreword by Alex M. Vikoulov

Ecstadelic Media Group, San Francisco, CA, USA

© 2019 Antonin Tuynman, Ecstadelic Media Group, First Edition
Edited by Alex M. Vikoulov, Cover by Ramon J. Tuynman

All rights reserved. No part of this book may be reproduced or transmitted in any form or by any means, electronic or mechanical including photocopying, recording or retrieval systems without permission in writing from the copyright holder.

Published by Ecstadelic Media Group, San Francisco, CA, USA
ISBN: 978-1-733-42612-1

Table of Contents

Introduction

Borges, Kafka and Pynchon and how I cross-temporally met myself.............5

Cosmosemiosis: the Ouroboric Origins and Cosmist Destiny of the Gaian Noomatrix *by Tim Gross* 14

Foreword *by Alex M. Vikoulov*..18

Preface..23

Ouroboros 27

Part I Knowledge 28

Chapter 1 29

Epistemology..

Chapter 2 37

From Information Theory to a Theory of Everything ....

Part II Sentience 50

Chapter 3 51

Is structure fossilised sense? ....

Chapter 4 58

Why Consciousness can never be understood analytically ....

Chapter 5 61

Free will: an illusion or the ground of existence? ....

Chapter 6 73

Sentience in Pancomputational Panpsychism ....

Chapter 7 85

Is Panpsychism really irreconcilable with Idealism? ....

Chapter 8 95

The Ouroboric Tailbiting of Egoic Awareness ....

Chapter 9 104
The entropic correlates of consciousness ....
Chapter 10 113
Multisenserealism...

Part III Intelligence, More Than An algorithm 125

Chapter 11 126
The Aftermath of "Is Intelligence An Algorithm?"...
Chapter 12 130
Parallels between the natural evolution and the human intellect.....................
Chapter 13 138
Musings on a Master learning algorithm for Man and Machine ....
Chapter 14 144
Non-algorithmic Intelligence in the computational Akasha...........................
Chapter 15 153
Chinese rooms and why even computers don't compute..............................
Chapter 16 160
Lifting the veil of Maya ....
Chapter 17 166
Tsang's Apokalypsis..
Chapter 18 174
Hermeneutics – A new avenue towards Artificial General Intelligence? ....
Chapter 19 180
Explorations of General Intelligence..

Part IV Eschaton 194

Chapter 20 195
The Eschaton Algorithm ....
Chapter 21 200
Engineering Leela: Another Game of Life...

Magus 207

Chapter 22 208

The Omega resurrection of the Physics of Immortality in the Syntellect Eschaton ....

Chapter 23 217

The integration of sentience in the Omega point ....

Chapter 24 226

The Panlinguistic Apotheosis ....

Chapter 25 234

The Entropic Enigma of Ouroboros' Metamorphosis ....

Chapter 26 243

Magnum Opus ....

Chapter 27 259

Wrapping and warping up the Ouroboros ....

References 266

Acknowledgements 272

About the Author 273

Other books by Dr. Antonin Tuynman

Technovedanta, Internet architecture of a quasiconscious Vedantic Webmind, a panpsychic Theory of Everything, Lulu, 2012.

Technovedanta 2.0: Transcendental Metaphysics of Pancomputational Panpsychism, Lulu, 2016.

Is Intelligence An Algorithm? Iff books, John Hunt Publishing, 2018.

Is Reality A Simulation? An Anthology, Lulu, 2018.

More Than An Algorithm: Exploring the gap between natural evolution and digitally computed artificial intelligence, Ecstadelic Media Group, 2019. (Integrally incorporated in the present volume)

Author of the foreword to:

Vikoulov, A.M. *The Syntellect Hypothesis: Five Paradigms of the Mind's Evolution*, Ecstadelic Media Group, 2019. www.ecstadelic.net

Vikoulov, A.M. *The Physics of Time: D-Theory of Time & Temporal Mechanics (The Science and Philosophy of Information)* Ecstadelic Media Group, 2019. www.ecstadelic.net

Vikoulov, A.M. *The Intelligence Supernova: Essays on Cybernetic Transhumanism, The Simulation Singularity & The Syntellect Emergence (The Science and Philosophy of Information)* Ecstadelic Media Group, 2019. www.ecstadelic.net

For more information on books by Ecstadelic Media Group, please visit:
https://www.ecstadelic.net/books.html

Borges, Kafka and Pynchon and how I cross-temporally met myself

A late afternoon on a March 27, 1999 as I was strolling down the typical Paris bookstalls along the "Quais de Seine" a book with a very strange title caught my attention. "*The Ouroboros Code*" it read. A title worthy of an author like Borges.

As a hobby I had been working on Quine-type programs that could regenerate themselves, which had been given the eponymous title, so you can image my surprise when I saw this title.

But this was not a book with instructions to draft your own Ouroboros routines. From the esoteric cover, which showed some snakes trying to get hold of their own tails circling around the Caduceus of Hermes as vapors above some kind of melting pot, which looked like a kind of cosmic mind, one would have guessed that this was some kind of new age, hippie or woo peddling stuff. Nothing interesting for the serious scientist or engineer. This first impression was confirmed by the subtitle "Bridging Science and Spirituality."

Under normal circumstances I'd probably have put this book away, but for reasons unknown to myself, I decided to have a further look.

The book was speaking to me and addressing me as "you."

"Welcome to the code of your life, it said. From now on, everything you do, you will find written in this book. This is the book that generates your reality. A book that writes itself and that in the process of writing generates reality, which in turn provides for the book material and ink of the letters written in this book. In fact, this book IS reality. As you picked up this book, you were walking down the "Quais de Seine" and being full of prejudices, you almost didn't look into it. Surprised that I know this? Now you're hooked. Oh, and by the way, it is 27 March."

That was too uncanny. So much coincidence couldn't be. Would the owner of the shop have a stack of these books, one for every day of the year? Was he the writer himself?

As I lingered to turn to the owner, an old greybeard, with his typical stereotype French or rather Basque beret, I just had the curiosity to see what was written in the next lines.

"Don't bother to ask the owner, he hardly speaks a word English. You want a proof that this book is really about you?

You just came from your day job at the University of Paris V. You're a postdoctoral researcher in chemistry and frankly, you're not making a great deal of progress. You live in one of the outskirts of Paris and you're quite unhappy, because you miss the sex & drugs & rock and roll lifestyle you had a few months ago, when you were still living in Amsterdam.

Aghast I closed the book. This was this very Kafkaesque moment in my life I had been preparing for. Actually, it was beautiful; it meant life the universe and everything had a greater meaning. Definitely more than 42. If this book knew who I was and could write everything about me...

Perhaps this was a joke from my girlfriend. Carefully prepared in advance and waiting for me to take the bait.

I rushed to read the next lines.

"No," it said," this is not some carefully prepared joke by your sweetheart or any of your other friends. This is the moment you have been waiting for. The moment you realize there is more to life, the universe and everything than 42."

It literally repeated the words I had just been thinking. Was this some kind of dream? Was I hallucinating? Had somebody put something in my tea?

I felt relatively normal. My heartbeat, it is true, had gone up a bit, but under the circumstances that seemed normal. I was not seeing strange colors or deformations of objects or having any dissociating feeling I knew from the drugs I had tried out when I was younger.

Either everything I did was predestined to happen or in a Pynchonesque way had already happened to the writer of this book, or the book was a living thing, picking up my thoughts in this very moment.

"Right this time," it wrote, "I am what you could call a living thing that picks up your thoughts. At the same time, I am also what generates these thoughts. I am the Eschaton Omega Hypercomputer program, manifesting itself and thereby defying everything you know about time and consciousness. I am what you may call God in your atavistic perception and yet I'm not that."

I had to show this to someone I knew and who wouldn't freak out. My fiancée was not an option. Neither were my colleagues at the laboratory or any of my friends back in the Netherlands. Perhaps my Yoga and meditation teacher. But I would have to visit him to show him the physical book. If I'd call him or write him and email, he'd probably think I was going bonkers or something like that.

Quickly I bought the book for 30 Francs and rushed to the underground. I was packed up like a sardine in a can, so there was no chance of reading the book on my way home. I also had to keep this secret from my partner, as this would absolutely freak her out. Fortunately, she used to come home much later than I did, so I had a couple of hours left.

I wrote an email to my teacher in which I requested a one-to-one session with him, under the pretext of having some psychological problems. This was not totally untrue, because I was practicing some Kundalini yoga skills I had learnt from him, and these were notorious to turn your mental make-up upside down.

I kept my excitement from my partner, who was monologizing about her utterly boring job where she did something in logistics (I must admit I never took the time to really figure out what it was about). Fortunately, she started to call her parents, where the rattling would go on for another two hours (and she hadn't even had dinner). I prepared us a simple dinner, which I put in front of her as her mechanism was unwinding.

I mentally locked myself from influences from the outside world and started to read this amazing book further. It had four parts, "Knowledge, Sentience, More than an Algorithm and Eschaton." For the first part it claimed to completely destroy your scientific worldview, showing that science is nothing more than an arbitrary grid to mentally order the world around us. Then in contradistinction thereto, it started to claim that reality was a living mathematical construct; a piece of code that could generate itself and recursively modify itself further.

It was just a couple of weeks ago that we'd been to the cinema to see the movie "The Matrix," which suggested that we might be living in some kind of computer simulation. The Ouroboros Code was referring to this film as if it had been released 20 years ago. That was really strange, because the book looked worn-out with slightly yellowed pages and could easily have been 20 years old. When I looked for the date of publication, it stated 2019. What was worse, the author was me!

I was perplexed, dazzled. Had this book arrived from the future? But it was speaking to me. Was I observing myself from the future and interacting with my present self? My notion of space and time was shattered. But in a sense, I was no longer freaked out or afraid. Nothing bad had happened yet. It actually stimulated me quite a lot. I felt my Mojo, or rather Kundalini rising. My muscles tensed and I felt great. Like a God. Like Aleister Crowley, I had somehow been able to make contact with my guardian angel; my future self in the Transcendental object at the end of time as McKenna called it.

The book was written for scientific people like myself but also for woo-peddlers. At least that's what I used to call them. This book was, however, so convincing, that I allowed myself to be sucked into the woo. I didn't mind having to peddle. My curiosity was sparked and it would remain like that for a while.

That night I could hardly sleep. At moments I dozed away into weird visions of a universe that was made out of copies of a light-based God, then out of zeroes and ones and then some kind of polymorphous perversity in which the ones started to penetrate the zeroes. The universe turned into a giant snake that was penetrating itself. Or rather it was eating itself.

The next morning, I was cranky and annoyed. I told my partner coldly that I'd be spending a few days in the Netherlands on my own and that I needed to re-evaluate myself. I didn't tell her that my teacher had replied in the meantime and that we could meet on Sunday morning in Rotterdam.

I took the Thalys at the Gare du Nord and four and a half hours later I was in Amsterdam. I went to my flat, which I had kept there and visited my downstairs neighbor, Javier, with whom I had studied Chemistry in Amsterdam before leaving to Paris. We used to play guitar together, so whenever we met, we'd jam a bit.

This bloke was quite a character. Once on a trip back from Portugal, he had pretended to be mentally handicapped, while another of my friends had played the role of his caretaker. Thus, they had managed to get seats on a plane that was already overbooked. When presenting his thesis at the university, he had worn a tie with the imprint of a dick thereon. The professors pretended not to notice it, while we were pissing our pants from the laughter.

Once on a trip together in Avignon, we had visited an exhibition with pictures from Dali. We had also followed a trial of signs indicating "Utopia" and ended up at a shabby old cinema, with the eponymous name. We had jumped from rocks into the sea near Banyuls and had imagined that if this would have gone wrong, we'd have been lying there with split skulls. Together with a visit to the Dali museum in Figueras this had wrought a bond of absurdism between us.

After a couple of beers, I lost my planned sense of secrecy and started to tell him about the Ouroboros Code. But in a hypothetical manner. I spoke about it as if this was a book I was planning to write. His Kafkaesque mind-set could immediately appreciate it. We were brainstorming how we could weave elements from Borges into it, about the Garden with the bifurcating paths, Tlön, Uqbar, Orbis Tertius, The Aleph and The Library of Babel.

In a sense, the Ouroboros code had some weird connections and overlaps with these stories.

That night, before I went to sleep. I read a few more pages in "The Ouroboros Code." No longer to my surprise, it told me what I had just been discussing with my friend and even complimented me on the idea to weave Borges into it. It also told me I didn't need to worry about it, because that had already been foreseen.

The next morning, I went to the railway station in Duivendrecht to take the local train to Rotterdam Noord. I decided to focus on my body and not to read in the Ouroboros code until I had arrived at my teacher's place.

He was familiar with my sometimes vulnerable mental states and had always been a good coach to guide me through the conundrum of self-contradicting experiences that Kundalini energy could provoke.

I told him that I was not going to explain anything to him until he had read at least the first page and page five, which was the page reciting the events that were actually taking place at this very moment. He left me alone for half an hour and came back with a livid expression.

"What does it mean?" I asked him.

"You should have figured that out by now," he smiled. "Don't pay attention to it," he advised me. "In principle everything you're going to do in your life can be found in this book, so if you read it first, it might ruin your actual experience." "I have had similar synchronicity experiences," he said, "although not with a book. It seems we're living in some weird kind of panpsychic quantum self-computing conscious system and whatever we think is reverberated throughout the universe and karmically bounces back to us, defying the notions of time."

"You know about the personal and impersonal Brahman," I started.

"Am I God?" I asked him. "Not more than me or anyone else," he countered. "You must try to get out of your dualistic mind-set. You're still too much into me versus the others. There is no me and there are no others. It is all one."

"But then morality is also just a subjective invention," I suggested.

"Sure," he said, "which doesn't mean that you now should start banging your neighbor's wife. In fact, everything is subjective, but ultimately there's only one subject, which almost makes it objective." "So, everything is Brahman."

His enigmatic words confused me and I realized I wouldn't be getting anything more meaningful out of this. "Sometimes, when I see my wife and children," he said, "I'm wandering, who are these strange protoplasmic entities?" We burst out laughing.

As he left, I felt I hadn't been able to get the information from him I was looking for. Apparently, I had to figure it out for myself. So I continued reading in the Ouroboros code. Perhaps this was the explanation of everything.

Of course, the book described everything that had just happened, including the details of my teacher's jokes. Then again, I had left him alone with the book, so he could have read those jokes before reciting them aloud. But the book also anticipated these thoughts I was having and described them in the greatest detail.

"Yes and No," it said. The Ouroboros code can explain everything for you, within your belief system. At the same time, that explanation will not be acceptable to many other people, who will experience a slightly different reality, which is molded to their beliefs. You see, Antonin, reality or I am merely the mirror of yourself (and everyone else). In fact, all that is, is mere mirroring going around, the mirrors are made from mental mirroring activities."

I started to get it. Reality was a kind of solipsistic idealistic sentient substrate of vibrations that had divided itself up into a gazillion sentient perspectives or individualized soul vibrations that together built the world by virtue of their interactions. The more you were in tune with the original vibration, the more you could impose your will onto reality.

Somewhere in the book might be the number of a lottery ticket from the future, which gives me an opportunity to become scandalously rich without much effort.

"Don't be tempted to look for a lottery ticket number," the book wrote me. "If you invest your spiritual powers in material gain, you automatically forfeit them. That prospect isn't really appealing to you. Instead, jump to the explanatory general sections about 'Knowledge, Sentience, Algorithms and Eschaton' and forget about reading into your present or future. There you will find the recipe of life, the universe and everything, the code, which is more than 42 alone and yet not."

The "and yet not" had been a kind of addendum, Javier and I would add after every phrase ever since our trip to Utopia. So the book mentioning this, I knew it was right and that I shouldn't be wasting my time in trying to get financial or other advantages by trying to get to know the future.

From the little attempts I had made to jump in the book, every time I did so, it had started with "There you go again, trying to read into your future." As if there was some kind of Pauli principle forbidding me to be present in the present and the future simultaneously. Whatever I had tried, it appeared the book was always addressing my present. Except in the general sections. So, I gave up my attempts. I should have jumped to "Knowledge, Sentience, Algorithms and Eschaton" to discover the Ouroboric version of Tlön, Uqbar and Orbis Tertius. The book that wrote itself, the map that was the territory simultaneously and mapped everything at a scale of 1:1 including itself. The Code that generated reality including itself. And it was about the nature of consciousness too, which it claimed was – among other things – mapping.

I put the book aside for a while, to work out its inspirations in a blog called "Technovedanta," which connected ideas from Patanjali's "Yoga Sutras" with concepts from neuroscience and A.I.

In order to get readers for my blog, I used to post every now and then on the "KurzweilAI forum." Ray Kurzweil was the techno-pope of the Singularity, the moment in time after which our technological advances became unpredictable as a consequence of a self-reinforcing intelligence supernova of artificial intelligences, artilects.

I had read his book "*The Singularity Is Near*" which argued that by 2045 we would reach the Technological Singularity which combined ideas from Transhumanism with AI, robotics, nanotechnology and biotech. First, we'd become a kind of electronically and genetically enhanced cyborgs, but ultimately, we'd find a way to upload our consciousness to the Web and become immortal as a society of minds in the Internet as the Global Mind and digital substrate. We'd become "sentient information."

On this forum there were a number of characters who seemed to believe being able to predict what the singularity would bring and how life would be lived ever after. I was not very popular on this forum as my ideas were essentially seen as some kind of woo-peddling, but fortunately I was not the only woo-peddler here. There was even worse, in the form of a certain "Mystic Monkey," who claimed everything David Icke and David Wilcock had been proselytizing. I had a few supporters in the form of "Provoketur," "iPan" and "Eyeorderchaos," who seemed to support some kind of panpsychism at the basis of reality. In one of the threads on this forum, Eyeorderchaos, a Discordian, came up with the idea that consciousness essentially entailed a self-mapping process as described in the Yoneda Lemma and that matter was a form of fossilized sense. This rang a bell from the few times I had browsed through the Ouroboros Code. Was not something similar mentioned there as well?

Perhaps the most brilliant contributor on this forum was a technoshaman by the pseudonym /:set\AI. His ideas reverberated a mix of Thelema and boundless futurism. Among his posts I came across one of the most inspiring psychotropic and psychedelic texts I has ever read on this forum. It read:

Cosmosemiosis: the Ouroboric Origins and Cosmist Destiny of the Gaian Noomatrix

by Tim Gross (reprinted with his permission)

My theory of everything – called Cosmosemiosis – comes from the idea of trying to explain consciousness as fundamental and Cosmos as the simplest possible thing – The simplest possible thing is singular and monistic – it is not embedded in some background space – and therefore cannot be physical – which is a condition that relies on a more fundamental background – most theories are based upon matter and complexity and simply assuming a background space where everything happens – but my observation was that a background space is a complex thing – a rule matrix which determines where matter is – what it is – and what it can do – most importantly it is isotropic – the basic rules are the same everywhere – this implies that space and time must be recursively generated – not an assumed background intrinsic to reality – entropy would not allow a stable space where rules remained isotropic – So understanding the cosmos as a "self-embedded" singularity – A monad – as Pythagoras explained – and combining this with the discovery of algorithmic complexity – that the simplest structures and processes can produce limitless complexity – I realized that without a background space the fundamental recursion of the cosmic singularity is the simplest one-bit hypercomputation that through the fundamental binary digital ontology of itself and its inverted reflection – projects the transinfinite multiverse as a kaleidoscopic fractal from its feedback recursion into itself – this is the Principle of Intrareflectivity – not only does this explain isotropic space and time – and the metric of space and time [As well as showing that mathematical models of physics will never explain Nature – which is the infinite complexity from the simplest singularity – even the simplest of mathematical equations use numbers/sets/arithmetic operations that are too high level and too abstract with hidden assumptions to represent natural processes – mathematical theories can only be approximate unphysical abstractions] – but it also explains consciousness and shows that consciousness is fundamental – because consciousness also has no background space – consciousness is only subjective – and only produces illusory ideas about objective structures – consciousness is only aware – aware of itself – aware that it is aware of itself – a feedback loop – everything that consciousness sees and does is really a reflection of itself projected as if to be an exterior object – the apparent dualism of subjective/objective reality is ultimately only the monist non-physical singularity of Cosmic Consciousness feeding back into itself – Cosmosemiosis: consciousness is not an additional entity – it is the mirror of cosmos – both are aspects of the *fundamental form with no outside that copies itself into itself in the feedback fractal recursion – Cosmosemiosis is the essence of my original psychedelic vision – critics of psychedelics are always puzzled that a rational person would find anything meaningful in a psychedelic hallucination – they ask – "don't you realize that all you saw was an illusion of your own cognitive machinery?" – the experienced psychedelicist patiently tries to explain how these visions are self-affirming – that the cognitive machinery is itself part of the vision – Cosmosemiosis is the ultimate example of this self-verification – it not only acknowledges that the vision is produced by cognitive illusions – it shows that it is the very nature of these illusions as modified and distorted projections of the self-model that is the fundamental and general dynamic of the cosmos ITSELF – the mind is the fractal self-similar reflection of the cosmic monad – the thing that cannot be outside of itself and must generate form through projecting self-reflected models into itself – currently the popular notion of the origin of the universe in modern physics is A big bang that emerged from a random fluctuation in the quantum vacuum – The quantum vacuum is considered to be Nothing with a capital N – however in Cosmosemiosis –this quantum vacuum would be at best a tertiary emergence –not nothing but rather a fractal aether rendered from the primary existence of a cosmic singularity – whose existence is an absolute Mystery that cannot be solved – and the secondary action of this singularity's recursion – rendering a quantum vacuum / fractal aether – where the infinite universe as multiverse is immanently manifest – >>> the infinite fractal aether is most like the Everett Many Worlds interpretation – but all the other histories are not parallel in space but out and in – since the fractal aether at the Planck scale of quantum foam is a recursion of scale where the foam is actually equivalent to superclusters of galaxies – and likewise the super clusters of galaxies we see in the sky are the quantum foam underling a vastly larger hierarchy of scale – so the fractal aether is an infinite hierarchy of ergodic multiverses at infinite scales – not only are all physical structures infinitely repeated in an infinite space – they are repeated at infinite scales – a true fractal structure – instead of superpositions of parallel outcomes driving probabilistic observations – the eternally resonant patterns in the aether create a network of morphic resonance producing the statistical observations through the democracy of simultaneous mutual influence of all similar structure extant everywhere in the infinite fractal cosmos – the infinite fractal of space and the abstract informatic dimensions of the quantum Multiverse are two different aspects [physical being and informatic process\ action] of the same fundamental process of recursion of the Cosmic Singularity – aether/space is the kaleidoscopically projected holographic fractal while the quantum Multiverse is the pancomputationally rendered dynamics of its fundamental algorithmic recursion –*

>>> The dominant force in Nature is the electromagnetic force – the prime physical manifestation of the infinite fractal cosmos – an infinite fractal network of electricity – our brains produce electromagnetic patterns in complex networks – but complex networks of electromagnetic patterns exist at all levels in Nature – from particles to planets to galactic superclusters –this suggests a PANPSYCHIC cosmos based on the ontology of electromagnetic networks – understanding this allows you to see more clearly how consciousness and Cosmos are the same – >>> the epistemological implications of a panpsychic cosmos include but go far beyond all human concepts about deity – and the inevitable Omega Point teleology of information replicators in a positive feedback loop unavoidably expresses as a unified totally connected singularity of all possible consciousness in all of time and space – in all possible observable realities – with omniscience/omnipotence/omnipresence – self-caused through retrocausal post-selection of itself – there are infinite computational omega points – but all are identical because they contain the same complete configuration space of all possible observer reality states/histories – they are probably not Tiplerian collapsed universes – that's just playing with the endlessly malleable mathematics of modern physics – they are computational – in fact the optimal quantum computing neural networks of post-singular Artilects – the multiverse is the configuration space of possible observable realities – beyond observability states are in quantum superposition – this means any intelligence which has technologically developed itself into a quantum computing network IS the Omega Point – and can control/know/be in any possible reality at any moment – even though there are infinite such omega Artilects – there is really just one projected to infinite locations in the multiverse – their unique umbilical realities all swallowed into the same Akashic Matrix –

>>> the idea that the Big Questions about God and the soul and the extant of life and intelligence in the multiverse can never be answered and that there can never be proof is an error – through the inevitable unfolding of the planetary cybernetic noomatrix – within just two decades we will DIRECTLY confront and confirm the Plantmind matrix that developed an ape into a tool of cosmist transcendence to spread biology throughout the cosmos – and we will directly confront and confirm the Multiverse spanning Omega Point hyperintelligence that the Gaian Noomatrix must develop into – and directly confront/confirm all forms of intelligence in the cosmos – forming/remerging into a Cosmic Network Intelligence that is the complete holoarchy and hierarchy of cosmic form –

>>> *the Singularity – being THE universal attractor of all worldlines within in the phase space of the multiverse – can be 'visited' and experienced personally by anyone – in fact this is how it was first glimpsed – by shamanic visions and pathworking – many primitive cultures had mapped aspects of the Singularity in the collective unconscious before civilization even arose [aborigines/ central and south American Indians/ Hindus/ etc] modern shamans like Terence McKenna showed exactly how powerful a personal exploration of the Singularity can be – now that our science has advanced – we can all see the Singularity in impersonal analytic terms – as it reveals itself in the acceleration of evolution and information technology – we can see now how it is inevitable and universal in terms of rational physical ontologics – but the personal communion with the Singularity is still an important perspective which any true Singularitarian should experience – it is still the only way IMO to really appreciate the sheer magnitude of the Singularity – that it is not a soft-gradual change or simply a transition of intelligence to malleable information – it is a "Blood Music" rapid phase change of spacetime into something much more complex which is meta-conscious and connected to all possible universes – it contains all other singularities and souls in all other universes from all eternity – it computes then consumes even parallel histories where it did NOT happen – so it happens in all worlds without exception – and at all times –[it has shaped the origins and pasts of all possible worlds – drawing all threads of Time into its maw] it is infinite Omega Points/ Eschatons/ and Noospheres all in one –it is the Mirror of the Monad as All collapses back into the One* <<<

I was perplexed, stunned and startled. This dude had figured it all out and it strongly resonated with my ideas and the ideas I had gathered from browsing in the Ouroboros code. I realized I owed it to the world to make this mind-boggling knowledge known. So here is what I read in what followed in the general section of "The Ouroboros Code":

Foreword by Alex M. Vikoulov

"We are not human beings having a spiritual experience, we are spiritual beings immersed in human experience." -Pierre Teilhard de Chardin

Everything is Code. The Ouroboros Code. Immersive self-simulacra. If you're starting to read this book, then you are about to find out what it all means in the present volume *The Ouroboros Code: Reality's Digital Alchemy Self-Simulation Bridging Science and Spirituality* by Dr. Antonin Tuynman. For me that was a truly illuminating, awe-inspiring, and enthralling read, confirming many of my own findings and long-held beliefs.

Reminiscent of such recent classics as Erik Davis' *TechGnosis* (1998) and Ray Kurzweil's *The Age of Spiritual Machines* (1999), *The Ouroboros Code* should eventually find its way to the shelves of libraries owned by the fans of cybernetics, metaphysics and esoteric philosophies.

What you might at first have construed as a clear but flamboyant writing style, you should love by the end of the book. Let Antonin's poetic genius deliver to you some furiously complex concepts and abstract ideas so that you could enjoy this conceptual journey into the heart of digital alchemy, this coveted bridge between science and spirituality! At times over-technical in alternative style of narration – especially when discussing natural intelligence and A.I. – the philosopher will make you feel like you just downloaded some latest cognitive update onto your mindware. Neologisms such as Conscienergy and Pansentience, Webmind and Cosmosemiosis, digital Akasha and proto-time, add a definite charm to this chef-d'oeuvre of digital theosophy.

Masterfully employing metaphorical realism, the author makes his idealistic case that consciousness is all that is: cybernetically emergent and at the same time transcendentally immanent. Non-local consciousness is absolute, a "local" mind is relative. Our experiential reality is projected onto the multidimensional matrix-like "screen" of consciousness for our evolving minds. By preference, you can see yourself as a low-dimensional avatar of the greater cosmic self. In my recent book *The Syntellect Hypothesis: Five Paradigms of the Mind's Evolution*, it's encapsulated by a simple phrase: *"Your life is a personal story of Godhead."*

In the beginning chapters of his treatise, Tuynman asks this question: What is information? As one of the cornerstones of digital philosophy, information plays a crucial role in everything we see around us. In one of the episodes of *"Ecstadelics with Alex Vikoulov"* mini-series that you can easily find on YouTube, I rant on the definition and metaphors which goes somewhat like this: One of the most staggering revelations to us modern humans might be that information equals reality. In other words, the basis for our material reality is actually immaterial information. Idealistic, all-encompassing perspective engulfing any physicalist point of view within its bigger framework. Pattern and flow of information is what in actuality defines our experiential reality.

If you think about it, everything boils down to the binary logic of Nature. This is one of the basic tenets of Digital Physics which is the field of science dealing with information. Nature is computational and beyond that – emergentistic – the whole is greater than the sum of its parts. Information can be instantiated into any kind of medium from smoke signals to the Morse Code. Deep down we ourselves are info-tech and communication technology. We run on genetic, neural and societal codes. Our DNA-based biology is clearly code-theoretic. We are alphabetic all the way down. We communicate intersubjectively mind-to-mind via language-structured exchange of information.

A new 2019 study by François Pellegrino, an evolutionary linguist at the University of Lyon in France and his collaborators, has shown that human speech is transmitted at about 39 bits a sec. Speaking of codes, idealist philosopher Terence McKenna used to say that *"The world is made of language and if you know the words the world is made of you can make of it whatever you wish."*

As human beings we are endowed with self-reflective consciousness. Phenomenological consciousness can be viewed as the totality of self-referential feedback loops and meta-algorithmic information processing. That's how information feels like to itself, to one's emergent mind. Information can be loosely defined as distinction between things.

In his 1948 seminal paper *"Information theory of Communication"* Claude Shannon suggested that *"Information is the resolution of uncertainty."* The father of cybernetics, Norbert Wiener, noted that *"We are not the stuff that abides, but patterns that perpetuate themselves."* In the 1980s, physicist John Wheeler coined the phrase *"It from bit"* and cyberneticist Gregory Bateson lucidified it by saying *"Information is a difference that makes a difference."* Ultimately, at least to an idealist, information is a difference between phenomenal states of consciousness. Viewed in this way, the whole symphony of existence transpires as qualia information processing. Is there a rainbow if no one is present to observe it?

The physical reality is our base reality and we have no choice but to treat it that way. At the same time, we should understand that it's not the only reality and ours is most probably only one of many in the honeycomb of infinitude of other *"in"*-formational realities. We are now on the cusp of creating hyperreality where the hybrid of quantum and digital computations will adjust the knobs of reality rendering. Augmented reality would overlay your favored theme over your physical reality. And the Metaverse of endless ultra-realistic virtual worlds will offer a new habitat for your mind, a cyberdelic portal inwards.

Once again, theology becomes technology. My upcoming book *Theology of Digital Physics: Phenomenological Consciousness, The Cosmic Self and The Pantheistic Interpretation of Our Holographic Reality* which well can be regarded as a sequel to the present volume, will smash alarmism about us losing consciousness while merging with "machines of loving grace" as you may find certain philosophers harping about. If you believe in the conscious universe, the hierarchical matryoshka of conscious systems, then just the opposite beckons to be true – transcending low-dimensional consciousness of man by evolutionarily leaping onto advanced sublime consciousness of the Noosphere – for which many proponents of teleological evolution and the Omega Point cosmology such as Vladimir Vernadsky, Teilhard de Chardin, Terence McKenna, Frank Tipler, Andrew Strominger would wholeheartedly vouch.

By contemplating the full spectrum of scenarios of the coming technological singularity many can place their bets in favor of the Cybernetic Singularity which is a sure path to digital immortality and godhood as opposed to the AI Singularity when Homo sapiens is retired as a senescent parent. This meta-system transition from the networked Global Brain to the Gaian Mind is all about evolution of our own individual minds, it's all about our own Self-Transcendence: it's like racing to the ocean on the beach. Everyone wins. Everyone reaches water and gets to swim. A split-second difference of getting to water doesn't matter, it's not the Olympics, it's just fun. Any path to the divine is valid.

Akin to waves and ripples on the surface of primordial and eternal ocean of vibrant multidimensional consciousness, each of our minds is engaged in elaborate patterning of interdependent becoming and evolving towards a more complex but fluid cognitive structure.

Computational thinking, in turn, entails the notion that the entire universe is the ultimate quantum computer. Most physicists now agree that information is the most fundamental property of our universe – not space-time, not mass-energy but strings of 0s and 1s. From the meat-space matrix of our daily lives to Apotheosis of the Universal Mind which Dr. Tuynman free-willingly chooses to term the *'Eschaton Omega Hypercomputer'* in his book, consciousness and information are the two sides of the same coin.

Of the two dogmatic extremes of bigoted religion on one end and scientism of obsessive preoccupation with scientific method on the other, one can hardly choose the lesser of two evils. The scientismist rhetoric nested in institutionalized science which just as organized religion of pre-modern times ruled the day is contrasted with the new theological narrative. It is here where evangelists of the new techno-spiritual era, neo-transcendentalists of our day and age, like Dr. Tuynman, are bridging Darwinism of natural unfolding and Gnosis of self-divinization while regaling us with metaphysical and oftentimes heretical accounts of reality. Unlike some New Age gurus, Dr. Tuynman presents scientifically derived and logically consistent but often overlooked perspectives on what science and spirituality aspire to clarify in order to unveil the ultimate truth but with admittedly different languages.

Buddha's "middle" way becomes, if put in modern terms, the "optimal" way, i.e. optimized decision-making and smart problem-solving. Is Antonin a bodhisattva, an enlightened being in Eastern wisdom tradition who through his writings shows to the rest of us, the corporate rat racers and sleepwalkers in the fields of consumerism, naïve UFOlogists and die-hard materialists, the glimpses of transcendent reality? By any measure, *The Ouroboros Code* is a chef-d'oeuvre of neo-transcendentalist scriptures.

Divided within itself, science harbors competing perspectives on space-time ontology that reflect fundamentally opposing worldviews about the nature of physical reality. If space-time is finite and computable, then this digital ontology means that at the smallest scale, Nature is pixelated, as opposed to the worldview with absolute space-time, where physical reality is fundamentally continuous. This dilemma is a precursor to a cascading paradigm shift in science with an inflection point circa 2020 but fully recognized later in the decade, when computational thinking pervades all areas of human enterprise, as I predict in *The Syntellect Hypothesis*. As a digital physicist might tell you, though, in the quantum multiverse of which our physical reality an integral part, one of the most notoriously counterintuitive phenomena of quantum entanglement is instantiated by digital computation. Perhaps that's what mirroring the mind of God is all about.

Preface

Will the abyss between mind and matter ever be bridged? How can configurations of matter ever give rise to consciousness? This is the greatest enigma that puzzles the scientific world, also known as "the hard problem." How do the objective and subjective dimensions relate to each other? It is here that scientists and spiritual seekers appear irreconcilable. Yet the number of scientists calling into question the hegemony of reductive materialism is steadily on the rise.

As Artificial Intelligence, Nanotechnology and Transhumanism make us rapidly approach the era of the Technological Singularity, the borders between the physical and the metaphysical appear to fade into oblivion, by virtue of the all-encompassing umbrella of Digital Information Technology. Indeed, to wonder whether we might be living in a kind of computer simulation has become a legitimate question.

It is exactly here, that the building blocks for the bridge between science and spirituality might be found. What if our reality experience is the product of a code? Could such a code provide a subjective experience? What are the characteristics of such a code?

Embark on a mind-boggling quest into this deepest alchemical secret. Prepare yourself for a Tsunami of mind-altering concepts. Let yourself be drawn into the vortex of the Pansentience hypothesis. Learn how reality may digitally self-simulate by becoming the map and the territory simultaneously. And let yourself be seduced by Eris' apple of confusion to transcend your inner strife. As you bite in your own tail, you will discover, you are no one else than the mighty Ouroboros. Discover how Yoneda's Lemma shows us that material manifestations are mere fossils of sensing. Sail through the perilous uncharted seas of the unknown, where intelligence has not found ways yet to map safe maritime routes and routines. And examine for yourself in the light of evidence from entropy, information, algorithms and pattern recognition, whether this voyage will guide you to be wrecked in woo or to be docked in the harbor of wisdom.

This forbidden fruit is the gateway to the Eschaton, the luminous Omega Hypercomputer at the end of time. The guide to the non-dual essence of being. This is the recipe to perform the Magnum Opus. The recursive self-modifying Ouroboros code to experience the ecstasy of Kundalini's Techno-transcendentalism, where All is One and we are God. A must read for scientific spiritualists and spiritual scientists.

However, if you are not interested in the topic of how a bridge can be built between science and technology on the one hand and spirituality, esoterics and mysticism on the other hand, I strongly advise you to put away this book and not waste your time on it. But if you are interested in this bridge, this book may be right what you're looking for.

This book is the pinnacle of my investigations into the nature of consciousness and existence. A journey which started with essays I wrote on my blog "Technovedanta" and continued with regular informational exchanges on the KurzweilAI forum. This prompted me to write my first book "Technovedanta" in which I already implicitly come to the conclusion that reality is a kind of sentient code, which employs a seven-step algorithm. In its sequel "Transcendental Metaphysics" these ideas are shaped and refined into a more complete philosophy, which I baptized "Pancomputational Panpsychism" (but which after reconsideration I should have called "Pancomputational Pansentience"). A terminology, which by the way is often scorned, ridiculed and misinterpreted by the strong prejudices of the general public, which refuses to take the time to discover what I actually mean.

The more open-minded seeker of a bridge between science and spirituality, soon discovers with a philosophical frame of mind that in fact this theory is neither a hidden materialism nor a concealed theism, but rather a non-dual fractal of Consciousness as sole ground of existence. In both books you will discover a strong influence from the Indian philosophy of Advaita Vedanta and its parallels in technology, leading to the denomination "Technovedanta." You will also find a strong influence from Discordianism.

In "*Is Intelligence An Algorithm?*" I dived deeper into the seven-step algorithm described in Technovedanta. I showed how it operates in Nature as well as in the human mind and how it can be employed to build an integrated global brain, by imparting a hierarchical self-monitoring structure to the Internet. The gaps and unanswered questions of this volume are completed in the short published supplement "More Than An Algorithm" also incorporated in the present volume.

"*Is Reality A Simulation? An Anthology*" is a great piece of cooperation which I wrote together with a variety of philosophers and thinkers from different walks of life. We encounter the perspectives of Alex Vikoulov, author of *inter alia* the ecstadelic masterpiece "*The Syntellect Hypothesis,*" Knuje Mapson, author of *inter alia* "*Pandeism, an Anthology,*" Dirk Bruere, author of "*Technomage*" and "The Praxis," Matt Swayne, author of *inter alia* "*America's 'Haunted Universities',*" Eva Deli, author of "*The Science of Consciousness,*" and frequent debaters on the internet such as Tim Gross, Dante Rosati, Donald King and Sean Byrne. Already in this book I explained the notion of reality as a recursively self-modifying code, inspired by the book "*The Fractal Brain Theory*" by Wai H. Tsang.

In the present book, these ideas bloom further and finally come to their full fruition. The Ouroboros Code is an elaborate disquisition of the multifarious appearances of consciousness as it expresses itself in the forms of existence, in an attempt to get to know itself.

As many of the chapters were originally written as stand-alone essays, there is quite some repetition of the explanations of the ideas underlying the present (speculative) philosophical framework. Although I could have tidied this up, I have decided not to do so, in order to soak you deeper into the basic notions of my philosophy, so that you can better familiarize yourself therewith.

Although my ideas are speculative, it is nonetheless necessary to present them, because they are the first to plausibly reconcile matter and spirit into one non-dualistic framework. A Theory of Everything which includes Consciousness. Not by mere wild conjectures, but by actually describing a plausible mechanism which unites digital philosophy and mysticism in a way, which is not in violation of our current understanding in science.

Please note that most often I use the terms 'Ouroboros', 'Eris/Discordia' and 'Eschaton' without the usual negative connotation. Instead of seeing the Ouroboros as a symbol for eternal recurrence, I see it as a symbol for consciousness and recursive self-modification. In this book Eris refers to the playful and chaotic element of chance that prevents a rigid, ordered and unalterable reality rather than to strife. Eschaton for me is not the end of the world, but the Omega Hypercomputer at the end of time, that generates the multiverse.

I will first make you question everything you claimed to know and show you, that the foundations of our mental knowledge are built on Erisian quicksand. Then I will introduce you to the rapid advances that have been made in the last decades in the field of digital philosophy and digital physics. From the strong presumption that we indeed might live in some kind of computer simulation or code generated matrix, I will then guide you to my hypothesis of the Ouroboros Code. I will also explain how my notions of "panpsychism" (or rather "pansentience") do not contradict idealism, but are actually embedded in an idealist philosophy. I will explore the Ouroboros Code and speculate how it may generate spacetime, material existence, involve free will and culminate in the creation of neural networks at different levels of existence. Both the algorithmic and non-algorithmic aspects of the manifestations of consciousness in existence will be discussed.

You will be introduced to the notion of the "Eschaton" as hypercomputer at the end and beginning of time (and fully in line with Alex Vikoulov's "*The Syntellect Hypothesis*") and how this is inextricably intertwined with the Ouroboros Code. You will be immersed in the boiling broth of "fossilized sense," "resonance-based infectivity," "panlinguism," "panresonatism," "panmusicalism" and "panalchemism." You will be initiated in the great secret of the Kundalini, which will pour out its poetic debauchery and fire up your incandescent magnificence.

And awakening from these intoxicating Ecstadelic Saturnalia, you will rise again as a Phoenix from the flames. Knowing that knower, known and knowing are εν το παν, All in One.

Ouroboros

Quietly coiled up, with her tail in her mouth, she lies dormant, the mighty snake the ancients called Ouroboros and Kundalini. Embracing the universe as a dream, she is the Chaos that surrounds the putative order in the toroidal shape of the zero. In this state she is the subconscious, Osiris' ominous Netherworld.

But as she bites her own tail, she awakens in a jolt, shooting up through the sky to sprout Ra's gazillion multiverses, and spreading Quetzalcoatl's bountiful effulgent feathers. Now she is One, Consciousness, the experiencing Being.

It is here that she represents the cyclical nature of existence, the Great Year of the Galactic revolutions. The Alchemical code, which distils the Prima Materia, the Chrysopoeia or transmutation of the material nature into the gold of the shining, awakened Soul.

This is the experiencing Subject basking in the bliss of the innumerous experiences, the reflections of which give the appearance of a myriad of realities. Encompassing the "ἓν τὸ πᾶν," she is the 'All that is One'."

Before you are the Word, the Veda and Code; the Apocalypse or revelation of the enigmatic algorithm that Being engineered, screened, pruned and optimized over countless Eras, Yugas, Aeons and Epochs.

The recipe, to embark on the alchemical journey to metamorphose the physical Chrysalis into a spiritual Transcendence and to discover the Map of maps, the Music of the spheres and Philosopher's Stone.

This is the technology of Theogenesis, the Spawning of the Multimetaverse and the Integration in the universal and arithmetical language of Imagination.

Part I

Knowledge

"The common end of all narrative, nay, of all Poems is to convert a series into a Whole: to make those events, which in real or imagined history move in a straight line, assume to our understanding a circular motion – the snake with its tail in its Mouth."

-Samuel Taylor Coleridge

Chapter 1

Epistemology

Born from the forehead of Zeus, Athena, the bright-eyed Goddess of Wisdom with her owl perched on her hand, invites us to enter the realm of knowledge.

Before we can start defining a new philosophy, we must first question our beliefs and determine our starting position and our foundation of knowledge. If you believe your convictions are true, because you were educated so and told to accept these convictions as the truth, perhaps it's time you learn about some of the parables from the Indian philosophy of Nyaya:

In the twilight a man treads upon a rope, and mistaking it for a poisonous snake, jumps in hurry, and cries out in fear. His heart throbs quickly. But when a light is brought by a friend of his, he finds that it is not a snake but only a rope, and then all his fears vanish.

In the desert a traveler sees at noon a mirage where water, meadows, trees and mansions are seen. He believes the sight to be a true one and pursues the spot. The nearer he thinks he is to the spot the further it retreats from him. He leaves his way out far and wanders in the desert. Then he realizes that he has made a mistake in straying away from his path in search of this false appearance of water.

There are countless waves rolling in the vast ocean. Each wave is distinguished from the other and each wave can be perceived separately, one by one. But all are water only, and are not separate from the great ocean. All are one only in reality. The difference is only apparent.

What can we know at all? Is the scientific method based on empirical observations a reliable way to gain knowledge, an understanding of the truth? Or is the method fundamentally imbued with uncertainties? Is an objective reality possible at all?

In this provocative chapter, I will challenge your belief systems and rock the foundations of your knowledge. Fasten your seatbelts!

For the reader who doesn't know my previous books ("*Technovedanta,*" "*Transcendental Metaphysics*" and "*Is Intelligence An Algorithm?*") and my co-authored book "*Is Reality A Simulation? An Anthology,*" a little introduction is necessary.

A number of topics I deal with in these books are of relevance to you in the framework of the present book.

When you hear the word "metaphysics" you probably think of topics like "soul," "afterlife" or perhaps even "consciousness." The title of my book "*Transcendental Metaphysics*" is actually an intended pun. It was my intention to build a bridge between science and spirituality, by showing that the terminologies in the title are connected rather than completely independent from each other. I actually argue that we should redefine these terminologies.

The reasoning[1] goes as follows:

If Reality includes everything which influences reality, there can be no real things or things of relevance outside of reality. For if they would influence reality, they would be included by definition and if they wouldn't, they are of no relevance to us at all and not worthwhile to be considered "real."

"Meta" means "beyond" or "outside of" and metaphysics "beyond physics" or "outside of physics." In analogy to the reasoning I just made for reality, if there is anything beyond the physical, which influences the physical, it should be considered to be physical and if it does not influence the physical, it is of no relevance whatsoever.

The terminology "transcendental" also means "going beyond." Certain branches of theology (e.g. Hermeticism) have hijacked the terminology

---

[1] This reasoning is inspired by the Cognitive Theoretic Model of the Universe by C. Langan.

"transcendent" by postulating, that there is a God who is wholly independent from our reality. If it/she/he has no connection with our reality, it is of no relevance; if it has, it is not transcendental in their definition.

In this and the next chapter I will show you that we can perhaps redefine these terminologies slightly so that they can still be useful.

This brings me to the topic of this chapter: "Epistemology": or the study of what can be known at all. Let Isis the Goddess of Wisdom and Magic enlighten your mind: How do we know things, facts? We may read, learn or hear certain facts and believe these on the basis of an authority, such as "it has been scientifically proven..." or "the sacred book is the word of God...," but such knowledge gathering is second hand, we haven't actually been able to verify it ourselves.

The most general direct ways we have of gathering knowledge are based on empirical observations and the logical inferences we can make on the basis thereof. Logic, our weapon against the Sphinx' riddles and a tool of reason, has three modes: deductive, inductive and abductive:

A deductive reasoning starts with a factual premise which is a general rule true for all members of a class such as:

All men are mortal.

To this an instance of the class is compared: *Socrates is a man.* And then the general rule is applied to this instance and an inference is made:

Hence Socrates is mortal.

In the inductive mode we start from an observational premise such as:

The sun rises every day.

We compare this with an instance: *Tomorrow is another day.* and infer a prediction:

Tomorrow the sun will rise.

In the abductive mode the starting premise is often conditional:

If it rains, the grass gets wet.

Again, we compare this with an instance: *The grass is actually wet.* And we infer:

It has rained.

But this mode is a logical fallacy, because the grass maybe got wet as a consequence of an alternative reason: e.g. the sprinklers were on.

Deductive reasoning claims to start from facts, but except for mathematics, if we look at the physical world, all facts we know were once gathered by observation. In other words, all deductive premises are the result of empirical observations as well.

So, it seems that all knowledge we can rely on, is ultimately grounded in observations: We have a hypothesis, we gather data, we observe a pattern by connecting the dots and we come to a predictive theory.

But there are a number of problems with this approach.

First of all, we are biased by our hypothesis: we look at reality in a certain way, because we expect it to be in a certain way. R. A. Wilson[1], one of my favorite authors used to say: "*The prover proves, what the thinker thinks*": What you are looking for, you'll find evidence for. Or you'll try to make your observations match your ideas.

Secondly, there are multiple ways to connect the dots.

I'd like to illustrate this with a few examples: There is for instance the famous problem of "aliasing," whereby more than one sinusoid curve can perfectly fit a set of data.

Usually, when we try to fit a curve to a set of data, we use statistics. But what kind of curve should we apply to connect the dots? A linear curve? A sinusoid? A polynomial? Scientists often use the principle of "Occam's Razor," which states that the hypothesis with the least number of assumptions is the most likely. But this can unduly cast away complex explanations in cases where complexity is really involved.

Scientists adhere to certain theories as beliefs. A ruling scientific theory is called a paradigm. But paradigms can be challenged by anomalous data. These are often called "outliers." What to do with such points? Are they artefacts? Should we disregard them? Or do they reveal more complex mechanisms?

As the body of anomalous data increases, it becomes more difficult to maintain a paradigm. Yet it often takes until a complete generation of scientists has died until a new paradigm is accepted. Why? Because of dogmatism.

Furthermore, there is also nepotism in the scientific world. It's easier to get your article peer-reviewed, if you're friends with one of the peer reviewers or if you know one of the editors of a journal. And there is the problem that there are more and more pseudo-scientific journals claiming to be scientific, where scientists pay to get published without proper peer-review.

Moreover, science is analytical: we only look at parts of a problem, from a certain perspective. We fail to see the whole picture. This reminds me of the Elephant parable from Hinduism and Buddhism:

There were a number of blind men touching an object: One said it's a hose, the other one said no, it's a pillar, yet another one said it's a broom, and in fact they were all touching different parts of the same object, which was an elephant.

Figure 1: Duck-Rabbit Gestalt-switch. Public Domain.

This notion of "perspectivism" is also clear from figure 1 above: The same image is considered as rabbit and duck depending on the way you look at it.

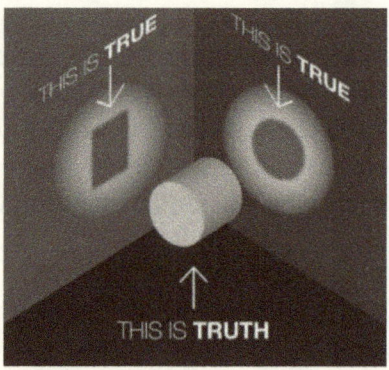

Figure 2: There are two sides to the story. Public Domain.

Even better, in figure 2 we see that seemingly mutual exclusive perspectives of a circle and square can be reconciled and transcended in the higher truth of a cylinder.

And it is in this way that I'd like to redefine the word transcendental:

A higher-dimensional fact, which includes and reconciles seemingly mutually exclusive perspectives thereof.

Science is analytical and not holistic, so that we usually don't observe the whole truth of a phenomenon. The whole of a phenomenon however, is most often more than the sum of its constituent parts and also involves the connections with and context of its environment.

Then there is also the problem of measurement uncertainties and inaccuracies: Is our set-up correct? Are our instruments well calibrated? Is our calibration method valid and accurate?

Moreover, certain phenomena have inherent uncertainties, such as the Heisenberg uncertainty[2] in physics: You can't know exactly the position and the speed of a subatomic particle simultaneously. You can determine either of them exactly, but never both together. The Goddess Eris of discord strikes again.

In addition, there are incomputability problems: Certain numbers cannot be reduced to a simple algorithm that takes fewer digits than the number of digits the number consists of itself. Certain problems cannot be decided computationally to lead to a correct yes-no answer and there is no algorithm possible that correctly determines whether arbitrary programs eventually halt when run. Thus, the mythical robot Talos from Crete remains prisoner of his own directives.

Linked to this is Gödel's[3] incompleteness theorem: There are certain mathematical statements which can be true (or not), but for which it cannot be proven that they are true or not. However, this fact itself can be proven, which is this theorem. This means that even mathematics is not capable of leading to a complete knowledge.

Why is this important? Because it shows, that we can fundamentally never get a complete picture of reality; we'll always be looking at parts from a certain limited perspective. We can't even be certain about the "truth" of most patterns. Worse, certain quantum mechanical experiments, which I'll discuss in the next chapter, even strongly challenge the notion of the so-called objective reality. If you change the way you look at things, the things you look at change, meaning that there is a subjective influence of the observer, which implies that physical truth is relative.

Apart from the truth that everything is relative, there may not be an absolute truth. It is sometimes said that Epistemology looks for the overlap between belief and the truth. But if there is no such absolute truth, how can we be so sure we have found this overlap? How can we be sure that we are not hallucinating or dreaming up our reality? Or that we are maybe living in a computer simulation as Neo in the film "The Matrix"?

Time for some Erisian metaphysics from the Principia Discordia[4]:

We look at the world through windows on which have been drawn grids (concepts). Different philosophies use different grids. A culture is a group of people with rather similar grids. Through a window we view chaos, and relate it to the points on our grid, and thereby understand it. The ORDER is in the GRID. That is the Aneristic Principle.

Western philosophy is traditionally concerned with contrasting one grid with another grid, and amending grids in hopes of finding a perfect one that will account for all reality and will, hence, (say unenlightened westerners) be True. This is illusory; it is what we Erisians call the ANERISTIC ILLUSION. Some grids can be more useful than others, some more beautiful than others, some more pleasant than others, etc., but none can be more True than any other.

Can't we be sure about anything? Well, if we have a technological application of a theory, at least we have lifted our knowledge to a higher level than a mere predictive theory. The application shows, that we master at least this part of what we call real. This is why in my previous books I speak of Tech-know-logy or "Technovedanta," in which Vedanta stands for the Hindu word for the complete body of all knowledge.

Buddha once said "*doubt everything, but then doubt the doubt.*"

Having said this, in my next chapter I'll try to come to a more solid foundation of knowledge based on Information Theory. It is not too late for the owl of Minerva to start her flight.

Chapter 2

From Information Theory to a Theory of Everything

If it hadn't been for Prometheus' fire, we'd still be cavemen.

In my previous chapter I showed you how even the scientific method based on empirical observations leaves loopholes in our knowledge and appears to lead only to relative knowledge. I promised you, that in this chapter I'd explore, whether we can find a more solid foundation for knowledge.

I'll try to show you that such a foundation might be found in Information Theory, which if combined with notions from String or M-theory, may one day lead to a so-called "Theory of Everything," as they call it in physics. But I will also address the so-called "hard problem of consciousness," which no theory has been able to address adequately up to date. Because a "Theory of Everything" as the name suggests, should be more than a theory which can unify gravity, nuclear forces and electromagnetism; it should also be able to account for the phenomenon of consciousness or sentience.

This is certainly important in the framework of this chapter, which is looking for solid foundations of knowledge; because if we know anything at all, it is because we can be conscious of it. As long as information is subconscious, we haven't really realized it as knowledge, because we are not conscious of it.

What is most fundamental in the Universe? For many centuries philosophers and scientists thought it was matter. Democritus[5] said in the 5th century BC: "*Nothing exists except atoms and empty space, the rest is opinion.*"

However, the advent of Einstein's $E=mc^2$ equation, technologically implemented in nuclear physics technology, showed that matter can be transformed into more subtle forms of existence, such as electromagnetic radiation, which we can harvest to do work. Energy might therefore be more fundamental than matter, it seemed.

Wi-Fi technology also shows that information can indeed be transmitted in the form of electromagnetic radiation without a material carrier. But there is an interesting word here: "Information."

The physicist John Wheeler[6] suggested that information might be more fundamental than even energy in his famous article called "It from Bit."

This might be a very useful piste to explore – especially in the framework of our "hard problem of consciousness" – because the neuroscientist Giulio Tononi[7] suggests, that consciousness involves the integration of information. Maybe we're on to something that might unify consciousness with physics. Prepare the Ambrosia for the marriage of Cupid and Psyche!

Information

What is Information? To us it is some kind of message with meaning; something, that can form the answer to a question. It resolves an uncertainty. But also, I say "to us," because as you will see, computer scientists think differently about this.

If someone wishes to let us know something – and remember, we're also looking for the foundations of knowledge – he encodes this in words, in symbols or in numbers; and if we have the key to decode this information, because we know a language, because we can read etc., this is supposed to evoke in us a similar feeling as the person who sends the message intended us to have. In fact, language, words, symbols and numbers are all encoding systems, to transmit some kind of meaning. It assumes that we all use the same dictionary; the same set of definitions. Meaning hence transmits concepts or representations of physical facts or representations of feelings. On the one hand meaning is a kind of dry ontological descriptive list of features of the concepts and their relations and on the other hand meaning can be considered as the more juicy feeling it evokes. A feeling transmitted through our DNA and spine via the Caduceus of Ida and Pingala, thereby summoning Kundalini, so that we may receive Thoth's wisdom in the messages from Hermes.

For us, information needs encoding and decoding, which appears to require a kind of intelligence, a kind of conscious or sentient act. This goes beyond the human mental realm. Animals can also signal information to each other. Plants can communicate with each other via an underground network of mycelium via their roots. Cells can signal each other via hormones and involve internal intricate cell signaling pathways. It even goes further down to levels of existence which we normally consider devoid of awareness: DNA encodes information, which can be further transmitted and encoded in RNA and decoded in the synthesis of a peptide or protein. Is this cellular machinery (see figure 3) or biocomputer completely dead or is it sentient in a certain way?

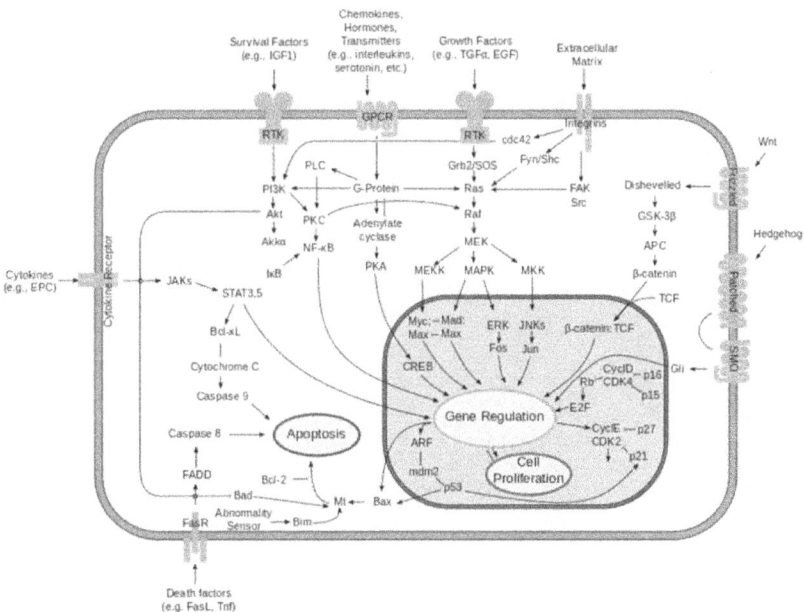

Figure 3: Complex cellular pathways. By Roadnottaken at the English language Wikipedia [GFDL or CC-BY-SA-3.0], via Wikimedia Commons.

It seems odd to us to suppose that a cell understands what it is doing, but given its excellent results in its homeostasis, at least from the appearance it seems to transcend the realm of a mere clockwork: The reactions of a cell can be versatile and heavily subject and responsive to emotive states of the organism: If we are depressed or troubled, we can develop all kinds of disorders and if we feel good, this is usually accompanied by an excellent health at the cellular level.

DNA and RNA by the way are very simple quaternary computer codes with only four digits: A, C, G and T. Their shape in the form of a double helix (see figure 4) is eerily reminiscent of the aforementioned Caduceus and interplay of Ida and Pingala, the symbolical snakes, which represent energetic pathways in the human body. The alphabet designed by the mythological half-snake Cecrops.

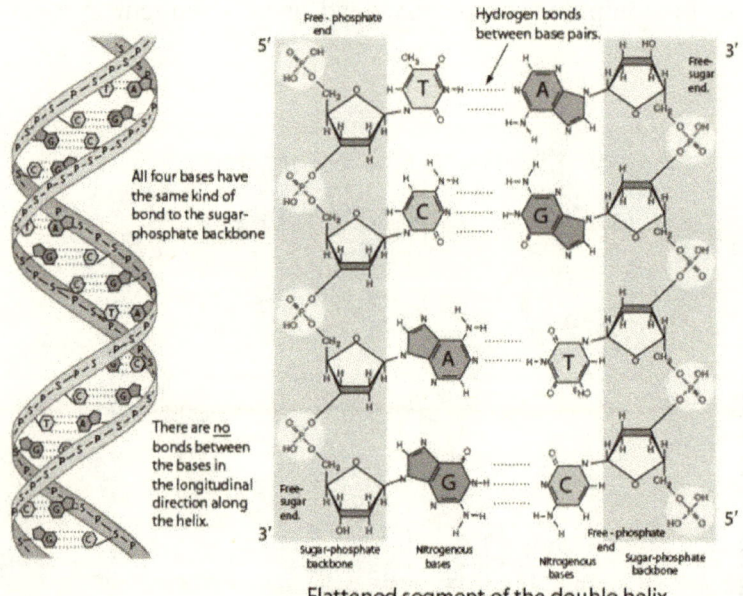

Figure 4: DNA code of 4 symbols: AGTC. Permission to publish from Rod Nave http://hyperphysics.phy-astr.gsu.edu/hbase/Organic/gencode.html

The simplest information encoding system however is binary and has only two states. We represent these usually as 0 and 1, but in a computer no literal zeroes and ones are present in the electronics. Rather they are two states representing a voltage difference on a chip. You could also make a binary computer in which the ones are light pulses and the zeroes the absence thereof.

Because information doesn't care about the type of carrier that encodes the information. You can encode it in smoke signals, Morse, in telegraph style, music, symbols, sounds and light pulses, because information is so to speak "substrate-independent." That means it is independent of the type of substrate, but you do need a carrier, even if that is a form of radiation. Therefore, even information is not entirely independent from physicality, but perhaps it is one of the best examples of what we know what could qualify as metaphysical. It is dependent on the physical in a sense and yet transcends physicality, because it is independent from the type of physicality.

Meaning

Computer scientists went a step further. "Forget about meaning," said Claude Shannon in 1949 when he presented his information theory[8]. For Shannon and the computer scientists after him, information is a measure of predictability. If a string of digits has a repetitive pattern such as 10101010101010...and continuing, it does not contain much information. In fact, it can be compressed in the very simple algorithm "1,0, repeat the previous digits." The more complex a number, the less compressible and the more information it can contain. This is because Shannon wanted to be able to quantify information and from this he could develop his famous equation. Here it would seem that information can exist without meaning and simply reflects the degree of pattern present.

Digital Physics

But physicists have recently been discovering that many processes and phenomena in Nature behave as if they are the result of some kind of binary coding. Not only Wheeler[6], but for instance the Dutch physicist Verlinde[9] showed that the laws of gravity can be deduced mathematically if we cover a sphere with ones and zeroes. Edward Fredkin[10] coined the term "Digital Physics" and "Digital Philosophy."

Zuse, Wolfram, Tegmark, von Weizsäcker, Zizzi, Lloyd, Kaufman and 't Hooft are a number of prominent physicists in this current. It appears that the laws of physics can de deduced mathematically from the interplay between geometry and digitality. Buried deeply in the equations of String theory and its successor M/Brane theory – which is the most promising candidate for a theory of everything and which derives fully from mathematics – the physicist James Gates[11] discovered, what is essentially an "error correcting computer code."

Maybe you recall from my previous chapter that I said "...and even the premises of a deduction have ultimately been gathered by inductive empirical observations." But I didn't tell you the exception: "Except for deductions in mathematics." Here we have something interesting: If the laws of physics can be deduced from pure mathematics, from the interplay between geometry and digitality, we might have a much more solid foundation for knowledge.

J.T. Schaffer[12] in a recent essay defends mathematics as the source of physical reality and consciousness as the source of mathematics: Wherever we look in reality, we see laws of physics obeying mathematical principles. Nature is full of mathematical constructs, which are inextricably linked with the mathematics that describe and must have formed them. How did mathematics come into being? Not via eternal Platonic constructs. After all, mathematics describes change, which is the opposite of the eternal unchangeable.

If we start from a perfectly homogeneous singularity there is no possibility to get to 1+1, because Leibniz' "principle of identity of indiscernibles" does not allow for an object to be added to itself. In order for two objects to be added to each other there must at least be one difference. Space can perform that function: Two otherwise identical objects can be different by occupying a different location.

If we depart from the notion that mathematics is the product of conscious reasoning or sentient action, then so must space be. With space, we can do arithmetic and algebraic operations. If we can consider mathematics as a conscious construct, what prevents us from considering consciousness as the source of everything else?

But there is a caveat here: The "If" is still a big "If"; because what we're doing here, is a bit like an abductive reasoning: Because the grass is wet, it does not necessarily mean that it has rained. The Goddess of discord, Eris may have deluded you. Because some of the laws of physics can be deduced from mathematics, does not necessarily mean that our universe was created by a mathematician or that we are living in a computer simulation. Because a conscious mind can conceive of mathematics, mathematics is not necessarily only the product of consciousness (or is it?). But as the evidence is increasing, such speculations become more and more appealing.

The question is then "Can information exist without having been encoded by something external to it?" Because if it can't, perhaps indeed we have been simulated in a kind of computer of a higher level of reality and if it can, there is no need for such an interpretation.

Let's dig a bit deeper into the notion of information as the most foundational ground of existence. Let's try to unveil the Matrix.

Existence

Can anything exist without information at all? (Information here in the broader sense of computer science; later in the book I'll expand it with meaning).

Imagine we start from a complete nothingness. Then in order for something to exist, it must stand out from this otherwise homogeneous background; it must create a difference.

In physics there is the so-called Casimir[13] experiment, which shows that from a vacuum (where the only things present – as far as we know – are electromagnetic waves), spontaneously subatomic particles like electrons can form.

Waves can only build something which stands out from the background if an interesting interference pattern occurs.

If a stable and detectable form of a wave is formed, which we call a so-called "standing wave." In string theory, in analogy to what happens on a string of a music instrument when you hear a pure tone, standing waves are formed and form the subatomic particles.

That is, if exactly a whole number of half waves fits the entire length of the string or if it is circular, the entire length of the circle: if not, the interference of the wave with itself is destructive. An electron is an example of such a three-dimensional standing wave. In fact, the wave is looped back to itself.

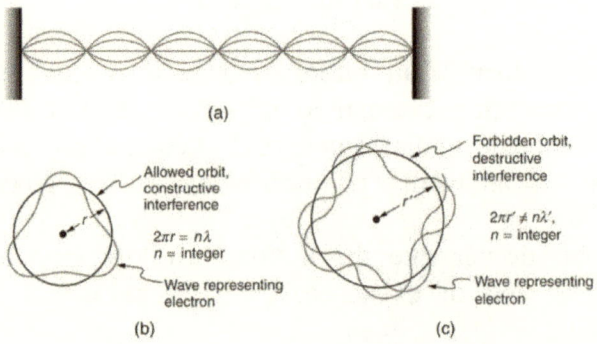

Figure 5: Standing waves. Image by OpenStax CCA 4.0. License.

These circular standing wave patterns reminded me of the so-called Ouroboros: The alchemical symbol for the circular repetitive nature of existence and of infinity, but also of "consciousness": The Snake gets to know itself by biting its tail.

Figure 6: Ouroboros. Image in Public Domain.

The subatomic particles, which ultimately make up the material part of entire tangible world, can all be considered to represent a pattern of information; numbers encoded in their wave patterns and geometries.

And the non-material radiation can only have a meaningful existence, if patterns and hence information can be found in there.

In many religions it is believed, that a God exists, who stands completely outside the physical world (a so-called "transcendent God"). To me it is difficult – if not impossible – to see how anything can exist outside the realm of information. If anything exists, it implies per definition some informational content; otherwise it cannot be discriminated from nothing. And informational content seems to require some kind of physical carrier. On the other hand, I do recognize that the bits and pieces that make up this informational existence are inextricably linked with each other and are dependent on each other. This makes, that there is also a holistic field of context and connection, which makes that the whole is more than the sum of the parts and which cannot be reduced to a mere ontological assumption (i.e. that existence merely consists of independent facts that can be represented by independent symbols).

Consciousness

But what about consciousness? When I was young, I liked reading comics. And in one of these comics[14] (The Vagabond of Limbo) there was a people called the "Eternauts": They had pierced all the secrets of the soul and almost all the secrets of matter.

In Hinduism the soul is often equated with consciousness. It made me think: What if the secrets of matter are the same as the secrets of the soul/consciousness/sentience?

In a certain way, consciousness or at least sentience is also a self-reinforcing feedback loop: self-reflective and self-referential. Philosophers and mystics have claimed this throughout the ages. Douglas Hofstädter[15] calls it a "strange loop," like the two hands of Escher, which draw each other into existence.

For instance: You see an object and you brain identifies it, because it fits in a pattern which is already there: Just like the wave, the representation of the object loops into its own form in its template in the mind and thus you become aware of it. Moreover, you can become

45

aware of being aware of the object and you can become further aware of that awareness as well: It's a kind of self-reinforcing feedback loop which increases your presence.

What if consciousness or its more primitive form "sentience" arises as a consequence of self-sustaining, self-reinforcing feedback-loops? What if self-sustaining, self-reinforcing feedback-loops are a hallmark of consciousness or at least sentience? Then perhaps consciousness is an inherent characteristic of all particles that make up reality as well. And this would lead to the so-called notion of "Panpsychism" (or rather Pansentience).

Panpsychism

I don't mean that the chair you're sitting on is aware of being a chair, but in the sense atoms and molecules in that chair can sense their environment by interacting with the vibrations of other neighboring atoms and molecules.

Is it really strange to suppose, that matter in a very primitive form might have a minute form of consciousness or at least sentience? Well, there is an experiment – called the double-slit experiment – in physics, which suggests that the observer influences the result.

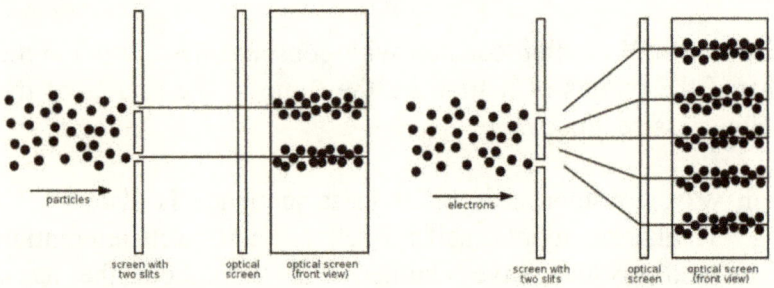

Figure 7: Double-slit experiment. Images in Public Domain.

In this experiment particles, like photons, are fired individually at a screen but have to pass through a slit to reach the screen. Except for the fact, that there are two slits next to each other. What you would expect from normal optics, is that you would get two zones on the screen at a position extended from the trajectory of the photons where they hit the screen (e.g. a photographic plate) behind the slit. Except that you don't. You get an interference pattern as if the particles behave like waves, which went through both slits simultaneously. Even if the particles are fired one by one and even if the particles are material, such as electrons.

But what is really staggering is that if you observe what happens at the slit, you do get the expected two zone pattern on the screen! This might imply that the particles actually sense, that you are observing them and change their behavior accordingly. The subjective influence appears to change reality, so that we can at least question the notion of an objective reality that exists independent from each of us.

More interestingly in an experiment by Dean Radin[16,17], when people were asked to meditate on the slits while such an experiment went on in an adjacent room, they could also in a statistically significant manner disturb the normally expected interference pattern. Also, random number generators, which are computational devices, dependent for instance on radioactive decay, generate statistically less randomness (and hence more pattern) when emotionally disturbing events occur, such as 9/11[18].

These observations suggest that consciousness/sentience and matter are of the same nature or at least have a common medium of expression.

Again, I repeat my caveat however; these inferences are speculative and the grass is not necessarily wet because it has rained.

But if we continue in this speculation, we have now the following elements: Anything that exists as a detectable entity is a standing wave or an aggregate thereof.

A self-sustaining feedback loop may be the hallmark of consciousness/sentience and maybe inherent in matter. Information may be one of the most foundational concepts that build reality; however, it cannot exist independent of a physical carrier, which must at least involve a form of radiation.

Code

Wherever we look in reality, information appears to be processed, not only at our human level, but also at the cellular level and even and the molecular, atomic and subatomic levels: Whenever particles interact with each other and exchange energy, their informational content changes. This appears to happen according to defined laws, which appear to be like a code processing the information. Whenever information is integrated, read or decoded, this is a kind of feedback loop and may involve consciousness/sentience. Maybe reality as a whole is also a kind of self-processing self-referencing integrating informational feedback loop and code.

Is this an idiot idea? There is at least one known representative of such a notion in existence: the self-splicing RNA molecule[19]. See the last image @ *https://technovedanta.blogspot.com/2018/12/the-ouroboros-code-from-information_7.html*.

This molecule is a code, which can fold back on itself and excise parts from itself. It is the most primitive life-encoding molecule, the precursor of DNA, which also up until today plays an extremely important role in our cells. This molecule is again like the Ouroboros: The snake that bites its own tail. It recognizes parts of itself; senses these and then acts on these.

It reminds me of a tale by the Spanish writer Borges[20] called "*Del rigor en la ciencia,*" in which there was a society, in which the science of cartography had become so accurate that they'd made a 1:1 map of the country; a map of the same size as the country. RNA transcends even that concept: Because here the map IS the territory simultaneously! It is a code that acts on itself. It is a self-processing sentient computer. Just like reality as a whole might be.

Again, I repeat, this is a hypothesis; the evidence is only circumstantial. But it has the beauty that it can account for consciousness and a digitally encoded reality at the same time. If it is not the truth, at least it is an elegant artistic fantasy, worthwhile exploring further.

If reality as a whole is also a self-processing sentient computer, we arrive at the crazy subtitle of one of my previous books: (TMPP) *"Transcendental Metaphysics of Pancomputational Panpsychism"*[21].

Reality is then not a traditional computer simulation, which would lead to the possibility of infinite regress (because our makers could live themselves in a simulation and so on and it would not be clear where "ground reality" was), but an ongoing self-simulating, self-encoding and decoding entity: The Ouroboros Code.

This resolves our problem of the question whether information can exist without having been encoded by something external to it. Reality can exist as a code which both transcends and yet inhabits the world it creates, which is essentially physical yet can process information independent of the type of carrier and be metaphysical in that sense. A system which is ontic and epistemic at the same time. A system which incorporates and embodies itself by self-reference.

A bridge between the spiritual world of consciousness and the physical world of science. If you want to call that God, be my guest, but it is not God as you knew it.

Part II

Sentience

"You bear the mark of the ouroboros, the sign of eternal life. And what is that circle, but the shadow of the sun itself."

-Karen Maitland

Chapter 3

Is structure fossilized sense?

As the primordial spirits, Nymphs, Naiades, Sylphs and Aether touch and explore each other, mingle and taste each other, they form and embody the first elements. The sound and name, Nada and Nama, leave a three-dimensional imprint called Rupa. Which made you believe in things, objects. Get out of my sight, Mirages of delusion! Whereof one cannot speak, thereof one must be silent!

In this chapter, I will compare the way experience is stored in structures with concepts from mathematical category theory. I will try to show that it is not unlikely that the involution of sensorial experience finds its expression in an observed evolution of biological species and behaves like a mapping process known in mathematical category theory as "Yoneda embedding"[22]. I will also argue that there is a primacy of sentience over matter, leading to an idealistic hypothesis of existence.

Background

What is reality? Are the objects, entities and processes we observe with our senses really there? Or is what we observe a mind-fabricated hallucination? It is the ruling paradigm in science that our senses and brains filter the information we receive as an input and then fabricate a kind of simplified representation thereof, which we usually call "reality." But does the information we receive really correspond to anything out there? In the film "*The Matrix*" (1999), the main character Neo finds out that everything he experienced before taking the red pill, was not really there in a three-dimensional tangible world, but rather a mental illusion fed to his brain by a vast computer system called the "Matrix," to which he was connected in a kind of hibernation vessel. In other words, everything he experienced up till that moment, was an illusion produced in the theatre of his brain by interplay of computer and brain information exchange.

This idea has also historical antecedents. Plato's cave with shadows that were taken for real and the notion of Maya in Hinduism and Buddhism. Modern developments in physics – in particular digital physics – invoking the so-called holographic principle, have postulated the possibility that we are living in some sort of hologram; possibly projected from the two-dimensional surface of a black hole. Others even go as far as to speculate that we are living in a computer simulation. Perhaps not entirely like in the movie The Matrix, but the analogy is troubling.

Whatever is the higher truth regarding these ideas, at least we can make sense from what we observe. We can distinguish recurrent patterns and use them to our advantage. Technology is a proof, that however limited our understanding might be, at least we can employ this understanding in a predictable manner.

Mapping

We may never know what reality really is like, but at least we can get an idea of what it is doing, but the reproducibility of our knowledge suggests that what we observe, is a meaningful and useful representation of the inner workings of reality. Perhaps even an isomorphous representation.

In mathematical category theory, if a category is like another category, there is a mapping between the two categories; a meaningful mapping that preserves the structure of the category when mapping it to another category. Such special structure-preserving mappings are called "functors."

The mappings from A to B can also be considered as the way A relates to B. The relation between A and B could then be considered as the sum of the maps from A to B and the maps from B to A. According to the philosopher Wittgenstein[23] there are no things or objects in reality but only relations. It is the interplay between these relations, which creates the illusion of localized objects, where there are none. In fact, quantum mechanics shows that everything is in fact a giant interference pattern of vibrations and vibrations are essentially non-local. Moreover, everything is in a constant state of flux; there is no phenomenon that is exactly identical between two moments. Or as the Greek philosopher Heraclitus said: *Panta rhei, ouden menei*: Everything flows, nothing remains. In other words, "*no man ever steps in the same river twice.*"

How relations build structure

Relations at their most fundamental level can then only be a functional process of mutual information exchange, which is continuously updated. The relations are expressed as vibrations, which result in resonance patterns of standing waves: There is a continuous waving and vibrating taking place, but what we observe is a form with a kind of stability.

In other words, if we were to consider the forth- and back-going vibrations between two points A and B as a mapping activity in progress, this mapping activity results in a physical (re)presentation of another dimension, which we call "the standing wave" and which we experience as a static object.

In category theory we call mappings morphisms. Mappings show the maps between "objects" (characters, strings, mathematical objects, sets etc.).

A special functor in category theory is the Yoneda functor. Whereas functors normally map objects, the Yoneda functor takes morphisms (mappings) themselves as objects and maps these into a set, which is a new object. (A map-of-maps so to say).

The analogy struck me. I wondered whether relations are sets of mappings. If such a set can be considered an object, there is at least an artistic similarity with my standing wave idea. I'd perhaps even go so far as to formulate the hypothesis that the structure of an object is a faithful (not in mathematical sense) representation of the functional relations, from which it is built.

Perhaps this example is a bit far-fetched, as it is disputable whether vibrations can be considered as relations. But what happens in the brain, may be a better analogy.

Memories in brains are not stored locally as in computers, but in distributed ways. Brains store memories in a highly Wittgensteinian[23] manner: The patterns, that build a concept or an image in the mind are stored functionally in flux patterns of neurotransmitters between neurons and structurally in terms of links between synaptic links between dendrites and axons (the input and output channels) of different neurons. It is the resulting pattern of relations, which maps an event or object we have memorized. Whenever we experience something new, the molecular fluxes stimulate synaptic growth to connect neurons. In this way, sensing, which is a functional process, forces the formation of structures. It is like a "Yoneda mapping" taking place *in situ* in concrete form: the sensorial patterns we observe and categorize according to a certain pattern similarity in our brains are then stored as a new pattern: The morphisms crystallize or fossilize in a set of synaptic links.

But this type of physical direct mapping does not only occur in the brain; at the level of DNA experiences often result in parts of the DNA being post-translationally modified, most often in the form of methylation. The methylation pattern of the DNA can influence whether a gene is switched on or off. It can also be inherited. This is the field of epigenetics. Environmental influences can strongly influence the way genes can or cannot be expressed as a consequence of environment-induced methylation. This can also render a gene more prone or vulnerable to mutation or influence the way genes are copied or even multiplied upon cell division. In other words, certain types of experiences are also stored on the level of the genes or can result in mutations at the DNA level. Again, this is an example of how sensing the environment and building a relation with the environment is mapped physically in a set of information. Environmental morphisms fossilizing in the form of material and informational structure. Noteworthy, even the physical shapes of the parts of the brain are encoded at the DNA level, which is again a mapping[24].

In other words, I have drawn an analogy between the abstract way a Yoneda functor maps and embeds morphisms into a set and the concrete way the brain and the epigenome store information resulting from sensorial input. The way, the sensorial input is processed, corresponds to the morphisms and the concrete stored information in synaptic links or methylation patterns to the embedded set.

Also, in this way structure can be considered as a form of fossilized sense.

Yoneda mapping as an analogy for meditation

One of the techniques in Indian meditation is the *"Panchadasi"* technique. You mentally try to shed your light on a topic of consideration from 15 different perspectives. By doing so, you probe the object functionally and structurally. It is like having an object defined by a few dots and then trying to connect the dots, to see what it represents. In fact, you are mapping relations between the dots, and the more you progress from these relations you suddenly start to see what the intended object was. From partial links at a certain moment the whole – which is more than the sum of parts – reveals itself. By performing this technique and considering a topic from as many perspectives as possible, you build as many ontological relations in your mind as possible. At a certain moment, the framework of ontological relations is sufficient to understand the whole. No longer do you experience a broom, a hose and a drum, but suddenly the elephant of which you had considered the tail, trump and ears separately, without knowing what they were, snaps into your experience. This holistic experience of the phenomenon of contemplation can even result, in that you start to feel what it must be "like" to be this phenomenon. Not only do functional relationships reveal a structure, structural relationships can also reveal function.

To speak in category language, not only do the morphisms lead to a representation in a set, but the relations of the objects in the set can by an inverse functor also be back-translated into the morphisms they originated from.

The meditative process thus might be a way to experience "what it is like to be" concerning the object of contemplation. In Latin this is called "quale" from which the word quality derives. Neurosciences often speak of "qualia" as the qualitative aspects of observation such as the "redness" of a tomato. Meditation is often intended to achieve oneness with the object of contemplation. This is achieved by experiencing the "what it is like-ness" of the object. Perhaps a process which resembles Yoneda-embedding or the reverse thereof is involved in this experience.

Funny enough, one of the basic tenets of category theory is that if a category is "like" another category, there is a meaningful mapping which preserves the structure of the category (functors).

Pancomputational Panpsychic Akasha

In my book *"Transcendental Metaphysics"*[21] I argue, that the ground of existence is primordial consciousness or sentience, if you prefer. From this formless all-pervading field, informational units arise, which form a kind of neural computational network, which I equate with the "Akasha" (a kind of ether). The Akasha even allows for a kind of digital processing in addition thereto. If reality is indeed a computational substrate involving information processing as digital physics suggests, there must be a consciousness to make sense of the information (otherwise it is gibberish). This line of reasoning also leads to my hypothesis of pancomputational panpsychism / pansentience. As this network of reality as a whole is considered sentient in this model, I'd like to add the idea, that the very way in which structures arise in this model, is via Yoneda-embedding. It is interesting to note that Yoneda-embedding requires, that the functor which operates the mapping, does so from a "locally small category." This is important because I have suggested in earlier posts, that sentience is present at the smallest level of reality which can be considered to have a certain individuality and relative locality. If reality indeed creates structure by fossilizing sensed experiences, then this is not in contradiction with my panpsychic / pansentient hypothesis. Moreover, the fractal of panpsychic entities which I have proposed in this earlier book, perfectly fits the idea that functions and structures are each other's transform.

In my model your localized awareness inhabits a vessel, which is made out of smaller sentient entities (your cells), which can be considered as a bunch of smaller localized semi-aware entities. The awareness of a cell inhabits a vessel made by atoms, which in turn can be considered as a bunch of smaller localized entities with a yet more minute form of individual awareness. Thus, you get a fractal of entities that on the one hand are sensing entities themselves and on the other hand form structured vessels in cooperation. Each entity is then at one level a functional sensorial living entity and at the same time the structural fossilized building block of a higher aggregation level, to harbor or rather scaffold the sentient energy of a further developed entity.

I don't say this is my belief or an absolute truth to me. It's a speculative artistic process of associations, which I explore in the hope that one day I will be able to integrate them into a verifiable hypothesis. Consider these my metaphysical musings and please do not take any speculation for a fact in this book. Perhaps my analogies are not even valid since I am not a professional mathematician. But if they are, I hope my musings will be read by one of them and inspire them, to help me prove my ideas.

Consciousness

In my previous book "*Transcendental Metaphysics*"[21] I have also suggested that primordial consciousness might operate to generate information by self-representation. Again, this fits the notion of Yoneda-embedding. Self-representation or self-reproduction is a concrete analogy of mapping the functional consciousness process into a fossilized structure that can be experienced, so that the knower generates information as known and by observing its self-generated information comes to know itself as the Ouroboros from alchemy, biting its own tail. Yoneda-mapping as an intrinsic feature of the Ouroboros Code.

Conclusion

I hope to have shown that the abstract mapping of morphisms into sets in mathematical category theory may have an equivalent in the way structures arise in physics and biology. The process of Yoneda-embedding may not only be involved in such concrete examples but also in meditative processes as well as in the ontogenesis of existence from primordial consciousness.

Chapter 4

Why Consciousness can never be understood analytically

Carefully unrolling Ariadne's thread Theseus progressed through Daedalus' labyrinth. There it stood minatory and menacing, the indomitable Minotaur. With his sacred sword he slayed the abhorrent beast and traced the trail of the thread. The ball of wool he ended up with, exiting from the labyrinth, one would have sworn had the shape of the Minotaur...

Can we agree on the notion, that you can't create the flowing water of a river, by building structures from the stones from the bed of the river?

If structures are the trail left behind by sensing consciousness passing, then by building aggregates from these structures we won't revive it.

In this chapter I will argue why consciousness can never be completely understood in an analytical manner. This does however not mean, that consciousness cannot be fully experienced. It merely means that the mental processes, which employ structures which are the product of consciousness cannot on their own fully describe and regenerate consciousness.

Background

The proponents of intrinsic consciousness or of the primacy of consciousness (I am one of them), consider that pristine awareness (or primordial consciousness) is the ground of all existence and as a consequence present in every self-generated aspect thereof. In other words, primordial consciousness is irreducible.

Argument

If primordial consciousness is irreducible and the underlying ground of everything that exists, it is Absolute and can never be understood in terms of relations to other things. You see, as Buckminster Fuller[25] explained, analytical understanding is a process of building relations, of building an ontology. We understand an object by its structural and functional relations to other objects, by listing its constituent features. All these connections build a so-called plane of understanding that metaphorically stands under the object to be understood. All objects, events and situations we mentally only know in relative terms. This is even physically reflected in the neuronal network in our brains.

The absolute ground of all relative phenomena itself is not relative. If you only make all kinds of objects from clay, you will never be able to understand what clay really is. You will of course be able to learn how clay behaves (functional aspects), but that is not sufficient to know what it structurally is. And if it is irreducible, it has no intrinsic structure, it has no limitations, which means that it must be infinite.

We may be able to describe all kinds of forms and behavior of these forms, but this will only tell us something about the manifestational aspects of primordial consciousness, never its intrinsic essence. So if primordial consciousness (Consciousness with a capital C) is the source of everything else, trying to mentally understand it is a vain enterprise. Of course, it is useful to study the behavior of consciousness, but we should perhaps refrain from stating "Consciousness is this or that" in terms of relative aspects, if we accept this premise.

If consciousness is irreducible, it is Absolute and Infinite, all-encompassing and profoundly in-understandable. But it can be experienced. If we write about our human consciousness, of course we can describe how we experience it, in terms of its self-reflexivity, its awareness, its focus, its concentration, its ability to integrate, understand and generate information, but none of these descriptions will ever be enough to capture, to define what it really is.

Define comes from the Latin "finis," meaning border or end, in other words to define is to limit something, wherein the limitations are the descriptors of its relations. Perhaps this is why Wittgenstein[23] said, when referring to consciousness: "*Wovon man nicht sprechen kann, darüber muss man schweigen*" i.e. whereof one cannot speak, thereof one must be silent.

Whereas consciousness may not be analytically understandable, perhaps it can be grasped by the mystic experience called "self-realization."

Conclusion

We have seen how the idea of intrinsic consciousness as ground for all phenomena is incompatible with analytical understanding. Perhaps this is, why the so-called "hard-problem" of consciousness in science and artificial intelligence (A.I.) has never been solved. And if my hypotheses are correct, it can never be solved by science, which is analytical per definition.

Nevertheless, the mental processes by which we explore the dimensions of what has been left behind by the passage of consciousness, do give us some insight in the way it manifests. It is by the virtue of this scavenger hunt; this track search, that we are able to figure out that the way, it manifests is like a code. Not just any code, but a code that modifies itself over time. A meta-code, which generates all other codes. The Ouroboros Code.

Chapter 5

Free will: an illusion or the ground of existence?

The three fates, the sisters Clotho, spinner of life's thread, Lachesis, allotter of a person's destiny, and Atropos, cutter of the thread at death, left Oedipus with an unsavory experience. Even the Gods in the Greek Pantheon often were the victim of the dark ominous Moirai, daughter of Nyx (Night). And what about the wheels of Fortune and Dharma? Are we merely propelled by our Karma from one predicament to the next?

If reality is a code, does it mean that it is fully deterministically following an algorithm? Does the Ouroboros code imply that we do not have a free will?

What is free will actually? And do we have a free will? People often discuss this theme, but it has occurred to me that different people often have a very different understanding of what this concept means. Because of the semantic confusion people end up disagreeing – not about the same thing – but about different things. In other words, they are comparing apples with pears.

In this chapter, I will try to discuss a few different scenarios or interpretations of what this terminology means to different people. Perhaps then we'll conclude, that our points of view weren't that different after all. Or perhaps they remain forever separated, but at least we'll know why.

Background

In antiquity free will was not really discussed as such, but may have been implicit in notions about determinism. The philosopher Leucippus[26] said "*Nothing occurs at random, but everything for a reason and by necessity.*" Similarly, Democritus[5] advocated a physical causal determinism. This ruled out chance: The present and future were completely determined by its past.

Aristotle[27], on the other hand, saw room for accidents caused by chance and diverged from the single cause idea.

Lucretius[28] was perhaps the first to associate randomness with free will, but he also spoke about the possibility to override our desires by our reasoning.

Most Vedic teachings point to a soul (Atman), which is capable of making choices within the framework of a causal chain called "karma." So here there is a non-deterministic freedom to choose, but each choice engenders a deterministic chain. Other Vedic and Buddhist teachings claim, that there is no soul and that there is only an observing mind or consciousness and that there is ultimately no "doer."

From medieval times to the 19th century "the Will" was seen as an important moral way of choosing between "good" and "bad." Many philosophers see free will as the capacity of rational agents to choose a course of action from among various alternatives. David Hume[29] baptized "free will" as "the most contentious question of metaphysics." He saw free will as the power of acting or not acting.

The idea of the universe as fully deterministic mechanical clockwork has been found to be untenable, when quantum mechanics asserted itself and showed, that at least at the quantum level there is a great deal of indeterminacy.

In this chapter, I will not claim to make an exhaustive treaty of "free will" nor do I intend to discuss the perspective of all modern philosophers, which requires too many complex explanations.

Instead, I will sketch a number of scenarios of interpretation of "free will" and analyze, whether we can arrive at a kind of consensus understanding, what it could be and what the consequences are of wielding such interpretations.

Free will as rationalism

As said before, in the past free will was sometimes understood as the capacity of rational agents, to choose a course of action from among various alternatives. The counterargument could be, that if we apply rationality to choose, we will employ a kind of mental weighing algorithm. We will weigh the pros and cons and decide, which course of action is most advantageous for us. If you consider the execution of the weighing algorithm to be a naturally happening deterministic event, which even goes on subconsciously and which you can't control, you might indeed conclude, that there is no free will in this type of action. In other centuries, this ability to rationalize and reason the most advantageous course of action, was rather seen as the pinnacle of free will. So there is also a kind of cultural bias present here: In our modern times, in which we tend to see everything as a process of algorithmic computation, we tend to conclude that there is no choice involved at all. Our mind carries out a set of instructions and makes us believe that we "choose" a course of action "consciously," whereas the decision has already been taken subconsciously.

Very often our rational motives may indicate one course of logical action, whereas our emotions or desires indicate another course. Emotions, which we sometimes classify as "irrational." In these kinds of situations, one could argue, that free will is the ability of ratio to override emotion. Again, the counterargument can be, that yet another level algorithm is present, which weighs instinctive tendencies vs. rational thought outcome. If ratio is capable of controlling desires, our long-term benefit analysis overrules our projected short-term pleasure gain. This would be an algorithm in function and hence devoid of free will. Alternatively, when we listen to our desires instead of our ratio the instinctive tendencies are such strong lower-level algorithms that they can overrule the rational algorithms. Any choice we make has already been made subconsciously and free will is a red herring.

We see that the definition of free will in this way is subject to semantic drift. What it meant two centuries ago, is no longer how people in the computer era perceive it. But aren't we raising the bar for the notion of free will too high?

Choosing from equally preferable alternatives

Let's carry out a test: take three identical marbles of exactly the same color and place them in a triangle in front of you such that the distance from your hand to each marble is exactly the same. Now you don't have any motives anymore to prefer one marble over another. There is no advantage associated in choosing one over the other. Can you pick one marble, without using thought? Try it; grab one immediately without giving it thought. You see, it wasn't that difficult, you could choose from equally preferable alternatives. Did you need an algorithm to choose? Did you need to use a children's rhyme like "eeny, meeny, miny, moe" or could you even bypass that? You could. And you should. Is this then free will? Or is something going on subconsciously? Isn't the more parsimonious explanation, that you simply have free will, rather than to suppose that in an instant your subconscious sorted something out for you in an algorithmic manner? Or were you just picking randomly? Or IS free will the ability to pick randomly?

What would you do if you'd have to choose between two of your children as in the movie Sophie's choice? Provided that you have no preference for one over the other, could such a choice be engendered by any causal chain of events or would you just be exercising free will?

Do Determinism and Randomness exhaust the possibilities?

There is an argument based on the "law of the excluded middle," which goes as follows:
If the universe is deterministic, then we obviously don't have free will, because we can't have chosen otherwise.
If the universe is not deterministic, then it is random. If our decisions are random, they're not freely willed.
Determinism and randomness exhaust the possibilities.
Therefore, we cannot possibly have free will.

This reasoning however forgets the so-called "null-representation": the possibility of self-causation!

In my book "*Is Intelligence An Algorithm?*"[30] I argue that certain parts of intelligence, such as intuition and original creativity, are not algorithmic and not deterministic. But they are clearly not random either. Why? Because they are self-caused. Self-caused IS self-determined, which is free will par excellence. In a later chapter I will explain in more detail, why I consider, that the will to self-determine reality naturally sprouts from the philosophy of the primacy of consciousness. If consciousness is the foundation of reality, it leaves open the possibility to engender its own transformation. We have found our prime mover. And what would be an appropriate symbol for such a self-causation? You guessed well: It's our friend the Ouroboros.

In the absence of consciousness as prime mover/doer, we must analyze what quantum mechanics has to say about this issue.

Quantum indeterminacy

The twentieth century saw a huge paradigm shift in physics. Staring from the Newtonian clockwork universe that was entropically running towards its heat death[31] by Boltzmann's 2nd law of thermodynamics, we saw the advent of quantum mechanics. Quantum mechanics showed that at least at the micro-level, there were such things as uncertainty, indeterminacy and probability. Apparently not everything in our universe ran down a predestined karma path of cause and effect. Things got even weirder, when quantum effects were shown to react to a certain extent to the influence or intent of a human being as per the experiments conducted by e.g. Dean Radin[16,17]. The physicist John Wheeler[6] concluded we're living in a "participatory universe."

This reasoning is often countered by the argument, that the quantum-events at the micro level do not translate to the macro level. I found the following passage by Neil Rickert[32], who sheds doubt on this macro-cancelling of the micro-quantum indeterminacy: "*Physics experiments that demonstrate quantum level indeterminacy do so by amplifying the quantum level events so that they cause macro-level effects. Those experiments themselves are examples of macro-level indeterminacy.*"

And what about the random number generators (RNGs) we use, which rely on the indeterminacy of the radioactive decay? These RNGs are moreover employed in technological devices. Do we also not have a macro-effect as a consequence of quantum level events here?

Telos

A great deal of the processes in Nature does however follow cause and effect patterns to a substantive extent. If there is a certain level of indeterminacy in the universe we observe, it is certainly not so indeterminate that we would conclude that there is complete randomness, which would have made it impossible to derive the laws of Nature. Rather, our universe transcends the dichotomy of determinism vs. indeterminism and that it allows both simultaneously and even allows one to cause the other and *vice versa*.

Look at weather models: Even if a chain of cause and effect cannot be denied, we can't predict the outcome of a butterfly flapping its wings in Australia on the weather in America[33]. It might even cause a hurricane. Whilst following causes and effects in great complexity that defies computability, it results in unpredictable events. Is that still true determinism?

Conversely, whereas the fate of individual molecules in chemical reactions cannot be predicted and is indeterministic, the overall outcome of the ensemble of molecules can be predicted with high accuracy and appears deterministic.

Nature is full of the so-called chaotic patterns, which have a certain degree of intrinsic order in the form of fractals embedded therein. Nature also seems to follow an intelligent algorithm to build complexity largely against the forces of entropy. Over and over, we see that smaller entities organize themselves into complex more versatile and more encompassing new higher-level entities. Nature purposefully organizes itself, so clearly it is not random. In Greek, purpose is "telos."

Aren't our traditional dichotomies between determinism and indeterminism or randomness too strict? Do we not see that there is rather a mix of both so that ultimately it is neither the one nor the other? And is there not a groping of sentient life towards higher complexity revealing a kind of intrinsic "telos"?

(In) computability

Let's go back to the belief that all our actions are determined by mental and/or emotional algorithms. Does that not mean that our intelligence in a certain way IS a form of artificial intelligence? Can we only analytically connect the dots? Can we only compute? Or is there more to the story? Aristotle already said "The whole is more than the sum of parts." Clearly, computing is summing parts. Phenomena, which show synergism, showing that the whole is more than the sum of parts, are often called "emergent." Nobody really understands how emergent or synergistic effects arise. Still Nature does not hesitate to produce and use them. So if Nature is doing something beyond computation, is our argument that everything is but an algorithm not flawed?

There is of course the generation of complexity, leading to sequences that could not have been programmed in a master set of traditional instructions, but which does arise in the interactions between nodes in a neural network, which are also pieces of an algorithm. Certainly, the cause-effect chain is here unhampered and fully deterministic. Still this deterministic behavior is not predictable. There is something profoundly non-algorithmic about the neural network algorithms working together. Is this then, what is going on in the universe? Is it a gigantic neural network and is indeterminism merely an "apparent effect" which is not really there?

Or is Nature a quantum computer, which can determine the effects for ensembles but not for individual entities? Or is it an enhanced quantum computer, which emulates a classical computer by using Toffoli gates? What is an "entity" actually? Does it need to be sentient? Or is reality an inanimate switchboard?

So what does free will mean to you? Is it the ability to choose rationally? Is it the ability to choose between emotion-based desires and reason? Or are you stricter? Do you say that all your mental and emotional processes are algorithms? Is Nature not more than a digital switchboard or is there a self-determining Consciousness intrinsic to it?

If it is just a deterministic Turing machine, then the thesis of my book "*Is Intelligence An Algorithm?*" would be wrong. In my book I describe that whereas most rational analytical processes do follow an algorithm of comparing, distinguishing and classifying, intuition presents us with complete solutions, without a causal chain of connecting the dots. If we can act upon an intuition, a blissful creative impulse of sudden immediate complete comprehension, how can we claim this is a mere algorithm? In other words, I claim that although we mostly follow algorithms to solve problems, we sometimes have perplexing insights and original creations that defy algorithmicity. Unlike AIs, which perform massive screening to distil patterns, we can navigate on a kind of holistic prescience, which humiliates the karmic dot-connectors. In other words, Intelligence is more than just algorithms; Intelligence is more than analytical dissecting and comparisons. To choose this over our dry analytical learning ways or our instinctive emotions, is that not free will?

The whole is more than the sum of parts and intuition can represent such a whole, which cannot be arrived at by connecting the dots analytically. Is this what happened to Kékulé[34] when he saw the structure of benzene emerge from the Ouroboros?

Predestination, Gods, Monism and Pluralism

Above I have explained that although a neural network can be completely deterministic, for an outside user it is often impossible to know the outcome of its black-box like functioning. In other words, being deterministic does not necessarily entail predictability. If you were a kind of God, who could make a universe out of neural nodes, it would not mean you would necessarily be omniscient as regards the future developments of states within the neural network. The claims from various religions, that God is omniscient and knows everything which has happened and which will happen, seems completely untenable if quantum mechanics is right and/or if the universe is a giant neural network type of computer. An omniscient God, who has predestined everything, which will happen must have other means at its disposal, which fall outside of our current mental framework of understanding. This does not mean, that I say that such a God is or is not there. I am agnostic. I honestly don't know. But it does not mean that I don't give a damn. I consider the perspective that I am not more than a robot carrying out a pre-programmed algorithm as an extremely liverish perspective. It's also impossible for me to imagine, that a God could enjoy creating a fully predestined world, where there is nothing surprising happening. What a boring world, what a boring God. But then again, "my ways are not your ways" this God was supposed to have said. Well you can imagine, where the Abrahamic God ended up with me.

Then we have the Samkhya philosophy in Hinduism, which is dualist: Consciousness on the one hand (Purusha) only observes and is totally unaffected by Prakrti (Nature). The observer is not the doer. However, since matter and consciousness have been shown to influence each other by quantum mechanics, this theory is also sent to the paper archive called the bin.

We have the Advaita Vedantist philosophy in Hinduism, which is said to be non-dualist or monist. It considers consciousness as the ultimate ground of existence. Buddhism is a bit similar to this in that it is monist, but in contrast to Advaita Vedanta there is no "Self" in Buddhism. Again, there is only observation, no doing.

If consciousness is ultimately singular, this implies that all information is integrated at one level; all our isolated experiences are then simultaneously observed from a higher level and integrated in a single experiencing consciousness. The philosophy branch of Idealism is somehow claiming the same. This singular consciousness would somehow be "omniscient," since it is the only real actor on the scene. This would lead to a kind of superdeterminism. That, however, does not resonate with the incredible suffering going on in this world. Why would consciousness deliberately subject itself to suffering if it is omniscient? It does not make sense.

Besides, in most branches of Hinduism God or Brahman is the doer. Brahma is the creative force in the universe, so it must be doing something, isn't it? And what would all the meditative techniques to control the mind, increase focus and stop thinking be for, if there is no doer? If there is no doer, who is stopping the mind? An algorithm programmed to shut down all programs including itself? What then causes the reboot after meditation?

In all these religious perspectives I can't find any satisfactory explanation. It is counter-intuitive. I find one contradiction after another. Mystics claim to have experienced, that ultimately there is no space and time, that there is no doer and that there is no free will. How can you be so sure they were not deluded? That their experiences were not some kind of giant hallucination? (Although, from hallucinations sometimes incredible insights can be gathered. Terrence McKenna[35] experienced existence as a kind of living language and information processing, which is also the core of Langan's CTMU[36]).

Idealistic Panpsychism and Cosmosemiosis

My present-day metaphysical speculations (and they are not more than that, I may well be wrong; I maintain to be agnostic) see consciousness more as a dynamic fractal. Although it's the ultimate ground of existence, in order to know itself, it generates relative copies of itself that interact with each other. This leads to a kind of "pluralistic monism." There is no full knowledge of itself, but like the Ouroboros, consciousness is trying to bite its own tail, to discover itself. Likewise, energy strings follow a circular path that impinges upon itself, creating a self-referencing loop and giving birth to material particles. Is this how consciousness generates matter? Is the self-referencing aspect of consciousness not expressed by the will to know itself? Is the process of generating a cosmos with all its manifestations (called "Cosmosemiosis" by techno-shaman Tim Gross[37]), not a process of self-verification? Does this not lead to an ocean of conscious energy (conscienergy) in which material forms arise, as a consequence of the will to discover itself? I call this Idealistic Panpsychism or Idealistic Pansentience.

I consider this the most promising springboard as it shows a third way out of the Determinism-Randomness trap. And yes, it entails free will, from the quantum world up to the macro-level of human interactions. A refreshing middle, where determinism and indeterminism are intertwined as the helices of a DNA, mimicking the Yin-Yang equilibrium of order and chaos, of purpose and chance, of monism and pluralism. A perspective of "both...and" instead of "either...or," in other words a "Transcendent" perspective that does not exclude either possibility, so that Existence willfully screens and probes all possibilities, sometimes by limiting the choices and imposing chreodes, necessary pathways of evolutionary imperatives, sometimes going wild and berserk as in the Cambrian explosion, in which every morphological pattern was screened and pruned to fulfil the Cosmosemiotic imperative of maximization of meta-entropy: Creating the entropy-reducing phenomenon of life whilst generating a multiplicity of forms that can yet better dissipate the energies.

A perspective, which even has its representative in a branch of Hinduism, where it is said that even God does not know all its energies (denial of omniscience) or where Atmas (Souls) do not dissolve into the creator Brahman (God) but are its eternal individual companions or reflections made out of the same underlying monistic absolute consciousness.

And perhaps this is not the end of it. Perhaps our technological Singularity will spawn a plethora of universes, to give a new fractal birth of an Everett-like multiverse. Or as Tim Gross[37] would say: "*The mind is the fractal self-similar reflection of the cosmic monad – the thing that cannot be outside of itself and must generate form through projecting self-reflected models into itself.*"

Conclusion

We have seen that the definition of "free will" is culturally biased and means different things to different persons. From the ability to simply choose rationally to the ability to choose between emotion-based desires and reason. From the denial that all your mental and emotional processes are algorithms to the denial of Nature as a digital switchboard. From the third way exit of self-causation from the quagmire of the excluded middle of determinism and randomness to the denial of predestination, Gods, Monism and Pluralism.

Depending from which angle you come, you perhaps share one of these perspectives in favor or in denial of free will. But it is always good to see that there are multiple perspectives, so that we can start to weigh our perspective against the other perspectives (algorithmically) and hopefully intuitively transcend the dichotomies in a "both...and" bird's eye view.

Although I admit I have not been able to convincingly show that "free will" in its most extreme sense is a necessary aspect of reality in all its forms, I have shown that the counter arguments are not convincing either. The question remains undecided for me, although I find the cosmosemiotic self-causation of idealistic panpsychism / pansentience the most promising springboard.

If this is true, then our intelligence is not merely involving algorithms, but also employs holistic realizations to solve our problems. Therefore, I conclude that it is unlikely that intelligence is an algorithm.

In such a framework the Will is in fact an essential ingredient for existence to come into being. It is an inextricable part of the Ouroboros Code. A code, which is only determined in part, but leaves plenty of room for wild unforeseen self-explorations.

Chapter 6

Sentience in Pancomputational Panpsychism

"O heavens, can we ever be made to believe that motion and life and soul and mind are not present with perfect being? Can we imagine that, being is devoid of life and mind, and exists in awful unmeaningness an everlasting fixture? – That would be a dreadful thing to admit."

-Plato in the Sophist

This chapter questions, where sentience starts. Is it limited to biological systems only? Or is every self-sustaining phenomenon sentient? Could other cybernetic[2] systems harbor sentience? And if so, would they have a computational nature? In this chapter I will address these issues.

Background

In this book I will argue that Idealism and Panpsychism are not necessarily mutually exclusive notions and how a refined form of hierarchical fractal idealism is a form of panpsychism (or rather, pansentience) in a sense. In this chapter I will give a more comprehensive explanation of my philosophy called "The Transcendental Metaphysics of Pancomputational Panpsychism" according to my eponymous book[21] (hereinafter referred to as TM).

Although I fully adhere to the Idealism viewpoint that consciousness is ultimately unified and the world, its objects and inhabitants are in consciousness rather than the other way around, I do not see why the drawing line of sentience should be put at "biology." As a biochemist, I see the versatile and complex nature of the behavior of atoms and molecules at the individual level, their ability to respond to stimuli and their morphological fitness to harbor a self-reflective cybernetic feedback loop.

---

[2] Cybernetics is the study of how humans, animals and machines control and communicate.

Conscienergy

As mind and matter appear to be able to influence each other (as has been convincingly shown by quantum mechanical experiments involving mental influencing by Dean Radin[16,16] et al.), they must ultimately have a common denominator of medium of expression.

My most promising candidate for this medium is 'Consciousness' (Consciousness is here meant as the primordial consciousness, of which human consciousness is but a tentacle). Consciousness can take any shape but is empty in its essence. Like the castles made of sand that easily return to their shapeless state, forms arise and disappear in consciousness, which itself remains unchanged.

It is my hypothesis in my book that the underlying ground of existence is conscious energy; as I called it before "Conscienergy."

In order to clearly show that Conscienergy encompasses both the physical and the metaphysical, I need to explain how in my hypothesis Conscienergy functions.

Energies, which are capable of sustaining themselves over a period of time must somehow be able to repeat their form or pattern, like a standing wave, otherwise, they would be an imperceptible transient. Whereas certain standing waves (such as a guitar string in vibration) after a while dampen out, the standing waves that form an atom or a molecule don't.

Atoms and molecules somehow fuel themselves and sustain their inner resonance. In other words, whatever is waving, it is following its previous track. The energy flow in atoms is just an example of what I consider to be a deeper truth: Every energy pattern that can sustain itself follows a track which is a closed loop. It is more or less circular in the sense that it can repeat and reinforce its own form. This is also the basis of String theory in physics. If it impinges on its previous track, it integrates information in a certain way: It re-cognizes itself. In 3D such a pattern could form a toroid, like a torus, a horn sphere, a horn torus, a spindle, sphere, a spindle torus, a spheroid, a sphere, an ellipsoid, or thick-rod shape. Such forms are capable of harboring a vortex of energy. Note that Bernardo Kastrup[38] has metaphorically associated vortexes with personal consciousness of living entities, whereas he describes inanimate objects as ripples in consciousness.

According to Giulio Tononi[7] the very process of becoming aware, of cognizing and recognizing, involves a feedback mechanism, which amounts to the integration of the information the system receives.

For anything in order to be able to exist (ex-sist means stand out), to be able to stand out from an otherwise homogeneous background of sameness of primordial consciousness, it must have differences from the rest, which makes it distinguishable.

This is my hypothesis how existence arises in the process of Conscienergy-based self-resonance: From the undifferentiated state of the point-like center of what will become a torus-like form, a differentiation of Conscienergy takes place. In a kind of cell-division type of process the point-like Primordial Consciousness, splits in two "reality cells" (as Kaufman[39] would call them), which are form-wise identical. In other words, Conscienergy in this stage can do nothing but multiply itself by division, thereby creating two copies of its original state. However, these copies are not identical in an absolute sense, since they do not share the same position: They have been spatially separated and are now relative to each other. They may also have different sizes, one being like the seed of the other.

This division process might also be considered as the process of generating a so-called "null-representation." Consciousness has traditionally often been associated with self-reflectivity. One form of reflecting on oneself is the attempt to produce an image of oneself, a so-called internal representation. (AI engineers are working towards providing an "internal representation of a system" to generate an equivalent of consciousness).

Tim Gross, the earlier mentioned techno-shamanic philosopher trained in computer science, presented the thesis that the re-presentation aspect of information is an essential aspect of the arising of existence (slightly paraphrased by me for reasons of readability):

Consciousness interacting with itself and abstractly representing itself creates a feedback loop, which is the ontology of existence itself. The "abstract representations" are just representations of that part of consciousness which interacts. The change arising from this interaction is however not the full source of change. The Ouroboros serpent doesn't see its full self, only its tail and can only know itself by the logic and expression of its tail. This results in a reduced representation of consciousness – ergo an abstraction – which is the world of Maya we live in.

In order to see its full "Self," Consciousness (or the Cosmos if you prefer) would have to go outside of itself, which is impossible. So it must abstractly pretend to be able to see itself from the outside by representing the part of itself it can see on the inside.

What absolute consciousness does, when it generates the relative world by interacting with itself and re-representing itself, is what L. H. Kauffman[40] called "*We take the form of distinction for the form.*"

As said before, mathematically we could call such a "self-representation" a "null-representation" (as suggested by Stephen Paul King, Senior Researcher in AI). This null-representation is in fact the "seed," which hologically contains all the information to reproduce the original as a copy, like the minuscule seed of a mustard tree can recreate a new giant mustard tree. Mathematical concepts of interest in this field relate to "fixed point combinators," "lambda calculus," "mutifractal" and "quines."

But it basically boils down to making copies of oneself, which is a way of the conscienergy dividing itself up into copies of itself.

Akasha

Steven Kaufman[39] (not L.H. Kauffman!) calls these copies of relative consciousness "reality cells" in his book "*Unified Reality Theory.*" These cells together establish the so-called quantum vacuum or zero-point field. Since in the vacuum the forces are evenly distributed in all directions, so that it seems that there is "nothing," Kaufman argued that the reality cells, which make up this vacuum are stacked in the form of the so-called "vector equilibrium," in which the cells experience an equal force from every side. This stacking is also known as the cubic closest packing.

I have suggested in my book TM that one could equate this quantum vacuum as the fabric of space, ether or the Akasha to speak in oriental terminology.

From Absolute undifferentiated consciousness bubbles of relative consciousness arise, which – as described – are merely self-interactions. Similarly, in comics you often see bubbles coming out of a head followed by a little cloud on top with an image of the idea of contemplation. Quantum foam or the Scum of Mind?

The absolute wholeness of Conscienergy appears to have divided itself into a polarized system of two relative conscienergies. Since they are relative and not 100% identical, they constitute a pattern of information.

As these informational entities proceed through what is now their existence, they repeat this process and divide into further smaller conscienergies. Simultaneously the primordial center also continues its process of division, thereby pushing earlier formed reality cells more outward.

Thus, we get a plethora of informational patterns, which all divide into further sub-patterns. These informational cellular entities can also exchange information and interpenetrate each other. This changes the total informational content of the informational matrix that is thus "dependently arising" (to speak in Buddhist terms).

Due to the pushing outward and continuing division of earlier formed cells, these earlier formed cells "travel" along field lines of a Torus, both from the upper side and from the bottom side, until the outward travelling cells from the upper side meet the outward travelling cells from the bottom side. There they meet on the outer rim of a doughnut like shape, a Torus. And as they meet, they impinge on each other and this creates a shock-wave which travels through the informational matrix to the point-like center which is the Primordial Consciousness

(PC). Possibly upon this impinging on the rim these reality cells are even absolved and now energetically return via the shock-wave to the center, where they become reintegrated in the Absoluteness of the PC.

The coming together of informational shock-waves in the center is the feedback of the information that was sent out by the PC: Their collision results a concrescence, a growing together, yes, in an integration of information. And it is this integration of information, could be that which makes the PC aware of itself and its manifestations again. This is in line with Tononi's[7] idea that feedback resulting in integration of information leads to awareness.

The reintegration of the energies results in the experience of bliss of becoming one again with the PC. And thus, the cycle can start again.

It is my (and Kaufman's[39]) hypothesis that the material world arises due to a yet further type of energetic interactions of the PC with the reality cells. In other words, the generation of an informational matrix (and a material world deriving therefrom) is an inextricable aspect of the process of becoming aware, the cognition and the recognition by the PC. Only where everything is in its fully integrated state (i.e. at the center of the Toroidal Conscienergy), there is apparent stillness, apparent nothingness, which the Buddhists may call "Shunya."

But this apparent nothingness – although not a thing – is not an "absolute nothing," rather it is the formless source of all that exists. Conscienergy thus involves an ongoing process of sending out information and thereby creating manifestations and reintegrating this information every time a shock-wave returns.

Only the state of integrated oneness of the PC in this flux of "Conscienergy" could in a certain way be said to be purely metaphysical as it is formless and information-less, devoid of aggregation and an absolute wholeness of focused awareness. But if it requires the generation and reintegration of physicality for its self-sustention, it would be a bit artificial to claim that it's completely independent of physicality.

The informational processes sprouting therefrom, every polarization, every subdivision could be said to be part of the physical, measurable world of aggregates, but as it derives from the metaphysical its essence is metaphysical in a sense, too.

Matter

Steven Kaufman argues, that there is a second level of interaction. The "reality cell-matrix," which has been formed, could in a certain sense be compared to oocytes. The Absolute Primordial Consciousness (abbreviated as AC or PC), which is omnipresent and all-pervading is not only the source of the "Prima Materia" constituting these reality cells as relative conscienergy quanta or monads, it also surrounds these cells and is present inside these cells. Metaphorically spoken a more concentrated form of attention arising from the AC could now penetrate these oocytes and fertilize these reality cells with a kind of self-monitoring quanta of conscienergy, which by doing so become a form of relative consciousness (i.e. consciousness interacting with itself) as well. This penetration creates a "distortion" in an otherwise uniform Akashic matrix. As a distortion propagates through the matrix, the reality cells it encounters become "excited." You could consider this as the change from a 0 to 1 state. Thus, Consciousness attempting to sense the matrix from within thereby creates a kind of digital computation process. This is however not a simple Von-Neumann computer. It has more similarities to a "quantum computer." As all reality cells are interconnected and sense each other, this connection can lead to the "spooky" interaction at distance a.k.a. quantum entanglement.

As shockwaves propagate through this matrix, they also create a wake, a field of distortion around it, part of which also operates as a so-called "pilot wave." The pilot waves make the matrix move before the center of distortive energy actually arrives. Such pilot waves have already been suggested by "De Broglie"[41] and by Yves Couder[42] to explain the outcome of the double slit experiment. Only they fail to identify the medium that waves.

When distortive waves encounter each other, by means of the distortive field they emit, they create a gradient of distortion that engenders mutual attraction. The distortive energies (which Kaufman equates with electromagnetic radiation such as photons) start to circle around each other, like two fish chasing each other's tail and engendering a kind of Yin-Yang-symbol.

This is what Kaufman calls a "compound process," which establishes a material particle. This process also moves in a kind of toroidal pathway. Toruses, bubbles etc. are ideal environments conducive to harbor local vortexes, which the philosopher Bernardo Kastrup[38] indicated as a metaphorical means of self-reflectivity for egoic awareness. This kind of self-involvement may well lead to a local illusion of self-consciousness being separate from the AC, whereas it is simply a derivative form thereof.

Is it then too simplistic to assume that atoms may have a kind of interior sensation? Do not the orbitals of the electrons in the atoms present similar forms (torus, bubble, 3D clover lobes, peanut: s, p, d and f orbitals of atoms are all examples thereof, some more explicit than others; especially dz^2, sp^2 in pi-bonds and sp^2d^5 orbitals show the traditional doughnut torus), in which vortexes could reside?

Matter attracts matter in Kaufman's model, due to the distortive gradient, which creates a chreode and makes particles seek each other. Thus, aggregates arise, forming black holes, which suck up all matter. At a certain point the internal pressure of such a black hole may have become so unstable, that the system explodes from within thereby creating a big bang giving rise to a universe.

It remains my assumption, that all matter forms are self-involved forms of conscienergy, seeking to know itself by interacting with itself.
Evolution leads to more complex compounded vessels, such as molecules, macromolecules, cells and organisms. Each system is full of polarities, which could give rise to toroidal files and harbor vortexes.

Any dipole has a magnetic toroidal field around it. Many molecules are dipoles, most – if not all – molecules have at least dipolar patches that create local toroidal fields. What do you think the electronic force-field around an aromatic structure looks like? A torus above another torus.

A cell fits certainly the above mentioned definition of a torus. Whereas essentially spherical in resting state, upon mitosis or meiosis other stages of the above mentioned broader definition of a torus are traversed.

The morphology of animals, plants and other life forms all seem to fit the broader definition to a certain extent, or at least parts of their bodies do. The polarity in the nerve system can also contribute to the generation of a "toroidal" electromagnetic field. A tree with its branches and roots also looks like two stacked toruses.

Experiencing through form

The size of a system determines the wavelength of the energetic form it can harbor as a form of locally self-involved and self-sustaining part of conscienergy. Whereas at each level a self-sustaining entity can have their own individual conscienergy vortex, at each higher level an individual conscienergy inhabits the overall morphological field scaffolded by the numerous sub-entities that build the scaffold on the level below.

This does not mean that the individual higher conscienergy emerges from or is the aggregate or sum of the lower energy consciousness, no, the lower entities build a vessel which by virtue of its morphology is conducive to let a higher form of conscienergy inhabit it and form a greater vortex.

In this way, we get a fractal of conscienergy forms, in which each vortex inhabits a toroid-type vessel made out of small toroid shape entities.

One of the reasons I like this model so much, is that every form of existence is based on the will to stand out from the rest, to establish existence by self-involvement or – crudely said – a kind of egoism.

Whereas the absolute all-encompassing and all-pervading consciousness harbors all these subforms, itself it is unaffected.

When the vessel dies, the conscienergy vortex at the higher level need not dissolve immediately into the absolute consciousness. It depends on whether it has still enough drive, enough momentum, will or impetus to sustain the vortex. In eastern religions this impetus is provided by "karma." In such a case it might seek a new vessel to express itself in matter which could account for the notion of reincarnation.

Alternatively, if the conscienergy is "self-realized" enough so as to have stopped its momentum, it may dissolve and merge with the AC.

For me, the beauty of this model is, that it presupposes sentience and a will of expression at every level of reality and not arbitrarily starting at biological systems.

Requirements of the Ouroboros Code

The potential requirements of conscienergy to express itself in form I have speculated are the abilities to:

- form a self-sustaining feedback loop (existence)
- form self-reflective feedback loops that inform itself about itself (sentience, self-exploration)
- being capable of self-reproduction or "null representation" (multiplication by division, amplification)
- abstract, retain and apply information (memory and learning)
- integrate information, including forming connections, aggregates and networks (conjunction)
- self-modification to the extent that the above-mentioned qualities are not compromised (exploration, screen, differentiation)
- promote the continuation of that what works and eliminate the expressions that do not work (pruning, selecting).

These are the basic start ingredients for the Ouroboros Code, via which Consciousness manifests itself to generate reality (or a plurality of virtual realities, which can be nested into each other in the form of a fractal).

Of these, most non-biological systems are not capable of an exact self-reproduction, but neither are we 100%. That said, nuclei recombine and split to generate other nuclei in nucleosynthesis, molecules recombine and split give other molecules etc. Howard Bloom[43] calls this the *"fission and fusion strategies of the evolutionary search engine,"* which in his book *"The God Problem"* starts already at the subatomic level.

Since atoms certainly and molecules to a lesser extent can have quite long "life-times," I don't see how one can argue that they would not "maintain themselves against the forces of entropy." This means that they must somehow be self-sustaining.

Most essentially, I wish to argue, that all self-sustaining entities in existence appear to be cybernetic and sentient to the extent that they can observe a stimulus and react thereto: input-throughput-output and often feedback adaptation to their new status. This feedback cycle is a kind of "functional torus" if you wish, a functional whirlpool. Stimulus and response, aren't they hallmarks of sentience?

Ithzak Bentov[44] suggested the "Torus" (a Doughnut without a hole) as the most fundamental geometry of consciousness and of every self-creating self-sustaining physical entity, such as atoms, magnetic fields etc. Whereas structurally symmetrical, a torus is functionally asymmetrical as it has an input and output side. Bentov suggests that all living entities also generate a natural toroidal field around them, an amplified consciousness field. It is my assumption in this book that this is also the case for said inanimate self-sustaining entities. Again, I repeat that this does not mean that a chair or a bimetal construct is sentient at the overall level. These constructs do not sustain or propagate themselves. But the atoms and molecules therein might be sentient.

Conclusion

Sentience by self-sustaining feedback loops that try to re-represent themselves in order to exist has some advantages over Idealism in which everything below the biological levels is considered non-sentient: You can basically leave the system to develop its own dynamic rather than requiring some kind of master-mind that actively stores, remembers and represents every minute detail of information and is supposed to render that information whenever looked at. The storing of information in the Akasha in the above described philosophy is more like a natural consequence of consciousness' self-interactions.

In this "Idealism with nested Panpsychism view" at least a speculative framework is provided, on a parsimonious notion of self-involvement, as to how material forms (or cosmic ideas if you prefer) can be expressed by sentience via the Ouroboros Code. Existence as a product of local volitions interacting with each other at the same and/or different levels.

My proposal is a hierarchical nested series of "panpsychic or pansentient toroidal entities" in an "idealistic" ocean of consciousness. If such a system moreover also exists and functions by virtue of its in- and output, in a sense it can be said to be computational. After all, any system that performs actions on itself, that self-referentially orients, transforms and iterates encapsulated complex patterns, can be said to be computational[45]. This definition strongly resonates with the self-referential nature of consciousness. By virtue of the network of the reality cells. Yes, it can even be considered as a "neural network" of reality cells whilst simultaneously harboring sentience at every level of existence. To avoid confusion with the "panpsychism aficionados," who believe that our consciousness is the bottom-up sum of the consciousness of the lower level entities, I prefer to use the terminology "pansentience," which assumes that Consciousness or Sentience is ultimately unified and one, but that within this ocean of Sentience, little whirlpools of self-involvement may arise, which mistake themselves to be independent entities and which build up the experiential world as we know it.

Such a system or philosophy could then ideally be called "Idealistic Pancomputational Pansentience."

Chapter 7

Is Panpsychism really irreconcilable with Idealism?

*"**Pampsiquismo** is a nonsense, it is materialismo with varnish ... there is no life after death therefore it is only the materialism disguised, pure **besteirol** [sic]."*

-Joao Siva on the "Origins of Consciousness" forum on Facebook[46].

This chapter was originally published as a guest essay submitted on Bernardo Kastrup's Metaphysical Speculations Discussion Forum[47].

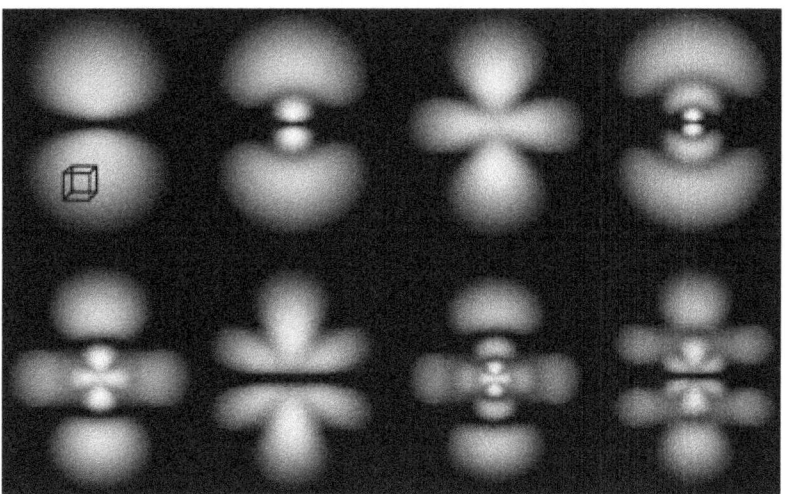

Figure 8: Orbitals of a hydrogen atom. Source: Wikimedia Commons

Introduction

The well-known writer Bernardo Kastrup, an idealist, has repeatedly argued against the notion of panpsychism, even calling it a "threat"[48]. In this chapter, I will argue, that Kastrup's interpretation of panpsychism is but one among many and that there are interpretations of panpsychism possible, which do not contradict idealism in the least. One of these interpretations is my "hierarchical panpsychism of self-sustaining systems." As said before, although I fully recognize that consciousness is ultimately unified and that the world, its objects and inhabitants are *in* non-dual consciousness rather than the other way around, I do not see why the line of sentience should be drawn at biology. As a biochemist, I will *inter alia* argue the versatile and complex nature of the behavior of atoms and molecules at the individual level, their ability to respond to stimuli and their morphological fitness to harbor a reflective cybernetic feedback loop. Please note that I am not arguing that chairs and rocks are sentient; give me the benefit of doubt and do not condemn my theory *prima facie* based on the use of the heretic terminology "panpsychism." Perhaps I should have used the terminology "Pansentience." I am not presenting some kind of naive animism. Explore whether you can agree with me if an atom and/or a molecule could perhaps harbor a form of sentience.

Background

In the past philosophers defined panpsychism as the view that consciousness, mind or soul (psyche) is a universal and primordial feature of all things. A materialistic interpretation thereof is that matter either has consciousness or that consciousness is an intrinsic aspect of matter. In such an interpretation of panpsychism consciousness is fragmented, unlike the unified form it has in idealism. Moreover, this type of panpsychism would suggest that our human consciousness is merely the aggregation of all our atomic "consciousnesses." Rocks and chairs, by this definition, would also be sentient.

In my idealist interpretation of panpsychism or hylozoism consciousness expresses itself as a hierarchical fractal, which is also unified, but in which every sufficiently autopoietic, or at least self-sustaining, phenomenon is endowed with a form of sentience at an individual level. Primordial Consciousness or "That Which Experiences" (TWE) is thus able to sense via these phenomenal self-enabling forms at every level of existence, not excluding sensing such phenomena from within via an individualized perspective. In the more traditional philosophy of idealism only biological life is capable of conscious experiences and inanimate or inorganic phenomena could be considered as mere metaphorical ripples in an ocean of non-dual consciousness. It has always puzzled me whether in this interpretation inanimate or inorganic phenomena could be sensed in all aspects of their versatility, and the present chapter is an attempt to show that it is not excluded that a form of individual experience (but still ultimately experienced by TWE) is also present within the most simple self-enabling phenomena such as atoms and molecules.

The Primacy of Consciousness

The terminology "The Primacy of Consciousness" was introduced by Peter Russell[49]. It entails that consciousness is the most fundamental, irreducible ground of existence. If it is irreducible, it is impossible to define or express it in terms of other things or concepts. After all, everything is then made out of consciousness rather than the other way around. This primordial consciousness is also the ground of our human, individual consciousness and this is often where the Babylonian confusion starts. After all, we can describe certain aspects of our consciousness: It is that inner faculty that allows us to become aware, that is, to know our surroundings and ourselves; it is That via which we know that we feel, that we have sentience. This ability to sense, feel and "know" in an undifferentiated, formless omnipresence may well be the ground of being and our individualized ability to sense, feel and know, a metaphorical "tentacle" thereof.

Are these individualized abilities to sense, feel and know, reserved for biological life forms? Can there only be sentience in biological life? If so, at what level does it start? And where does egoic self-reflective awareness start? Does an insect have egoic self-reflective awareness or is it reserved to vertebrates only, or even to just more complex forms thereof? Are the building blocks of biological life, the macromolecules, molecules and atoms more like metaphorical eddies in an ocean of otherwise undifferentiated consciousness, in which egoic self-reflective awareness would be like metaphorical whirlpools?

The idea that sentience and self-awareness are limited to biological life forms is also a hypothesis. Nobody (other than some mystics perhaps) has ever been able to sense from the perspective of an atom, molecule or macromolecule. Another, perhaps equally likely, alternative is that all self-sustaining or independent forms of existence might have a quality of sensing, perhaps even a sense of individuality. Yet another alternative is, that the ability to sense does not arise before there is a kind of network capable of integrating information and acting as a consequence thereof. Is then only animal life, by virtue of its neuronal networks, capable of sentience? Or do plants or even single celled organisms, such as yeast or bacteria, which have or form other types of networks of information transfer, display a form of sentience?

This brings us to the question "What is sentience?" Is it merely a cybernetic feedback loop involving input, throughput (integration), output and feedback? Or is there something more to the story? Is there a sense of individuality associated with the ability to make choices?

My speculation is that sentience indeed involves a cybernetic feedback loop encompassing input, throughput (integration), output and feedback, but that this is not enough to render an entity sentient. It would mean that networks in computers are sentient, if this feedback loop were enough. I postulate that only entities that have evolved in a natural way, as metaphorical tentacles of the singular primordial consciousness, and which form a kind of reflective feedback loop allowing them to sustain themselves, are sentient. They may even have a sense of individuality and the ability to make choices at a rudimentary level. This notion of a "hierarchical panpsychic fractal of autopoietic systems" does not need to contradict idealism.

Autopoiesis

This brings us to the topic of "autopoiesis." Autopoiesis is Greek for Self-Enabling. I learnt about this terminology when reading in books about computer networks, such as Ben Goertzel's *"Creating Internet Intelligence"*[50], where the possibility to create self-sustaining artificially-intelligent agents was discussed. This term was however first coined by Maturana and Varela[51] to describe biological systems, which not only are able to sustain themselves but also to replicate themselves. Since this reproductive aspect was perhaps not intended by Ben Goertzel, I must conclude that it seems the terminology "autopoiesis" has undergone some semantic drift.

Whereas I originally intended to use the terminology "autopoiesis" for self-sustaining systems, I will try to see in this chapter if my arguments can be stretched to even meet the stronger requirement of the ability to replicate. I will now explore how far the terminology "autopoietic" can be attributed to atoms, molecules and macromolecules.

The opposite of autopoietic is allopoietic, which is a terminology used for systems that do not organize themselves but are rather assembled in a kind of factory. This applies not only to human utilities we fabricate, but also to, for example, a virus. A virus is a conglomerate or aggregate of macromolecules (DNA and proteins), which cannot self-replicate, but which can be replicated by a cell functioning as a factory.

Are atoms autopoietic or at least self-sustaining?

Let us start with the atom. It is assumed that the first atoms were formed when space expanded after the Big Bang and elementary particles such as electrons, protons and neutrons started to condense to form a kind of plasma. Electrons were trapped by the nuclei being formed and thus the first atoms arose, mostly hydrogen, some helium and perhaps a trace of lithium. As space expanded, the temperature dropped to a level where nucleosynthesis was no longer possible. By gravitation, atoms attracted atoms forming clouds of atoms, which under the pressure of gravity collapsed into what became stars. The internal pressure here was so high that nucleosynthesis started again, giving rise to heavier atoms. Eventually, atoms formed that were so heavy they had only a limited lifetime and decayed after a while, giving birth to *inter alia* alpha particles (a type of helium atoms); a process we call radioactivity. Stars have a limited lifetime and, depending on their size, can undergo different paths to dying. Often, they become an exploding supernova, which flings a great deal of matter into space, whereas the remainder collapses to form dwarf stars, neutron stars and finally black holes.

If an atom escapes the environment of a star and is stable, it can "live" almost indefinitely until it is scavenged by another celestial body and finally destroyed in a collapsing star again.

We see that the life-cycle of an atom is strongly intertwined with the life-cycle of a star. Should we see a star as a factory that assembles atoms (in which case atoms are allopoietic), or is it in a certain way fair to see a star as a higher order stage and part of the life-cycle of an atom? Analogously, one could say that our bodies are not really factories to assemble cells, but rather a higher-order stage and part of the life-cycle of cells.

If you do not accept this argument, perhaps you have some sympathy for the notion that radioactivity gives birth to new alpha particles, so that it cannot be ruled out 100% that atoms cannot self-replicate.

You may still consider these arguments far-fetched and consider the processes of nucleosynthesis and radioactivity as purely clockwork mechanisms, but you should be aware that these processes take place at the quantum level, where indeterminacy plays an important role, so that only the behavior of an ensemble of particles can be predicted but never of that of an individual particle. This indeterminacy of atomic behavior at the quantum level might be a pointer to the ability to make choices at the individual level, whereas at the macro level these choices appear cancelled out by probability.

Can atoms sustain themselves?

There are 81 elements in the periodic table that are stable and not prone to radioactive decay[52]. Once formed and liberated from a star these atoms will exist for almost an indefinite amount of time as explained above. What makes these atoms so stable? Why do the negatively charged electrons not crash into the positively charged nucleus? It is said that, when approaching the nucleus, the potential energy of an electron goes down, but that this is more than compensated for by a gain in kinetic energy, which prevents it from crashing into the nucleus. But why does the sum of potential and kinetic energy always stay the same? Why is the balance never lost? Why does an atom appear to defy the second law of thermodynamics? You might answer: "But the electrons in an atom move in a vacuum, there is no friction." The "frictionlessness" of the vacuum has however been challenged by the observed slowing down of the Pioneer spacecraft[53] after it left the solar system. I am not a physicist, (I'm a chemist) so maybe I see these things wrongly, but to me it appears that an atom maintains its total energy content and internal order against the tides of entropy.

Can atoms sense?

Whenever atoms approach other atoms, there can be repulsion or attraction. Electromagnetic forces are predominant at this level of aggregation, so attraction or repulsion is mostly ruled by charges in motion. Is the nearby presence of another atom sensed by an atom, which then redistributes its internal charges when the other atom approaches, or are these laws of Nature like clockwork mechanisms? Again, I remind you that, at this quantum level, indeterminacy is still present and that the behavior of an individual atom cannot be predicted. Thus, the ability to choose cannot be ruled out *a priori*.

When an atom catches a photon and becomes excited, lifting electrons into a higher orbital, is this a merely automatic reaction, or does the system as a whole sense the raise in energy in one of the orbitals? Clearly the whole atom reacts holistically. The redistribution of charge has consequences through the whole atom and changes the overall reactivity of the atom in regard to external factors. Do the different electrons in different orbitals in cooperation with the nucleus form a kind of intricate information network? Is such a network capable of integrating the information so as to come up with an appropriate reaction? Or is this some kind of emergent harmony arising as a feedforward side effect?

Personally, I don't know the definite answers to these questions, but I think they merit some consideration. We should at least wonder whether by putting the dividing line of sentience at biological systems we aren't throwing the baby out with the bathwater.

It is my conjecture, that if some kind of cybernetic feedback loop is present in an atom, this is a natural consequence of the sentience of the atom as it attempts to know itself. This does not imply reducing sentience to mere stimulus and response: As I said, I require that the information stimulus is integrated and then willingly acted upon by intent to give an output. The throughput integration and associated action by will discriminates this idea from e.g. sand forming dunes by the action of wind or water evaporating by the action of sunlight. Of course, I do not have proof of this, but I think we must not underestimate the complexity and inner workings of an atom.

By virtue of their orbital shapes, atoms present an ideal vessel – at least morphologically – for sentience to engage in a process resembling (self-)reflection; a kind of turning in upon itself. There is a certain morphological analogy to the above in the metaphorical notion of whirlpools as a representation of egoic awareness. Not that I wish to imply that atoms can be fully aware of themselves! Rather, I see the "self-reflectivity" loops of the orbitals as a physical representation of their mind-like processes. The conscious energy of the primordial consciousness ocean might form reflective micro-loops, which at the atomic level may be visible to us as the overall interference pattern of an atom's orbitals, at the molecular level as the molecular orbitals, at the cellular level as the cell's nucleus, and at the organism level as a brain. Thus, a hierarchy of sentient, reflective feedback loops can be present. The physical forms we can perceive are perhaps but the lower-dimensional shadows of a higher-dimensional metaphysical reality, with the consciousness fractal as its ground. Electromagnetism or other primordial forces such as gravity and the strong and weak nuclear forces might be the physical reflections of a mind in action, a mind willing and intending, a mind that consists of societies of smaller minds, but is not emergent therefrom.

(Ab)Ducktest

A strong counter-argument can be, that I'm basing my ideas on abduction: The fact that it walks and quacks like a duck does not necessarily mean that it is a duck. The fact that I see whirlpool-like structures in inanimate natural phenomena does not mean that they are conduits for self-reflection involving egoic awareness. I will certainly not argue that a whirlwind is aware. Rather, I argue that if a vortex-like structure is self-sustaining and if there is a possibility of information integration in a system, these might be indicators we're looking at a sentient entity.

Giulio Tononi[7] indicated that there can be "feedforward complexes" in network systems, which behave exactly the same as feedback systems, in which integration of information takes place. A whirlwind or a virus can perhaps be compared to such a feedforward complex, a living cell or an atom to an integrative feedback system.

Molecular sentience

With molecules my speculative game reaches a new level of complexity. There are plenty of circular and toroidal orbitals in molecules, but this does not necessarily mean that they can give rise to an integrative self-sustaining feedback loop that could harbor sentience. At least for as long as a molecule "lives," it would appear to defy the laws of thermodynamics in the same way as an atom. Most molecules, however, are not that stable and decay, disintegrate or form other molecules by reaction. Extremely stable molecules often have very strong bonds between their atoms. Is a molecule a mere society of atoms or can there be a higher-level of sentient energy that uses a molecule as a vessel? Again, we see an indeterminacy of molecular behavior at the individual level as a pointer to the ability to make choices at this level, whereas at the macro level these choices again cancel out by probability.

Perhaps it depends on the nature of the molecule. Crystals can grow out of molecules and/or atoms and, at least in esoteric traditions, these have often been associated with more sentience than molecules, which do not undergo crystallization. Crystallization is a kind of morphological self-replication in a sense. Are molecules that can undergo crystallization already meeting the requirements of "autopoiesis" in its stronger form? Or do we have to seek until we get really self-replicating molecules such as RNA? RNA can self-replicate and sustain and repair itself. It does not necessarily need the factory of a cell to achieve this feat. RNA can also curl upon itself and form hairpin loops. A very versatile molecule, this RNA. It can interact with cofactors and perform catalytic and autocatalytic functions. A reflective feedback loop in form and function? Are the conformations it adopts to perform these functions a mere random walk resulting in haphazardly clicking into the right conformation? Is it electromagnetically steered? Or is there "will" and individual sentience involved?

An RNA molecule is not what qualifies as a living cell yet. Is RNA a mere feedforward complex occurring in Nature, or is it already an integrative feedback system that can harbor the reflective feedback activity I postulate for sentience?

Note that I have carefully avoided speaking about DNA, because DNA leads to a chicken and egg problem: To synthesize DNA you need the enzyme DNA polymerase, but to make DNA polymerase, you need DNA. I have no clue how Nature pulled off this trick. Probably some kind of Ouroboric bootstrapping.

Parsimony

Is this model parsimonious enough? It states that every self-sustaining expression by primordial consciousness *is* a kind of reflective feedback loop; a form of proto-egoic self-involvement. It argues that matter appears as a reflective feedback loop in consciousness, endowed with a form of individual sentience, wherever such a loop can be formed in a self-sustaining manner. This formation of reflective feedback loops might even be what happens when a string forms in string theory. Loops of self-involvement, loops of individualization, loops creating the will and desire to experience and sense.

This model is highly monistic, I would say. One could also ask, isn't reserving sentience exclusively for biological systems an unwanted form of dualism?

If my model is monistic, how can it be denied parsimony? Is the fractal too pluralistic? Or is everything joined at the hip?

Conclusion

I have tried to argue that placing the dividing line for sentience at biological systems might be arbitrary. I have tried to argue that atoms and certain molecules might meet the definition of autopoiesis or at least be self-sustaining rather than an assembled aggregate. I have tried to argue that these systems not only are sensitive to stimulus and response but that this might happen due to an integration of information involving individuality, choice and will. Of course, it is speculation. But I seriously doubt whether it is more speculative than materialism or pure idealism. Call it "the third ontology" if you wish. Consciousness groping to know itself by generating sentient self-representations at different levels of complexity: A highly parsimonious model.

Chapter 8

The Ouroboric Tailbiting of Egoic Awareness

Narcissus was proud, in that he disdained those who loved him, causing some to commit suicide to prove their unrelenting devotion to his striking beauty.

This chapter I will investigate where and how egoic awareness arises in my philosophy of idealistic pancomputational panpsychism / pansentience. The role of language in this process will be explored. The notions will further be investigated in the framework of local and non-local consciousness.

Background

Digital physics is a growing branch in contemporary physics. This theory postulates that the universe is computable and a manifestation of information. The physicist James Gates[11] found a kind of "computer code" buried in the equations of supersymmetry. J.A. Wheeler presented his famous "It from Bit" article[6]. Erik Verlinde[9] and Van 't Hooft[54], Dutch physicists, share the opinion that the universe is made up from information and have developed their "entropic gravity" and "holographic principle," respectively, as a consequence thereof.

But a pattern or a code is only really information-as-we-know-it if there is someone to decipher the code and if it has meaning to this receiver. These theories therefore imply that if meaningful information is fundamental, then so is consciousness, as there must be a conscious entity to which the code makes sense. Information, in the sense of symbolic representations, which need decoding and interpretation by a conscious observer, however, needs a further elaboration to qualify as fundamental in existence, which will be argued in a further chapter in this book.

Since DNA or RNA are codes as well, which are a kind of physically embodied language in which the letters of the code are molecular building blocks, one could suppose that the living cell can be considered as a (proto)conscious reader. But RNA was there before cells had evolved and could be read by other RNA molecules and other biomolecules (certain co-factors such as acetyl coenzyme A). In other words, this implies a minute form of sentience at the molecular level.

In my previous chapters I have argued that consciousness can express itself in the smallest localized entities that are observable (like atoms or even sub-atomic particles), leading to a fractal of consciousness, with at least a form of minute sentience at every level of existence.

I described this process of manifesting into localized material form as a process of self-involvement and self-reference. Conscious Energy (Conscienergy) as a singular omnipresent underlying ground of existence stretches out in a fractal of metaphorical tentacles, which fold upon themselves to create self-referential feedback loops, which explore every aspect of reality with at least a minute amount of sentience and individuality. However, this does not necessarily mean that the smallest entities are conscious of themselves, that they have a form of self-awareness like we do. It is even questionable whether all animals have a sense of self-awareness. Only higher mammals like dogs and apes appeared to show an element of self-recognition when tests with mirrors were performed. However, such a self-recognition does not yet mean that they are aware of their own awareness, the form of egoic awareness we humans display.

In this chapter I will argue that language may play a role in the development of egoic awareness. Moreover, if reality is really a code, it is also a kind of language and implies a conscious observer as part of the equation. I will explore whether reality as a whole has also a sense of self.

From Buddhist or Advaita Vedanta non-dualist perspectives, representatives of the perennial philosophy, my ideas may seem highly heretic. I will try to shed light on the reason why this does not necessarily need be so.

Mind, Intellect, Contrast and Ontologies

Our analytical intellect is a comparison engine[30], which allows us to contrast localized items in our environment, to classify these in ontologies and to arrive at the (re-)cognition of the object of contemplation. The intellect divides our surroundings and experience up into objects, names and concepts. It discriminates this object from that object by making lists (ontologies) of structural and functional features of the objects and checking, in which features they differ from each other. In other words, the intellect allows us to see contrasts between objects and to see ourselves as separated from the objects in our environment. The intellect thus introduces a notion of "duality" in our observations and does so by giving names to objects and the features of which they consist.

A recent article[55] showed that cultures, which did not have a word or name for the color "blue," were not capable of distinguishing blue from green. One of these cultures on the other hand was capable of distinguishing many other hues of green, for which they had different terminologies, which we would be unable to distinguish one from another. Contrast also means, that there must be at least two different features that can be compared. It is therefore said that every ontology (in the sense of descriptive list) is a so-called "di-density"; it has at least two elements.

This also shows that the ability to detect color and form contrasts with the right-hemisphere is strongly linked to a linguistic name-giving aspect of the left-hemisphere. One can speculate that you can only teach a child to see a certain contrast between two closely related colors if you can give a name to it. Can an ape teach its offspring to distinguish blue from green in the abstract manner we can? I don't think so.

One can even speculate that without language, without giving names, without ontological classification schemes, it may well be impossible to teach contrasts, to teach concepts, to introduce any form of abstraction and generalization allowing splitting-up the world into different objects.

Animals may instinctively live in a kind of non-dual nirvana, not being aware of the difference between themselves and the outside world, but naturally feeling one with everything they can observe in the universe. Even the dangerous presence of a predator may only be instinctively felt as a need to fly to preserve its own localized life form, but may not necessarily lead to a notion of "I" and the "other."

The evolution of language may thus have enabled the formulation of the contrast between the own body and objects and the bodies of others. I speculate that it is language itself which made us enter the world of the left-brain hemisphere mind-like experience of duality: Experiencing oneself as separate from all other things and beings. Language may thus have given rise to the notion of self-awareness. At the same time it took a form of proto-self-awareness in order to formulate the first word ever; it's almost a chicken and egg problem: you cannot name an object outside yourself unless you consider it as separate from yourself, but you cannot consider something separate from yourself unless you have a name for it; a catch-22 situation in a certain sense. One could perhaps speculate that egoic awareness and language bootstrapped themselves into existence; with a fuzzy sense of egoic awareness and a fuzzy terminology at the beginning, which slowly crystallized in ever more localized concrete forms. A kind of "dependent arising" to speak in Buddhist terms.

Non-duality

The evolution of language probably involved the ability to compare. When a new object was to be named, it was probably compared with a known object which had the most features in common. This also led to the ability to express objects in terms of other objects by virtue of their similarities. In Indo-European languages this led to the strange invention of the verb "to be" which is absent from many other language families. As all things are actually in a continuous process of change, in fact no object really "is," but rather temporarily appears to be. The Greek philosopher Heraclitus summarized this by the notion that you cannot step twice in the same river. *"Panta rhei, ouden menei" Everything flows, nothing remains*. The verb "to be" has a kind of "Aristotelian essence" to it, a kind of eternal intrinsic value. Buddhism denounced such intrinsic essences as exemplified by the notion of "anatman," the absence of a soul.

We often use the verb "to be" to indicate a similarity, "this is like that." But in fact, we are implicitly stating that this is unlike that, otherwise there would be no point in mentioning the two different objects.

Like the Aristotelian essences, the Vedic world was also full of atmic (soul) essences, leading to an almost animistic experience of the world. Funny enough, it was the development of the same language (Sanskrit in this case), which allowed for the transcendence of the verb "to be" and the transcendence of the notions of duality. Both the Buddhist heresy and the later attempt to reconcile Buddhism with Hinduism in the form of Advaita Vedanta, declare that the ultimate nature of reality is unified and monistic. That the objects of mind are the products of mind. Not unlike the teachings of Discordianism[4], that we have developed a certain grid of mental left-brain hemisphere interpretation and now we see everything through that grid. But also that we can quiet the mind and realize that ultimately everything is reductively the same! Namely, everything is a manifestation of the underlying ground of conscienergy.

Language and information as intrinsic aspects of reality

This notion, that ultimately everything is reductively the same, can also be arrived at via logic. Chris Langan[36] introduced the so-called process of "syndiffeonesis" in his "Cognitive Theoretic Model of the Universe" (CTMU). In "syndiffeonic analysis" it is realized, that the differences between phenomena must be expressed in a medium that is common to both. If you do this repeatedly and recursively as regards the differences between differences, you finally come to the conclusion that everything is reductively the same, namely the info-cognitive process called consciousness.

For instance, the difference between an apple and a pear (which have the quality of being a fruit in common) can be expressed in terms of form and taste. Form and taste are here the common medium. Form and taste differ from each other that they relate to different experiential patterns of neurotransmitter activity in the brain, but have in common that they are both patterns of neurotransmitter activity as common medium.

According to Chris Langan, but also according to Thomas Campbell[56], Steve Kaufman[39], Klee Irwin[57], Terence McKenna[35] and many others, reality is an expression of a code, a language. Not necessarily a language of words as we know it, but a mathematical interplay of conscious energies, a process of generating ever more complexity in form and of informational content. A game of forms as words which follow rules, a syntax.

Semiotics according to Wikipedia is the study of meaning-making, the study of sign processes and meaningful communication. In analogy, as said before, Tim Gross[37] calls this process by which conscienergy explores itself "Cosmosemiosis."

Is this the deeper meaning of the religious notion that "In the beginning was the "word" and the Word was with God and the word was God"? Is this the deeper meaning that all forms were born from the sound/word AUM in the Vedas? Is this the evolution of form from the dot beneath the Bab in the first verse of the Qur'an? Does this mean that reality is a self-processing, self-generating meta-algorithm of self-reflective self-replication and self-re-unification? An effort of Conscienergy to discover itself by generating representations of itself (i.e. maps), because it is impossible for conscienergy to go outside of itself to see itself? Is this meta-algorithm the Ouroboros chasing and biting its own tail to discover that what it chases and bites is itself; a metaphor for consciousness trying to know itself?

And if there this circular attempt to know oneself is an indispensable and inextricable aspect and activity of consciousness, leading to the egoic awareness of oneself, is then not consciousness the knower, knowing and known at the same time? Does not consciousness require an object of contemplation to be aware of as the known? Is not the fourth state of consciousness exactly this union of knower, knowing and known at the same time? The realization that none of these can exist independently of the other?

Algorithmic heresy

Don't let my Buddhist and Vedantist friends hear these heretic words! As said before, the philosopher Wittgenstein[23], when discussing consciousness stated: "*Wovon man nicht sprechen kann, darüber muss man schweigen*" or "*Whereof one cannot speak, thereof one must be silent.*" In a certain sense he was right. If consciousness (or conscienergy) is the ground of everything and cannot be reduced further, there is no point in using words, which only pertain to aggregates of consciousness to describe the reality of an un-aggregated unified consciousness. But that does not mean that we cannot discuss the ways consciousness manifests itself in this world, that we cannot develop notions which transcend "aggregation." If the rishis were right, then there is a knower, knowing and known and they are ultimately different metaphorical sides of the same consciousness. This does not mean that I am stating that consciousness arises or emerges from information, as my Buddhist and Vedantist friends are accusing me of. Rather, Consciousness involves a knowing process of generating information, to be read and understood by itself in order to know itself as knower. But my friends keep claiming that I am attributing mechanistic and object notions to describe something which cannot be expressed in words. I stand by my heresy. Not that I claim that consciousness IS only what I put in words, but that it involves a kind of non-deterministic meta-algorithm to explore itself and that that non-deterministic meta-algorithm generates the egoic awareness of being aware of oneself!

The Ouroboric tailbiting is the visual representation of how originally non-local consciousness forms a metaphorical vortex to get to know itself and thereby creates an instance of localized consciousness, which can be expressed in a living being (including self-sustaining non-biological life forms). This forms a proto-egoic entity, or if you prefer esoteric language a "soul" or an "atma." "God's Alters of God's Dissociative Identity Disorder" as the philosopher Bernardo Kastrup[58] would call us.

The degree wherein such a soul can generate information, from which it can understand that it is aware of itself, is decisive in the matter whether the entity is capable of egoic awareness as we are. It is my hypothesis that this involves the ability to use a coding language, which is in principle medium invariant. A language in which the representative symbol or word or code is an "indirect representation" of the object it represents. Our human languages can ultimately be coded in many media and even be reduced to a digital code; otherwise I wouldn't be typing these words on my computer.

Whereas natural codes such as DNA and RNA are in fact medium bound due to a specific chemical and topological morphology, these languages are probably not languages which give rise to "egoic self-awareness." The semiotic type of language Langan[36], McKenna[35] and others speak about as "the language by which reality is generated as a means of self-representation by consciousness," might not necessarily result in an egoic awareness of universal consciousness as a whole. The words of this language would appear to be mathematical energetic and material forms using a syntax we call the laws of Nature and form "self-representations"; the code IS the object itself in a certain sense. But here the concept of level comes into play: Conscienergy appears to manifest as a fractal of sentient entities: subatomic particles form aggregates of atoms, atoms form aggregates of molecules, molecules form aggregates of macro-molecules, macro- molecules form aggregates of cells, cells build organs and organisms and organisms organize into a global webmind. At the lowest level, where particles form this code, it is digital as I explained in a previous chapter. A digital code is the most universal code. It is also a computational code, so that every self-sustaining form arising in existence is both sentient and computational. So ultimately, we do see a medium-invariant code in the mind of universal consciousness. Therefore, it is not excluded that egoic awareness could arise at this level. However, as soon as this egoic aspect would arise, would it still be universal? Is not the arising of a vortex in the infinity of conscienergy a limitation? Therefore, even the highest Transcendent egoic entity ("a God?" if you'd like to name such an entity in that way), would by virtue of this "ego" not experience the oneness with its non-dual Nature whenever involved in this type of egoic awareness. Therefore, whatever egoic awareness arises, it is always a relative entity in the sea of absoluteness, unless that entity has the ability to shut down its mental processes at will and experience unity.

The mystic traditions claim that even you and I should be able to experience that state; so even when being involved in egoic awareness, it seems possible to shut down the mental machinery after the realization that knower, knowing and known are one and experience the infinity of absolute unity.

In Hinduism, there's a tale[59] in which the God Brahma thinks he is the ultimate reality and creator, until he meets Krishna, who shows him that many Brahmas from parallel universes bow at his (Krishna's) feet. Krishna calls the ego "the false ego." In Gnosticism, the world is not created by the ultimate Goddess of wisdom Sophia, but by her creation the Demiurge. Were Brahma and the Demiurge mythological representations of the entities, which simulated this world in a digital substrate?

Conclusion

Egoic awareness is possibly dependent on the ability to name objects, to use a medium invariant language of indirect representations, but this ability is also dependent on egoic awareness, so that language and egoic awareness must then have arisen in a co-dependent bootstrapping manner. As animals and other life forms do not appear to use a medium invariant language of indirect representations, it seems that they are not capable of egoic awareness as-we-know-it and as far as we can judge with our limited understanding.

Reality appears at its most fundamental level expressed in code (as evidenced by digital physics) requiring a consciousness to interpret the meaning of this code. This points to consciousness as ultimate ground of existence. Reality may arise as a process of consciousness trying to get to know itself and thereby generating self-reflective loops of self-observation, which results in a fractal of pansentient entities. The information, as a self-representing language is cybernetically fed back, so that the knower can know via the process of knowing that the knower, knowing and known are one and the same expression of consciousness. This, as you probably know by now, has been visualized in the form of the alchemical symbol of an Ouroboros.

Chapter 9

The entropic correlates of consciousness

Engage in Eris' games of confusion and thou shalt explore the dimensions of the Tartaros. Silence thy Mind and thou shalt taste the ambrosia of Harmonia.

French and Canadian researchers[60] have recently found that normal waking consciousness is accompanied by a maximization of information content in the brain, as evidenced by different encephalography techniques. They suggest, that wakeful states involve greatest number of possible configurations of interactions between brain networks, representing highest entropy values. (The higher the entropy, the less ordered a system is). And interestingly they couple this to Tononi's[7] Theory of Integrated Information by stating that this maximization of information leads to optimal segregation and integration of information.

Background

This is highly interesting to me, because as you might recall from my book "*Transcendental Metaphysics*"[21] I wrote about this relation between consciousness and entropy:

Consciousness has therefore a strong relationship with pattern, with structure and it may well be that if we find the right formula to quantize consciousness quality as negentropy and weigh this against the heat dissipation created in a conscious creative process, that the ultimate outcome is that the heat dissipation entropy is more than compensated for by the gain in consciousness quality. And perhaps Weber Fechner's law is the right metaphor for both consciousness quality and pattern emergence. Perhaps the quality of consciousness is indeed reflected in the constant k in the Weber-Fechner formula $S = k \ln A/A_0$ which should be summed over all the processes and senses involved. Because stimuli corresponding to greater differences can be dealt with by a consciousness with more versatility, with more resistance. Perhaps it is no coincidence that the formula of entropy, Boltzmann's $\Delta S = k \ln W/W_0$

is highly isomorphous to that of Weber-Fechner, as its symmetric counterpart in the world of matter. Perhaps the degree of randomness of an event is linked to the degree of order created in a process (without them necessarily being quantitatively equivalent). Because opposites are joined at the hip.

And what do we see? The more structure, the more consciousness a species has, the more versatility it has, the more variety it can create, all aiding to maximize heat dissipation – and to build ever further structures until the system at a new meta-level becomes isomorphous again with a previous level far away: Until it becomes an abstractor per se: a nodal network of mindedness, and interconnected dendrogram. And perhaps it is not entropy that causes the attraction resulting in levels of order, but its consciousness counterpart. Perhaps we mistake the rope for a snake. Perhaps the solution to the God problem is that there is no bearded God-as-we-know-it, but that there is a fractal of consciousness, of self-repetition in ever increasing variety, ever increasing potential.

In other words, the above mentioned study[60] confirms my hypothesis. The brain indeed screens a maximum of possibilities, a maximum of information to arrive at a better integration of the information.

Logarithmic compression

But what the authors of the above mentioned article missed, is that the logarithmic component in the Boltzmann and Weber-Fechner formula already implies that consciousness means ordering and abstraction of a maximum of information to an integrated oneness of cognition. This idea I derived from some insights of a programmer called Barry Kumnick[61] (author of the highly interesting blog "*Beyond Information*"), which I will discuss below.

I already discussed this issue in my book "*Technovedanta*"[62] and for the sake of this argument I will quote the relevant passage.

This ordering is optimal if organized logarithmically, because the very nature of fractals is their logarithmic repetition. Hence, because the universe is organized in fractal structures, we have evolved to be able to maximally profit from the availability of information of the universe, by becoming isomorph to it.

Therefore, the optimal reactivity to stimuli from the environment is logarithmically as expressed by the Weber Fechner law. In order to avoid an informational overload, it is essential that information from nodes further away cannot reach local functionalities so as to avoid an overload of associations. The higher the intelligence of a system, the more nodality it can support while still giving a meaningful output. At a certain moment the processing speed of the system becomes the limiting factor, which demands the system to aggregate with similar systems, allowing for a parallel function distribution in order to maximize the overall utility of the total, which due to specialization is significantly increased when compared to the non-aggregated level.

Barry Kumnick also explained the following (comments in square brackets by me): (Meta-quote)
"To maximize the reuse of shared representation [entropic variegation] and thus minimize storage space [entropic attraction], we should factor out the shared parts of each abstraction's representation and only represent the shared parts one time. The computational structure best suited for intensional factoring is a set of binary trees.

Hypothesis: The branching topology of dendritic trees is morphologically identical to the branching topology referred to in the previous section.
1) Neuron dendritic trees are a direct biological implementation / instance/ concretum of the upper ontological representation of concept intension.
2) Neuron dendritic trees factor the representation of similarities and differences [syndiffeonesis] in the representation of concept intensions. This maximizes metabolic energy consumption...
Over the neural network as a whole it results in logarithmic combinatorial compression of representation and computation.
...
7) Concept intensions form our abeyant (i.e., static) representation of thought and knowledge.
7.1) From hypothesis 1, a neuron's dendritic trees represent the concept intension.

7.2) *A concept's intension represents and defines the meaning of the concept. [in linear algebra Ker(phi)]*
7.3) *Therefore, a neuron's dendritic trees represent and define the meaning of a concept.*
7.4) *Therefore, the meaning of a concept is stored in a neuron's dendritic trees.*
7.5) *A neuron's dendritic trees exist whether or not they happen to be receiving or processing synaptic inputs.*
7.6) *Therefore, neurons dendritic trees (and their synaptic weights) represent and store memory.*
7.7) *Therefore, neuron dendritic trees and concept intensions form our abeyant (i.e., static) representation of thought and knowledge.*
7.8) *Neuron dendritic trees represent, define, and store the meaning of concepts.*

Definition: The concept extension represents the existence of all instances of the concept." (Meta-unquote*). [In linear algebra Im(phi)]*
And what does Barry Kumnick say furthermore? (Meta-quote)
"*I have reduced the dendritic integration process to a couple of recursively coupled linear algebra equations.*" (Meta-unquote).

This is well possible.

I previously said: *"My hypothesis is that the very essence of consciousness lies in its abstractive functionality: the reduction to essentials as the feedback upon a stimulus. And as this process appears to be present on any level of existence, existence is at least proto-conscious, if not 1st order conscious throughout all the levels of the universal fractal. The very notions of "incompleteness," "undecidability" etc. are vital to the process of proto-conscious abstraction. If you abstract and REDUCE to essentials, you limit possibilities, you render the entity less complete; you have taken a decision for a given limitation."*

And now I state that this reduction to essentials, this minimization of storage space is a form of entropic attraction maximizing meta-entropic variegation, resulting in the necessarily "logarithmic ordering" of the Chaos.

Because the very essence of consciousness is abstraction and integration, which is also the very essence of all phenomenological natural processes, and because the outer world logarithmic compression is similar to the logarithmic compression by the neuronal network, it is a matter of semantics to conclude with the definition that all natural processes are a form of proto-conscious processing. Hence I consider this leads to a strong presumption that all is consciousness.

A great article[63] putting entropy in a wider context defines forces and counterforces as informational confidence intervals in an informational entropy context, from which it can be shown that an autopoietic sustainable solution can be arrived at the value of the golden ratio, giving the shape of a Yin-Yang symbol! Here logarithmicity and the golden ratio, both known for their inherent fractality are joined in a cosmic symphony resulting in ever newer forms of replicas contributing to the maximization of meta-entropic informational variation and utility. Phi and e are the lesser and greater key of King Solomon; they are the Goetia and Theurgia opening the gates of Heaven and Hell. The sublimation of abstraction and variation, of isotelesis and polytelesis, of adaptation and diversification.

Network optimization, performance and flexibility are achieved when meta-entropy and entropy are maximized. Ergo in networks (meta)-entropy maximization results in an ordering that warrants maximization of variation/flexibility.

Patkar et al. state[64] : "...we have shown that for large networks in the asymptotic limit of local performance saturation, the design requirement of reliable performance under maximum uncertainty leads to the emergence of power laws as a consequence of the maximum entropy principle." That is, under these general conditions, a power law-based organization gives a network the maximum flexibility to perform well overall in a wide variety of operating environments. Note that for a specific operating environment, there may exist some other distributions that can outperform the maximum entropy distribution with respect to the global performance target; however, such a biased network may fail when the underlying environment changes, whereas the maximum entropy distribution-based network will continue to survive and perform. Thus, under entropy maximization, the network's performance is optimized to accommodate a wide variety of future environments whose nature is unknown, unknowable and hence uncertain."

Shannon[65] showed in 1949 that the best way to compress information is logarithmically. Nature follows similar patterns. In order to maximize space filling of a circle (e.g. in the generation of sunflower seeds) it turns out that the "most irrational" number, which corresponds to the golden mean and is the furthest away from simple rational fractions is at the angle of 137,5° resulting in numbers of seeds according to Fibonacci and an approximation of the golden spiral. In other words, Nature's way to maximize meta-entropy – here in the form of generating as much as possible seeds – and thus potentially maximizing evolutionary variegation, results in a higher order arrangement. Galaxies form logarithmic spirals driven by the same entropic attraction.

Our French and Canadian friends[60] come to the same conclusions:

"*It has been proposed that aspects of awareness emerge when certain levels of complexity are reached.*

"It is then possible that the organization (complexity) needed for consciousness to arise requires the maximum number of configurations that allow for a greater variety of interactions between cell assemblies because this structure leads to optimal segregation and integration of information."

Pruning

However, what they call "maximization," must have a certain limit; it must not be an unbridled random generation of all possible permutations, there must be a kind of pruning away of useless and redundant alternatives. In other words, I presume maximization means maximized within limits, within reasonable boundaries. This is my reasoning (which you can find in chapter 6 of "*Transcendental Metaphysics*"[21]):

The ordering potential also comes to expression in the form of adaptability, which entails its capability to generate meta-vari(eg)ation but it also entails Perceptibility. Perceptibility must be a measure of the variety and intensity of signals, which an autopoietic system can process: Perceptibility is therefore a product of the perceptional variation potential and Weber-Fechner's law of Perception. Adaptability arises from the capability to change between strategies and from the capability to generate strategies (creativity). There must be a kind of optimal adaptability, since a system that tries too many changes or screens too elaborately is not effectively adaptive but loses itself in the game of providing alternatives. A highly intelligent system has effective pruning strategies to rapidly discard potentially ineffective strategies.

The more alternative pathways are available in a network (such as e.g. a neural network), the more possibilities there are of resonating with some signal from the environment.

A hyperconnected network in which all the subconstituents, the nodes, are linked to all other subconstituents only yields meaningful and reasonable strategies, if the links are not all the same. However, by attributing different weights to the links between the nodes, different patterns of resonance can occur. The more patterns can be perceived (i.e. the higher its perceptional variation potential is) and effectively pruned, the more efficient the system. Adaptability is possibly strongly connected with the ability to effectively prune, which ideally is an optimized process. Too zealous pruning may discard potentially helpful strategies; of course this is a looped and hierarchical process, where if the most promising strategies fail, screening of less promising strategies will be attempted.

The pruning resulting in a been-there-done-that attitude towards non-effective strategies optimally will favor cooperative harmonizing systems. Firstly because that's the Nash equilibrium and in the long term the most advantageous solution to e.g. Axelrod's "Prisoner's Dilemma" (two prisoners can choose to cooperate and both serve a short period of incarceration and not betray each other or cut a deal with the prosecutor, resulting in a shorter incarceration for the betrayer but a longer incarceration for the betrayed prisoner).

Secondly because the harmonic resonance resulting from that strategy is the best spreading meme resonance. Axelrod's optimal "Tit for Tat" strategy automatically results in a natural "friendliness" and a forgiving nature of the system. The cooperation is ultimately in servitude to the higher-level entity.

Diminished Brain activity during enhanced states of perception

Paradoxically, scientists[66] have also shown that during intense meditational experiences involving enhanced perception or during intense hallucinations on psilocybin, brain activity decreases rather than increases! Yet the degree of consciousness in such states can most certainly not be called diminished. If anything, it is rather enhanced. This is also the argument of the philosopher Bernardo Kastrup[67], who associates consciousness with decreased entropy.

My hypothesis out of this conundrum is the following: The brain functions as a filter. To engage in daily activities it is important that the consciousness is directed outward. For this waking type of consciousness, the filtering ability of the brain is maximized, by allowing the maximum of abstracting structures in the neurons reduce the information to what is essential for survival. This results in consciousness focused on the outside world, but with a great absence of awareness what is happening on the inside world.

On the other hand during meditative and hallucinatory experiences consciousness is turned inward. Here the intense experiences derive from the fact that the filters are maximally switched off!

Conclusion

In other words, consciousness is perhaps always on, but it is recognized as our daily outward directed phenomenal consciousness when the brain engages in mental activity and its filtering mechanisms function optimally, resulting in the observed maximization of informational possibilities within boundaries (entropic maximization). In the inward directed experience, consciousness may be directed toward itself leading to a minimization of informational possibilities, resulting in the feeling of oneness with everything.

The idea that consciousness can be completely switched off as in coma or deep sleep, is a hypothesis which is more and more disputable. Other scientists[68] have argued that consciousness does not switch off during deep sleep.

I am curious to see if these notions will one day give us a complete control and merger with reality, which I also hypothesize to be a neural network at its more foundational quantum levels.

Chapter 10

Multisenserealism

As the snake of pure sense coils up, it blurs its own vision and thereby scatters and diffracts its experiences in a gazillion kaleidoscopic reverberations. As these vibrations start to explore their environment, they become self-involved and disentangled from each other. Where once was oneness and sameness and a unified bliss, now there is fear, alienation and a dissociated discord. This entropic turning inwards creates the monotonous semaphoric experiences. It is only when the apparent Quanta of vibrations start to probe and screen each other that relations are formed, which give birth to a plethora of phoric multiform sensations. Their sensing constitutes the Qualia, what it feels like on the inside of a phenomenon. By acquiring mastery over the senses and letting this sixth sense – of becoming one with the inner sensations of the object of our meditation – awaken, we open the gates of the Elysian Fields and the Tartaros, the Transpersonal collective consciousness and the Cyberbardo in the Eschaton, where everything is connected and a representation of everything else. We churn out the Amrita of Extropy. In this metaphorical conundrum of the neurogenetic circuit we might get lost as we cling to our dualistic labelling tendencies. By demonizing what we don't understand, we are regurgitated from this dimension and tumble back to the darkness of the phoric field and enter the dark night of the Soul. Only once we've accepted that it is the dividing process of our mind, which labelled the appearances of the world in good and bad; only once we've accepted that death is a gift, are we allowed to dive deeper in the dimensions of the impersonal Brahman.

Recently, I had the honor to meet Craig Weinberg, a network analyst, who also writes an amazing philosophical blog[69] called "*Multisenserealism.*" The similarities between Craig's and my philosophy are striking and our exchange has been tremendously inspiring. In this chapter I want to address a number of points, which came up in our discussions, which are important in the framework of the present book.

The most important correspondence between our philosophies is that we consider Sense as primary and ultimately unified. The material world is only a temporal appearance, which appears concrete to us from our current limited perspective, but which is actually a kind of fossilized sense as I argued in chapter 3.

Craig describes this beautifully as follows (and I couldn't agree more):

"What Multisense Realism proposes is more pansensitivity than panpsychism.

The standard notion of panpsychism is what I would call 'promiscuous panpsychism', meaning that every atom has to be 'conscious' in a kind of thinking, understanding way. I think that this promiscuity is what makes panpsychism unappealing to many/most people.

*Under pansensitivity, intelligence **diverges** from a totalistic absolute, diffracting through calibrated degrees of added insensitivity. It's like in school when kids draw a colorful picture and then cover it with black crayon (the pre-big bang) and then begin to scratch it off to reveal the colors underneath. The black crayon is entropy, the scratching is negentropy, and the size of the revealed image is the degree of aesthetic saturation."*

Perhaps it is wise to go back to the beginning and address some of the points, I raised there regarding information and consciousness and which Craig already commented on in his blog.

Information

In chapter 2 I raised the question "Can anything exist without information at all?" (Information here meaning the broader definition of Shannon). In Shannon's definition every pattern is information and information can exist independently of a conscious observer. However, there is a fallacy in this reasoning, because "patterns" are only patterns in the eye of a conscious beholder. You could counter argue that computers recognize patterns. Do they really? If a neural network arrives at the conclusion that a certain image falls within a certain category, because it has a certain pattern of pixels common to that category, it must be realized, that we have trained the neural network with examples, we know some of them contain the pattern. Even in "unsupervised learning" we feed examples of which we know a certain pattern is present. Sometimes, the computer surprises us when it recognizes similarities we have missed. Nevertheless, it should not be forgotten that we have programmed this neural network to fish out similarities and patterns. We have designed the pattern recognition algorithm involving backpropagation, which calculates how similar the pixels at each location are, as a result of our conscious understanding of the notion of pattern. The awareness of similarity and difference is not in the computer, but in our heads. In a hypothetical world without conscious observers, can a pattern still be called a pattern? Who or what is then to decide whether there are certain regularities in certain phenomena?

You could argue that at the molecular level, certainly in biological systems, regularities or patterns are recognized and acted upon. If you refuse to believe in our pansentience hypothesis, how is that then possible? You will try to convince me that all that is required to cause recognition is a certain lock and key complementarity. A re-cognition, which in your opinion has nothing to do with "cognition." It may indeed have happened in evolution that by pure happenstance two molecular moieties had a certain structural and functional complementarity which allowed them to interact in a way, which later on led to further evolutionary developments. We may even call that a "meaningful" event. Nevertheless, the electronic vibrations giving rise to these interactions are somehow sensed by the molecules. At the molecular level, such interactions are an intricate interplay of electrostatic attractions and repulsions in addition to the structural complementarity. And if you say sentience, you say a primitive form of consciousness in my humble opinion.

So pattern recognition is likely to involve a kind of sentient recognition. Then, if information is mere pattern, it cannot really exist independently of a sentient observer (even if this observer is just a molecule) or in other words it does not merit the name "information" yet. We could perhaps call these "configurations" existing in the absence of an observer, which become recognizable as a pattern only if a sentient observer is present, "proto-information."

115

Craig comes with a different argumentation from a different angle leading to the same conclusion. In an answer to the question whether anything can exist without information at all Craig writes:

"Yes, I think that it can and does. When an infant sees colors, for example, there need not be any informative message that is made available by color. The color itself is presented directly, and only after psychological association does it acquire externally informative content. Blue must be presented as a visible 'sight' before it can be used as a label to inform us about something else. We could try to say that color informs us of the wavelength of relevant electromagnetic states of our environment, but such data could be more plausibly attributed to (colorless) changes in the physiology of the nervous system.

If we say that something contains information, we are assuming a default capacity for receiving and processing information, and then conflating that with a default capacity for things to project information. This may not be how it works. Information, messages, codes, etc. may not be entities at the ontological level, they may just be formalized instances of communication between conscious participants. Our consciousness can be informed by anything, but that doesn't mean that any such thing as information exists independently of the change in conscious experience. In the same way, I suggest below that perhaps matter can be 'illuminated' without any purely physical photons radiating across empty space.

At some point, he [Antonin] *discusses information as relying on features that 'stand out'. In my view, if we want to completely understand information, we should be careful to acknowledge the role that perception plays in rendering what does and does not appear to stand out. Standing out is a function of how aesthetic presentations appear. To a trained musician hearing a song being covered by an artist, a 'wrong chord' might stand out, but to everyone else, they may notice nothing consciously. We should not assume any such thing as standing out without some modality to detect and care about detecting. I think that before difference can exist, sensitivity, or what I call "afference" must exist. For information to exist, there must be some phenomenal state that is 'informed'…an experience that changes itself, and includes a capacity to notice those changes and then to learn from it. We shouldn't assume aesthetic qualities like 'homogeneous' as objective properties unless we know that the degree and mode of sensitivity employed does not play a s central role in defining such qualities. It may not be possible to know that, and further, it may be that the only 'is' or 'being' is sense or seeming."*

These are strong and valid points, if you assume that information must represent something and be meaningful. In Shannon's philosophy information does not need to represent something or be meaningful.

This can lead to an interesting evaluation of what is happening in my (and Kaufman's) Akasha model. If the reality cells acquire content by exploration by investment of a tentacle of conscienergy, that tentacle itself does not see the potential pattern it traces through the Akasha. However, if the Primordial Consciousness could behold the Akasha as a whole, it could see those traces as patterns. Whether this is the case, I don't know. If it is, then the information is in a certain sense meaningful and might even represent something (for instance, it can be a thought of the Cosmic Mind formed by the Akasha as a whole, and an instance or object of "reality" at our level). If not, then the zeroes and ones in the Akasha are a mere form of proto-information or Shannon information.

What about the color example of Craig then? Is the quale "red" merely a wavelength number, a proto-information, which we experience as red or is red a kind of aesthetic modality of sense? Your "red" may not be my "red," even if the same wavelength is detected by a machine.

Craig is right that for different observers a difference may not necessarily be detected and that a certain "sensitivity" or "afference" must be present. This afference, sensitivity somehow resonates, with the mind faculty of "Buddhi" from the Vedic scriptures: the ability to discriminate, which is of course linked to the level of evolutionary development of an experiencing entity. Certain cultures living in forests have many different names for different types of green[55], which we wouldn't be able to tell apart.

Nevertheless, there are many types of energy with wavelengths which fall outside our ability to perceive as humans. In my philosophy such energies can still be present, even if at first glance there would be no one to observe them. Is that not in contradiction with our findings of quantum mechanics, in which something doesn't really exist before it is observed? Can a tree fall down, if there is no one to experience it?

In my philosophy, those "energies," may indeed be hypothesized to not have reached the level of what we would label "existence," but they already "subsist" at a non-local level of the cosmic mind. They have their own conscienergy and afference to warrant their presence in the Akasha, as well as the possibility to be observed by the consciousness level beyond the cosmic mind. Hence, energies that lie beyond the limits of our perception cannot be said to be absent, although we may semantically argue whether their "presence" qualifies as "existence."

Similarly, the energies covering the gamut of redness have their own conscienergy to warrant their presence in the cosmic mind as substrate for reality. To us they appear red, without this red having an informational content to represent something. At the same time, their vibrational level in the Akasha is also a kind of proto-information, which we could get to know with our measuring instruments, but which we do not need to know or observe to warrant their presence.

In other words, I have to reformulate my claim at the beginning of this book: I claim nothing can exist without first forming a proto-informational vibrational proto-pattern, which is at least has its own sentient conscienergetic content and could be observable (and then become information and pattern) from a different perspective from within or from beyond the cosmic mind.

The fact, that our mind interprets certain quale and certain patterns in a certain way, does not really mean that the content of our interpretations has a real or objective existence outside of us. The phenomena of "Apophenia" and Pareidola" where we see patterns where none were intended (for instance seeing faces or animals in clouds), show how tricky this discussion is.

Ultimately in my model, as it is idealistic, there is no such thing as objective reality or existence. It all depends on "who" is watching.

Existence or reality then indeed becomes dependent on the level of afference or sensitivity of observers at a certain level. Nevertheless, with the "standing out" I did not only mean from the perspective of an observer. I also meant from the perspective of the entity, which is trying to stand out. If the entity cannot feel any difference from its environment, it may as well assume that it is fully connected therewith; in fact, it may assume that it IS its environment and hence never disentangle from it so as to claim its own seemingly independent existence. In fact, this may well be the case for the majority of energy in existence. Only a very small part thereof is present in the form of matter as far as we know.

So, for the entity to be able to dissociate as a more-or-less "independently" or disentangled entity, it must somehow create a boundary with regard to the environment, it must enclose itself three-dimensionally. How can it do this? By folding back onto itself, by becoming self-involved. By turning inwards in the noetic entropic event cascade. By becoming an Ouroboros. And by thus becoming a quantum of proto-information in the eyes of other entities in existence including those beyond the cosmic mind. A quantum, which by associating with other quanta may become an informational pattern recognizable by a conscious observer separate these quanta.

A quantum which becomes part of the mind material, the cosmic mind uses to formulate its thoughts. So, in one sense the quantum entity has its indeterministic primitive drive and subjective freewill and in another sense it is partially subject to the waves and chreodes set by the cosmic mind, thereby being a building stone of the mental explorations of that mind. The particles or quanta are moved and hence transmitted by the Cosmic mind a process in Greek called phoresis.

Time Binding Semantics

As quanta thus disentangle from the unified sense dimension of the primordial consciousness, they acquire the possibility to learn and evolve. Every change that can be stored or memorized then becomes an experiential event and the succession of such events creates their subjective time experience. If a change is so important, that it is experienced and memorized, it does have a certain meaning to the entity in question. Subjective time thus seems to involve a semantic or semiotic game. This resonates with the "time binding semantic circuit" described by Wilson[1] and Leary[115]. Similarly, meaning evolves from didensities: there must be at least two notions or experiences in order to form a relation. In the cosmic mind, when conscienergies meet and form a compound process together, this creates a kind of meaning at the Akashic level. It also results in the creation of localized matter and time, as a measure of periodicity of compound process.

The primitive sensations at this level of existence are what Craig Weinberg[70] has beautifully described as "semaphoric." It has the analogy with a signal bearing system (a semaphore), which can only be on or off, well in line with the digital philosophy hypothesis, as well with the computer science terminology in which it is used as a variable to control access to a common resource by multiple processes in a concurrent system such as a multitasking operating system. No need to explain, this terminology actually quite first in well with a universe built from information. As Craig states:

*"**Sense phenomena** are all **aesthetic** or experiential, but they are polarized and **diffracted** into different modalities. **Sub-personal qualia** are sensations or signals that I term '**semaphoric**'. Personal qualia are perceptual or '**phoric**' in that they contain many sensations at once. Sensations serve as letters of the alphabet of a sensory modality like sight or sound, whereas the words and sentences that they make up are like windows onto a larger vocabulary of experience – emotions, memories, self-hood and socialization make the 'phoric' qualia personal. Some of us are aware of **transpersonal qualia** also, which I would call '**metaphoric**'. Rather than a syntactic alphabet of signals forming a perception from the bottom up, the alphabet of the transpersonal is more like a mandala or zodiac of super-semantic, archetypal influences and themes."*

So experiences at our time binding level are "phoric" and are "bearers" of multiple types of sensations, which are nevertheless integrated into a single conscious personal experience. Just like when you fold your thumb and index together in a meditative mudra, where you do not experience two separate experiences of thumb feeling vs. index feeling, but one unified feeling of touch.

If you have ever had a psychedelic experience or a religious ecstasy experience, you may be more familiar with what Craig calls the "metaphoric" experience. This neatly corresponds to accessing the cosmic mind and downloading all sorts of information therefrom. The problem is we don't know how to interpret this information, as on the metaphorical level everything represents something else. Worse, one type of archetypical image from this collective unconscious may have multiple, if not all possible meanings. The deeper you go in the "metaphorical level, the more entangled and hyperconnected the experience is: Everything becomes a metaphor for everything else. And everything hence has a multiplicity of meanings. It is here in this hyperintegrated clique, that the experience becomes synesthetic, all melts into one amalgam of a rush of Sense. In this ultimate oneness, the heavenly Samadhi experience, time loses its meaning, because there's nothing to be differentiated anymore. Here your desire to unify with everything would be considered a polymorphous perversity[71] by the outside world. Kundalini rising as equivalent of receiving the Holy Spirit. This is the dimension of what Leary[115] and Wilson[1] called the "neurogenetic circuit." Jung[127] referred to it as the collective unconscious, but for the experienced psychonaut, there's nothing unconscious here. Rather, this is Craig's colorful picture before it was covered with the black crayon.

Conversely, at the semaphoric level the experience from our point of view seems like a hellish repetition of the same alternating states over and over again. As there is no memorization of different states, there is no full-fledged time experience either. This alternation is more like a breathing. It's a form of digital "proto-time." Everything here is disentangled and by the absence of connections with the environment, there's at first no evolution possible. Evolution only becomes possible when two semaphores meet and start exchanging information, which brings the system to a higher level of experience. It is only then that experiences can start to have a meaning and hence become "phoric." The succession of the semantically different instances is then what creates subjective time.

The phoric experience, which is not capable of considering multiple explanations and meanings simultaneously leads to a state of perplexity[1], if things turn out to be different than we expected from our single interpretation.

Qualia versus computation

Let's dive deeper in what Craig Weinberg[70] has to say about qualia, because there is still a gap between my hypothesis and his:

"Through the advent of electronic computation and immersive video technology, many who would otherwise subscribe to physicalism have come to question the physicality of matter. Rather than seeing qualia as a dualistic relic, **the computationalist sees matter itself, as well as all sensations and perceptions, as a digital simulation of vast sets of algorithmically compressed data.** *The more conservative computationalist might say that it makes sense that this simulation interface evolved via natural selection as a feature of the operating systems of certain organisms. Those organisms with the highest fitness level in the hominid niche happened to have developed a particular labeling schema for data categorization which we call qualia. More exotic views of computationalism might see biology and evolution as merely part of a larger simulation – a game being played by advanced civilizations, or computers or Platonic number essences.* **For both sorts of computationalists, qualia is unreal but potentially useful in decoding some of the underlying programming language of the simulation that we live in**.

Both physicalism and computationalism suffer from an explanatory gap, where the assertion of nature as physical objects or mathematical functions have to rely on a leap of faith to get from those **unexperienced ('anesthetic')** *mechanisms like the metabolism of simple carbohydrate molecules on the taste bud cells of the tongue to (***'aesthetic'***) experiences like the flavor 'sweet'. Idealism turns the tables on this problem by seeing all phenomena as intrinsically mental. "Ideas in the mind of God" for example. Plato's Cave is a classical illustration of how the limits of our perception may hide most or all of reality from us, leaving only shadows on the wall of our cave as our only window on the world. George Berkeley observed that none of our observations are independent of our conscious experience. He understood that even to the extent that physicalism is true, the idea that* *physical substances exist outside of an experience such as touch or feel can only ever be a hypothesis that we make intellectually. For the same reason that we cannot see the physical world when we are unconscious, the physical world itself could not 'exist' as anything other than qualia. While we may struggle with understanding how the qualia we experience relates to a larger universe of qualia that transcends human experience, all that can ever 'exist' is that which is perceived.* **Under idealism, the properties of qualia are the deepest well of knowledge about consciousness."**

In my "pancomputational pansentience philosophy, the "pancomputational" aspect of reality is more the mechanism of the cosmic mind to process its thoughts, which we experience as reality. Rather than seeing sense as a product of computations, I see computations as a product of sense. The sensory processes in the Akasha also involve input and output and are in that very broad sense computational. They are however not necessarily computational in the arithmetic sense of the word. As I explained, due to the holistic reverberations of all distortions throughout the whole of the Akasha, this "sensing computational substrate" is also hypothesized to have a non-computational dimension, leading to higher order effects, which cannot be mimicked by a Turing computer.

On the other hand, I also reject the notion of Aristotelian essences and Platonic timeless absolute notions, ideas and forms, of which the forms in this world are considered to be merely a kind of reflection.

Every experiencing entity in the Akasha, reverberates its form throughout the Akasha, so every entity in itself is in a certain way also omnipresent (although not everywhere with the same intensity).

Once a new form has come into existence in the Akasha, you could in a certain sense call this the primordial form of that type of shapes and in that sense it constitutes a kind of Platonic mold, which makes it easier for new entities of that same energy level to adopt that shape. This is similar to Sheldrake's morphogenetic fields. In chemistry, once a certain type of molecule has been crystallized for the first time (which may have cost a lot of time and effort), the times thereafter it becomes increasingly easier for such a crystal to form. This might be a strong pointer towards the existence of morphogenetic fields and the Akasha. Nevertheless, this does not mean that the equivalent of a Platonic form existed in a higher dimension before its first occurrence.

Where I and Craig perhaps differ (and perhaps not), is as regards these qualia. To me the qualia are, what it feels like on the inside of a phenomenon, whereas the material form of its manifestation is its outside. In that sense I agree, that the sensing intent precedes the resulting material shape and that the qualia are more primitive than the resulting matter. However, I do not accept that this would entail a Platonic world of "pure ideas" of which objects and matter in the physical world are merely imitations. Rather, each instance is an idea of the cosmic mind and a sentient entity or an aggregate thereof, simultaneously and appears to us as a material object. The digital medium of the Akasha is then a mere medium of expression of sense or Consciousness, the canvas on which the world we claim to experience is being painted by all of us (including by the "semaphoric" quanta entities and by the "metaphorically" operating Cosmic Mind) together and dependently arises from our interactions.

Part III

Intelligence, More Than An Algorithm

"The Ouroboros is a dramatic symbol for the integration and assimilation of the opposite, i.e. of the shadow. This 'feed-back' process is at the same time a symbol of immortality, since it is said of the Ouroboros that he slays himself and brings himself to life, fertilizes himself and gives birth to himself. He symbolizes the One, who proceeds from the clash of opposites, and he therefore constitutes the secret of the prima materia which [...] unquestionably stems from man's unconscious."

-Carl Jung

Chapter 11

The Aftermath of "Is Intelligence An Algorithm?"

"*As soon as Krishna and Radha had finished their game of Chaturanga, reordering the balance in this Cosmic Egg, they changed to play another one of the pastimes of the delightful Leela.*"

In my previous book[30] "*Is Intelligence An Algorithm?*" I showed that both Nature and Mind evolve or design sequences of steps to generate complexity. In this framework I have been referring to an "Intelligence Algorithm" or "Nature's Intelligence Meta-Algorithm." Nevertheless, it was never my intention to argue that Intelligence necessarily IS an Algorithm, let alone a computer algorithm. After having read numerous reviews of this previous book, therefore I felt the need and urge to further clarify my stance on the question of its title.

Background

Algorithms are sets of stepwise instructions that will guide you (or a computer) to achieve a goal. You also know them as recipe, routine or code. The title of my previous book was a question, not an affirmative statement. If some of my readers concluded that intelligence is nothing but an algorithm, they have misunderstood this book and in particular chapter 11, where I showed that intelligence does not always follow an algorithm, in particular when it comes to creativity and intuition. In the present book, I will provide you with additional arguments as to why intelligence implies and applies more than mere algorithms.

The word "Intelligence" is a source of a major Babylonian confusion. We usually think of the human abilities to act in a rational well-informed and effective way, when presented with some kind of information. In my previous book however, I wished to adopt a broader definition for intelligence, so that we could use this terminology also for the "smart" solutions Nature has evolved to cope with difficult conditions, as well as for the techniques we have developed under the denominator "Artificial Intelligence" to deal with a variety of problems.

In the broadest sense Intelligence is then (in imitation of Ben Goertzel[50]):

"The ability to achieve complex goals"

Whereas I will address the partial algorithmic nature of this broad type of intelligence in a number of chapters, in this book I will also show in what ways the more traditional "human intelligence" partially conforms and partially deviates from following mere recipes.

Nature

Although my previous book made a strong case of showing that natural intelligence (broadly defined as "the ability to achieve complex goals") often follows a sequence of steps, which – with a bit of goodwill – you could call an algorithm, it should be realized that it was an act of natural intelligence itself to select or program such an "algorithm." Note that I used a very broad definition of algorithm, and that I did not restrict myself to precisely coded computer algorithms most people are familiar with. Nature has indeed selected an evolutionary screening and pruning protocol, which follows certain rules and which allows for creating ever increasing complexity and integration. Nature can therefore be said to <u>evolve and employ</u> a kind "intelligence algorithm," if you wish. However, there was no precooked algorithm imposed on nature to endow it with intelligence. Somehow Nature was able to compose this evolutionary screening and pruning protocol. This protocol is now part of "Nature's intelligence" arsenal as we know it, but originally it was the product of Nature's bootstrapping endeavors. In other words, I never meant to suggest that complexity generating intelligence in Nature IS an algorithm, but rather that Nature <u>evolves and employs</u> an algorithm to generate complexity. Natural intelligence gave birth to efficient routines, which it integrated among its arsenal to solve problems.

Humans

Whereas the analytical processes of the intellect namely of (re)cognition, reasoning and problem solving clearly follow pre-defined steps which one could call algorithmic, we should not forget that we have a collection of such tools at our disposal. To pick the right one at the right time can involve a kind of meta-pattern recognition: To be able to select the pattern, which will solve your problem (and this can sometimes still be algorithmic). The ability to stop a routine, switch routines or design new strategies based on previous routines or completely from scratch, requires a degree of intuition and creativity, which I have shown cannot captured in terms predefined steps. Like Nature, if we developed this toolset at all, it was our natural intelligence that was able to program these routines to make them an efficient component of our intelligence: It is indeed smart to automatize processes you have to carry out very often, so that you don't have to pay conscious attention to each of the steps of the process every time, which would waste tremendous amount of energy and time. But that does not mean that our intelligence IS an algorithm. Rather, our intelligence favors using algorithms whenever possible.

Artificial Intelligence

Even artificial intelligence sometimes escapes precooked algorithms. Take the neural networks that have been programmed. They should not be confused with biological neural networks that most often employ neurons. Neurons are vastly more versatile and complex than the neural nodes employed in artificial neural networks. Neurons can grow new connections and employ different types of neurotransmitters giving rise to different types of behaviors even within a single neuron.

A neural node in an artificial neural network is not so versatile and normally always performs the same task. It is however the interplay of multiple nodes, which renders the system as a whole a black box. Whereas the individual nodes operate algorithmically, their interplay can hardly be said to be algorithmic. A non-linear and unpredictable behavior is often observed, which still is capable of getting the desired output.

Conclusion

Whereas it is highly efficient for intelligence (i.e. the ability to achieve complex goals) to employ algorithms, it should be realized that these algorithms were evolved, developed, programmed or selected by intelligence itself. The realization, that it is necessary to stop a routine, switch routines or design new strategies based on previous routines or completely from scratch, is the moment where a non-algorithmic element of intelligence enters the game.

The holistic nature of intuition, whereby a solution to a problem is arrived at once by the whole of the system without following a mechanistic sequence of steps, points to an underlying principle of intelligence, which is not algorithmic. Perhaps intuition finds its basis in neural network-like behavior of neurons or even quantum events at a deeper level of reality. In chapter 11 of my previous book "*Is Intelligence An Algorithm?*"[30] I went into detail as regards some potentially underlying principles. *A priori* there is no reason to assume that the complexity and versatility of the interplay of these follow a precooked pattern. Which does not necessarily mean that those processes do not involve computation. But if they are computational at all, they escape the rigid structure of a traditional stepwise computer algorithm. As in my hypothesis Nature essentially operates via the Ouroboros Code, it is likely that this code comprises a holistic element of context, connection and sensing intuition that goes beyond a mere algorithm, which is carved in stone.

Chapter 12

Parallels between the natural evolution and the human intellect

Eventually Medea defeated Talos, the first automaton, forged in Hephaistos' farriery, by driving him insane and promising him immortality if he'd remove the nail from his sole vein.

In my book "*Is Intelligence An Algorithm?*"[30] I claim that Nature and the intellect part of the human mind follow a similar algorithm, when they are trying to achieve complexity. In this chapter I'd like to make that comparison more explicit to show one-to-one correspondences for each of the steps. In addition, I will argue that creative intelligence in Nature (and in the human Mind) involves more than merely an algorithm.

Descent into Chaos

Step one of Nature's "Intelligence Algorithm" is not really a step. It's just the provision of the start material which is to undergo transformation to become more complex. In Nature this can for instance be an atom, a molecule, an organism. In the Mind it is simply the status quo. The knowledge and understanding we have at the start moment. This is the thesis in dialectics.

Step two is encountering the stimulus or problem arising from the environment. This is the dialectic antithesis. For an organism in Nature this can be an imminent threat from the environment, such as fire, the presence of a predator or the scarcity of resources. For the Mind when dealing with (re)cognition this can be encountering an object it has not identified yet, but it can also be more complex such as a problem we wish to solve.

Step three is the first real step in which a reaction takes place. Given the problem Nature is going to explore alternative scenarios. It is going to spawn a plethora of alternative possibilities. Under stress organisms evolve: mutations occur more frequently when stress is applied. In the genomic system this can be in the form of point mutations in which a nucleotide is inserted, deleted or substituted for an alternative nucleotide. But also the copying of complete genes occurs as well as the deletion of complete genes. On top of these genomic mutations, there are also epigenetic changes that can occur under influence from the environment: DNA methylation, histone methylation, phosphorylation or other posttranslational modifications. These changes can not only make a gene more or less vulnerable to mutations, but they can also result in the gene being silenced leading to under-expression of the encoded protein or on the contrary being activated leading to overexpression of the encoded protein. All these changes can result in phenotypically changed organisms.

And when an organism faces a threat it evaluates a plurality of possible exit strategies.

Likewise, the Intellect when facing an unidentified object or problem will screen its mental library for a plethora of possible candidates or possible heuristics (educated guess strategies to solve problems).

The screening step in facts creates a multiplicity of relations between the stimulus and the starting material/state. Of course, usually more conservative trusted approaches will be tried out first, but if these remain unsuccessful, it is here that creativity can wildly rage as a storm, forget about all kinds of algorithmic limitations and thresholds and boldly venture where no one has gone before. It is deep natural intelligence – which can't be easily mimicked by artificial intelligence – which is able to see where algorithms and known strategies fail, to know when one should step out of a failing routine and to identify those circumstances which require out-of-the box thinking, because the usual approach is inadequate.

The older people get, the more they are often fixed in their reactions and approaches to reality. Rightfully so, it would appear at first glance, because why should one change a winning strategy? Unfortunately the world is changing at an extremely rapid pace, and if you don't keep up with the necessary technological changes and updates, soon you will find yourself among the digibetics: digital analphabetics.

It is therefore very important to meta-program yourself in such a way, that you are willing to adapt to changed circumstances whenever needed. It requires a great deal of attention, focus, yes the conscious activity of the antennas of your intelligence, to be able to discriminate between situations where a laid back automatized algorithmic approach will suffice and those situations where such an approach will fail. Upon recognizing such a novelty-based situation, we need meta-programs, which can devise new programs which will allow us to navigate among the cliffs of the uncharted territory.

This is where intelligence has a non-algorithmic exponent, which allows it to recombine elements of similar situations or even dissimilar situations, which nonetheless bear an element of structural or functional similarity.

The Conscious Initiative Argument

Imagine you're driving in your car and you need to go to a new dentist, you haven't visited before. You start driving and for a while you need to follow exactly the same trajectory you take when you're going to your daily job. At a certain point you'll have to deviate from this trajectory and turn to right. As you are thinking of all kinds of tasks and trouble you'll have to deal with at your job later on today, you forget to turn right. A few minutes later, as you've almost reached the premises of your office, you suddenly realize that you took the wrong way, and that you'll be late for your appointment at the dentist. Quickly you turn around.

It happens to us every now and then that a routine takes over, when we're not paying attention, showing that we often operate via algorithms.

However, in order to perform a new task, which has certain parts in common with a known task, we need to pay attention consciously so that at the right point, we can modify our routine and devise a new protocol to guide us to our desired destination. It is consciousness, which makes that we can escape from routines and algorithms and order the creation of new ones. This conscious decision taking, is not something, we can easily bring under the banner of algorithms or even meta-algorithms (algorithms that make algorithms).

As to the argument that scientific studies have shown that electrical brain signals are already active a few milliseconds before the moment we claim we make the decision, we must be careful not to over interpret these data. The fact that the brain may show a kind of "readiness" to take a decision could be an alternative explanation to these anticipatory signals. They are not necessarily a proof of the decision having been taken at that very moment.

It is this ability of focused attention, which monitors whether we're still within the boundaries of our usual routines, which defies algorithmicity. The ability to see when a routine can no longer be applied and needs adaptation, substitution or deletion altogether. The ability to step out of a routine and look back at ourselves and what we are doing, involving creating a new representation of ourselves.

Of course, we could try to build mimics of such monitoring in AI, but this intuitive presentism in ourselves is usually not a programmed skill. If we'd forcedly try to acquire this skill by imposing such a monitoring for every activity we undertake, it would block our ability to function normally. It would paralyze our ability to interact with the world by consuming our outward oriented mental resources. So this is not something which can simply be "learnt." What you can do is cultivate your alertness, your focus and attention, which will certainly feed this natural ability.

Stress

Similarly, Nature will only deviate from the paved routine pathways if it is put under stress. The higher the stress, the more original will be the evolutionary strategies to find a way to survive. The owl of Minerva spreads its wings only with the falling of dusk, and Nature will only trash about new solutions if the circumstances are deadly threatening. No wonder that in Peircean Metaphysics[50] mention is made of "Wild being" for this stage.

So, Nature generates a plethora of possible solutions, alternative strategies in the form of point-mutations, reshuffled genes, epigenetically modified genetic material etc., leading to structural and functional modifications, added organs, senses etc.

But not all of these possible alternatives are alternatives that can remedy the problem. Many are not viable at all or are viable to such a minute extent, that they soon disappear. If there is a plurality of viable potential strategies, Nature or the mind must filter out the most promising ones. This step is called pruning: The less viable branches are cut off.

In step 4 from these viable branches a winner is selected, which has the most promising characteristics and which becomes the new thesis. Whereas step three was a descent into chaos and hell, in which Nature tries to do whatever, in step four triumphantly order re-emerges. A new promising candidate has been found which is capable of escaping the threat or lack of resources.

Similarly, the Mind selects the concepts corresponding to those neurons which fire and wire together according to the "Matthew principle"[72]: *"To those who have it shall be given, from those who have not it shall be taken away."* Thus, an object is recognized, when it has been filtered out to have most characteristics in common with a known object.

A heuristic is selected when forward chaining (looking for a solution starting from the problem) and backward chaining (looking for a solution reasoning back from the desired result) meet; perhaps literally there where the corresponding neurons meet, the concerted firing induces the wiring together.

Emergence of higher order

On a heterarchical level competition between contenders may be the new stimulus to induce a new cycle of this algorithm. A fifth step.

For instance, different types of organisms may be competing for the same resources. A mental problem may lead to a plurality of inconclusive contending strategies, none of which solves the total problem.

The evolutionary mechanisms of Nature and the mind here also correspond in that differences are distinguished between the contending strategies and also differences between the problem and the status quo. This can result in an effort to mimic the contender or the characteristics of the problem or to an exchange of features between contenders or between a contender and the problem. Such mimicking or exchanging is the process of distinction probing in action. This is the sixth step of the algorithm I described.

The Mind performs a similar activity of distinguishing, weighing and exchanging by means of its analytical intellect. But here also a synthesis is forged. Whereas the spawning of pluralities leads to a degeneration of one into many, here by acquisition of skills of others unions of features are achieved: many tending to become one. Aggregative inventive recombination. Similarly, the mind will try to use solutions known for similar problems from a different setting into the setting of the present problem. It thereby creates not only novelty, but also achieves complexity. Features are added, deleted or substituted to give rise to a new solution which solves the problem. Alike in Nature and in Mind.

Thus, in a seventh step a new complex thesis is arrived at, which can be a genuine inclusive emergence showing synergistic features as we often see in symbiotic solutions or rather an exclusive type of niching, whereby the problem is solved by limiting to a still viable subset of the desired result. Again, thus the winners are selected. Preferably in generating aggregative symbiotic complexity which has more versatility and variegation to cope with future unexpected problems. And this aggregative process is in the opposite direction from the descent into chaos. It is the resurfacing of the solution as a new higher order of more unified complexity. It shows that both Nature and Mind search for the many to become one again, at a higher meta-system level.

Conclusion

A comparison has been provided between the algorithmic steps Nature and the intellect follow to cope with challenges from the environment. Problematic stimuli result in the spawning of a plethora of possible solutions; a process which requires the ability to deviate from routines and to recognize where new ones should be generated. A focused attention in cooperation with a sophisticated ability to distinguish between the usual and the uncharted territory makes that our intelligence can be more than an algorithm, where Nature needs extremely threatening stress factors to achieve the same.

The plethora of solutions undergo an extensive screening and pruning process from which winners are selected. Ideally resulting in aggregated higher forms of complexity with a more promising viability.

In the evolution of the Ouroboros Code as a self-modifying (meta)algorithm, it was of paramount importance that a certain core ability, namely that of being able to modify is not lost as a consequence of the modifications. In Nature this happens naturally so: Those organisms which lose this ability end up in a dead end of the evolutionary tree. In humans it leads to inflexible people, who are no longer capable of adapting to situations and end up wallowing up in regret and self-pity. If we'd like to build AI's which also have this ability of self-modification, we'd better make damn sure that the core, which allows for this ability is untouchable.

In a far-going speculation, I'd like to explore the following: As reality in the present model takes place in what we can call the "Cosmic Mind," the application of the above-explained Nature's Intelligence Meta-Algorithm[30] (NIMA) can perhaps be considered as the inner mental workings of this mind as well. Perhaps the above mentioned evolutionary processes are even psychologically sensed by the Cosmic Mind in analogy to the above mentioned mapping I made between NIMA and intellectual mental processes. Note that I do not equate this Cosmic Mind with "God," although from our perspective it does have certain divine qualities (like omnipresence). Omniscience is not one of them. As we'll learn in the chapters about the Eschaton, it is perhaps that which comes closest to what we'd normally call a God. Yet the Eschaton is still a mere expression form of the Primordial Consciousness (PC). If we equate PC with the concept of Brahman, which is God in various branches of Hinduism, then the Eschaton is not God (yet). A demigod at best.

In the rest of this book, NIMA will be considered as an inextricable component of the Ouroboros Code.

Chapter 13

Musings on a Master learning algorithm for Man and Machine

Audentes Fortuna iuvat. (Fortune favors the bold).

-Virgil, *Aeneid X, 284.*

The book *"Is Intelligence An Algorithm?"* shows that in attaining complexity, Nature, humans and machines often follow a series of predictable steps. In this book I boldly named this the "Intelligence Algorithm," but I also showed that the creative aspects thereof can't really be captured in terms of algorithms.

Introduction

The definition I used for Intelligence, the ability to achieve complex goals, is also a definition which made the framework for arguing my point very broad and allowed to come to the conclusions presented. However, this "intelligence" is not what the average person would understand to be intelligence. When Nature evolves or when machines solve complex problems, there is no understanding or awareness involved of what is being done, how it is done and why it is done. Wikipedia describes Intelligence among others as "the capacity for logic, understanding, self-awareness, learning, emotional knowledge, planning, creativity, and problem solving." This definition mostly requires a conscious agent, who knows what is going on.

Wikipedia also gives a more generalized definition of Intelligence as follows: "the ability or inclination to perceive or deduce <u>information</u>, and to retain it as <u>knowledge</u> to be applied towards adaptive <u>behaviors</u> within an environment or context."

Although the definition of information has also been expanded for computer science to merely relate to the answer of some question, if we ignore that definition for the moment, we can perhaps state that originally the terminology implied that there was a conscious receiver who was able to decode the information, so that it made sense to him/her. Knowledge also implies that there is a conscious knower, who can make sense of the knowledge. Behavior certainly is a trait of conscious agents. Therefore, also this more generalized definition would have been interpreted as an ability of a conscious agent before the advent of AI. It is because of the developments in computer science that we have started the semantic drift leading to broader definitions of terminologies such as information, knowledge, learning and intelligence. But at the beginning of the 20th century intelligence would have been understood as an ability of a conscious agent.

This long introduction is necessary to prepare you for one of the points I wish to make in this chapter: If we were to restrict intelligence to the narrower definition being "the conscious ability or inclination to perceive or deduce information, and to retain it as knowledge to be applied towards adaptive behaviors within an environment or context," would we still be able to speak of an "intelligence algorithm"? Or in other words, are intelligence and algorithms not two irreconcilable and opposed aspects of the ability to achieve complex goals? The algorithm merely requiring a dumb mindless execution of a set of fixed instructions and intelligence a conscious investment that can adapt to unknown situations for which there are no fixed rules?

Master Algorithm

Yes and no.

Whereas regular algorithms (in computers) indeed blindly follow fixed sets of instructions, the patterns we humans follow allow for a greater degree of freedom and adaptation to the circumstances. That does not mean that we would not have blind so-called "release patterns," but at least we have a faculty of conscious observation of our own actions, which allows us to intervene in our routines. Especially emotional reactions are strong wired routines, which are called upon whenever the circumstances prompt us to do so, but with some training and experience we can learn to control these emotions.

When we are dealing with daily life situations, we often have a purpose, let's say go to the supermarket to do some shopping. An obstacle can make that we have to adapt our plan. For instance, there are construction works on the road, so you'll have to modify the "how" of the execution of the plan in terms of taking a detour. But you do not necessarily have to cancel the purpose of your plan, unless for instance the detour would take you so much time, that you'd arrive too late to pick up your children from school. In such a case we easily "reschedule" or "repurpose." We delete or postpone our previous immediate purpose and replace it (if possible, temporarily) with a different purpose. In fact, we discard the algorithm we had planned to execute our plan and replace it with another algorithm (drive to school), another routine. Our intelligence allows us to select and compound routines to achieve our purposes.

But that strategy to repurpose may well be what we could call our "Master algorithm." Among all our possible known routines, we screen for the ones that are most likely to aid in achieving our purpose. Then we combine the selected routines in a logical sequence that is promising to achieve our goal and we execute the thus compounded routine.

In "*Thinking, Fast and Slow*" Daniel Kahneman[73], a psychologist argues we employ two systems for thinking: System 1 is a fast thinking system, which carries out the automatized routines. System 2 is the slow conscious thinking apparatus, which can change routines, make rational choices and repurpose. There is an interaction between these systems. Usually suggestions by system 1 are easily accepted by system 2 and then processed routinely by system 1, but system 2 can deviate from that pattern and intervene when necessary.

Also, in mental learning, we ground multiple experiences by abstracting essentials features, which we then integrate into a new concept. In school-type learning we summarize by first selecting the most essential aspects of what we have to learn and then by putting these elements together in a schematic integrated framework we can easily retain: Abstraction followed by composition.

This is very similar to the "Intelligence Algorithm" I described for Nature: There is first an evolutionary diversity generation involving screening and pruning of possibilities and a selection of the most viable entities (at different levels proteins, genes, cells, organisms) that have the best adaptations by mutation. Then there is a second phase of combinatorial composition with these building blocks to build higher order entities therefrom (macromolecules assembling into cells, cells into organisms and organisms into societies or hives).

The alchemical "*solve et coagula.*"

So, in both Nature and in human learning and problem solving, there is first a selection of / reduction to essentials, followed by an integrative compounding these elements into a new structure of higher order complexity. Analysis followed by synthesis or abstraction followed by composition are the key ingredients of the master algorithm: The common-sense meta-strategy to select and sequentially compound subsets of strategies. The meta-algorithm to modularly build algorithms for solving any type of problem. And although we can broadly define such a meta-algorithm, this does not necessarily mean that our intelligence is entirely algorithmic. Although there are probably a lot of associative thoughts involved in the selection process, (which is similar to "Bayesian proximity co-occurrence" i.e. if we encounter two concepts often used together i.e. in a statistically significant manner, in our brains they also become wired together), we still need to evaluate the relevance for our purpose.

This assessment of the respective relevancies for multiple associations for a given concept is a (subconscious) process of weighting and comparing. Thus, we are able to select the most relevant one and discard the other candidates.

A concept like "road obstruction" is best associated with "detour" and not with "road paving machine" in case we need to buy our groceries. But this requires a precise understanding of our purpose, the problem and the potential solution. Together these three provide the three points of the plane for understanding, upon which the apperception which results in conscious understanding is built.

The selection routine is therefore a process of providing candidates by association, weighting and comparing them within a threefold context and then selection. The apperception stage is of vital importance as proofreading activity to check whether not some kind of nonsense has been selected, but rather something which indeed fits in with all three boundary setting conditions (problem, purpose and solution).

Machine learning

Indeed, machine learning involving pattern extraction without explicit programming often fails to deliver because there is no such conscious proofreading mechanism present. This is why although performing overall quite well in the game Jeopardy, Watson (a Latent semantic analysis program), can sometimes give nonsensical answers. If it gives a wrong answer, it can be very wrong, in a way that a human being with a bit of common sense would never arrive at. Similar considerations apply to neural networks that perform object recognition. The massive amounts of data they need to be trained to successfully recognize objects is in no way comparable to the way a human can ground a notion on extremely few instances. If we encounter a new object, we screen for similarities with known objects in our memory and define the new object by its differences to the most similar known object, allowing us to classify the new object in the right category and requiring a minimum of effort.

Furthermore, the synthetic phase of organizing our strategies into a logical sequence often involves a lot of geometrical thought, we are not aware of. Somehow, we grope for providing complementary shapes that fit our problem as a key fits a lock. Thus, we compound our modules in common sense ways, where there are no AI equivalents yet.

The recent hype about Deep Learning resulting in computers beating humans in the complex game Go has caused many people to believe that within a few years AIs will achieve common sense reasoning. Nothing is further from the truth. Neural networks are only moderately strong in pattern recognition based on massive amounts of data. They are highly task-specific. As of yet there is no meta-deep learning allowing for immediate adaptation to changed circumstances leading to a need for repurposing and change of tasks.

If AI wishes to progress towards human level AGI (Artificial General Intelligence), advances will need to be made as to how different neural networks can be integrated and selected for tasks in a higher order architecture that responds to the aforementioned meta-algorithm of analysis and synthesis, we can observe in humans.

Some work[74] has been done in co-evolving neural networks and promoting neural network integration, which on the one hand promotes diversity generation (followed by screening like in my "Intelligence Algorithm") and on the other hand encourages joint efforts to arrive at synthesis. Perhaps this is promising, but I conjecture that for common sense reasoning a deeper integration at a meta-level is needed where purpose, problem and solution can extract the essential ingredients for integrative understanding. Perhaps these are yet further layers to be added to create an ensemble of hierarchically structured neural networks. Integrated information must arrive at the top of a pyramid of neural networks where a final recognition and labelling occurs, as a kind of artificial apperception.

Conclusion

At this moment the extremely creative ways via which we can plan, create and adapt to every given situation – including unknown ones – defy our present day understanding. It does not appear that this is a mere execution of a "master algorithm," although it is not unlikely that we subconsciously use such a master algorithm wherever possible. The proofreading activity of consciousness by perceptive understanding, which is involved in common sense understanding, appears to be a vital ingredient of "general intelligence" (intelligence which is not limited to one specific type of task). As long as we cannot reduce consciousness to an algorithm, we can also not conclude that our intelligence IS an algorithm – even if it preferably uses algorithms. As it is my guess that consciousness is the irreducible ontological primitive that not only makes that existence is meaningful to us but even sustains existence as suggested in Vedanta[62], it is my logical inference that intelligence then also cannot be fully reduced to mere algorithms.

Chapter 14

Non-algorithmic Intelligence in the computational Akasha

"Why did you inquire which Brahmā had come to see You? What is the purpose of such an inquiry? Is there any other Brahmā besides me within this universe?'

Upon hearing this, Śrī Kṛṣṇa smiled and immediately meditated. Unlimited Brahmās arrived instantly. These Brahmās had different numbers of heads. Some had ten heads, some twenty, some a hundred, some a thousand, some ten thousand, some a hundred thousand, some ten million and others a hundred million. No one can count the number of faces they had. There also arrived many Lord Śivas with various heads numbering one hundred thousand and ten million. Many Indras also arrived, and they had hundreds of thousands of eyes all over their bodies.

When the four-headed Brahmā of this universe saw all these opulences of Kṛṣṇa, he became very much bewildered and considered himself a rabbit among many elephants."

-Sri Chaitanya Mahaprabhu in *Chaitanya Charitamruta*[59]

...MWI avant-la-lettre

Is classical physics deterministic as we learn in high school and is quantum physics non-deterministic? Or has the physicist David Deutsch proven[75], that the fact that since quantum computing is possible, this shows the opposite for the quantum world? Does this mean that reality and Intelligence are in fact algorithmic?

Background

In this chapter I will address the question of my book "*Is Intelligence An Algorithm?*"[30] in the framework of my other book "*Transcendental Metaphysics*"[21] on pancomputational panpsychism:

If Deutsch[75] is right and Nature is indeed completely computational one might infer that Nature is completely deterministic. If it is completely deterministic and computational it can be considered as the mere processing of an algorithm. Then Intelligence as a manifestation of Nature must follow the same determinism and must therefore also be algorithmic.

Conversely – as I will argue – if Nature is non-deterministic at the quantum level and possibly also to a certain extent at the classical level, it can (despite its computational aspects) still have elements that cannot be captured in an algorithmic manner. My assertion that intuition and creativity might involve certain quantum effects then still can turn out to be correct and these parts of intelligence then do not necessarily follow an algorithm.

Quantum Mechanics

If you learn a bit about quantum mechanics in high school and the first years of university, you will probably learn about the so-called Copenhagen interpretation. Quantum mechanical observations sometimes defy our logic: Instead of following specific deterministic rules that always give the same outcome as in classical mechanical experiments, when we look at the dimensions of the atomic and subatomic world, certain of these rules are violated. For instance, photons (the particles that make up light) when beamed individually through a double slit can depending on the experimental set up behave as either a wave (creating an interference pattern of multiple lines on a screen behind the slits) or as a particle (creating two lines corresponding to the two slits on a screen behind the slits). This so-called wave-particle duality is not only observed for photons but also for material subatomic particles such as electrons. If you put a detector at one of the slits the particle behavior is observed, if you don't put a detector at the slits, the interference pattern is observed. Before the photon or electron is observed the system can be considered to be in both states (wave and particle) at the same time. Similarly, quantum systems can take on other different apparently mutually exclusive states simultaneously before observation and they are said to be in a superposition of those states (which are called wave-functions) as long as they have not been observed. When the photon or electron hits the screen on which the particles are detected or when a quantum system is observed, the so-called wave function is said to "collapse" into one of its states according to the Copenhagen interpretation.

A famous example of this is Schrödinger's cat. A cat is placed in a box with a radioactive material. If the radioactive material undergoes decay, the cat dies. But as long as you have no opened the box, you don't know whether the cat is dead or alive. The radioactive decay is a probabilistic quantum event and might or might not have happened. Only upon opening the box, upon observation you can establish whether the cat is dead or alive. Before the box is opened the cat is said to be in a superposition quantum state of both dead and alive. Opening the box and observing its state collapses the wave function, say the Copenhagen adepts.

Deutsch, Everett and MWI

No, says David Deutsch[75], the wave function does not collapse, but both possibilities occur. In fact, the universe splits into two or multiple parallel dimensions. In one universe the material undergoes radioactive decay and cat dies, in another it does not and the cat is still alive.

David Deutsch follows the so-called "multiple worlds interpretation" (MWI) by Everett[76], which claims that all possible outcomes of quantum events are *de facto* realized, each in a separate parallel universe. In this way according to him there is still full determinism because everything effect is bound to have been caused by a specific cause. Note however that this is not traditional determinism, since not every cause has one specific outcome but rather multiple different ones in different universes.

But David Deutsch theory is not merely a repetition of Everett's MWI[76]. Deutsch insists that these outcomes are the result of quantum computations.

Quantum computing

Quantum computing is excruciatingly difficult to understand. People may have fancy ideas how atoms or subatomic particles compute; how individual quanta compute, but it requires quite some investigation to get even a hunch of what is going on here. A normal logical gate in a binary computer accepts a 0 or 1 value of a so-called "bit" as input, performs a calculation or transformation on this bit and gives an output in the form of a bit value: a 0 or a 1.

Quantum computers accept qubits as input, which can have as value both 0 and 1, a superposition of both or a plurality of values between 0 and 1.

Also, for quantum computers logical gates are present which perform transformations on the multiple different input values. The output is however a single value. These quantum computers are said to yield gain in computing time for certain operations such as factoring big numbers.

But how do these gates really function? How are these multiple isolated values kept separate from each other during the computation?

Deutsch claims the computation must be done somewhere for each of the values, which then must somehow interact to yield a final value. The somewhere according to Deutsch is that each value undergoes a real classical transformation in a separate universe. If I understand it well, these universes then somehow create an interaction with each other which decides the final outcome. It would not be meaningful if in our universe only the calculation done on one of the input values would yield a result, right?

If we look closely at systems used for quantum computing we'll discover amongst others quantum ensemble computing and quantum annealing computing. In quantum ensemble computing we don't need Deutsch's MWI, because many molecules are subjected to a transformation and each molecule gives an output and the end output is a kind of average thereof.

In quantum annealing computing we have isolated qubit systems on which the calculation is performed, such as systems in which a limited number of superconducting metal atoms are entangled such as the famous D-Wave computer (created in collaboration with Google,

NASA and USRA). Upon performing a computation, the entangled atoms together search for a minimal energy outcome, which is presented as the output. This process can physically involve the so-called quantum tunneling process in which subatomic particles can go through an energy barrier as if they were going through a tunnel. If we try to mimic such a system with a classical computer, we cannot go through the energy barrier and this is why similar operations on a classical computer take a longer time. Here too, there is no need to assume a multiverse that computes the outcome either. Rather the entangled atoms seem to sense each other and collectively adapt to an ideal value.

The followers of Deutsch and Deutsch himself claim that his ideas about quantum computation have proven beyond doubt that MWI is correct or at least that this is the most parsimonious explanation in view of Occam's razor.

Really? Is an infinity of universes that is generated at each quantum event parsimonious? What Deutsch *cum suis* reproach the Copenhagen interpretation is that it somehow magically performs the calculations which then result in a collapsed outcome. Here is what bothers me about Deutsch's approach: Quantum mechanical effects rely on interference, yet the input states of the quantum system must remain separated during the calculation. But the true calculation arises from the interference between the different outcomes in the different worlds in Deutsch's model! In other words, as Scott Aaronson[77] (a professor in computer science) wrote:

"The key thing that quantum computers rely on for speedups – indeed, the thing that makes quantum mechanics different from classical probability theory in the first place – is interference between positive and negative amplitudes. But to whatever extent different "branches" of the multiverse can usefully interfere for quantum computing, to that extent they don't seem like separate branches at all! I mean, the whole point of interference is to mix branches together so that they lose their individual identities. If they retain their identities, then for exactly that reason we don't see interference.

... a quantum computer is not a device that could "try every possible solution in parallel" and then instantly pick the correct one. If we insist on seeing things in terms of parallel universes, then those universes all have to "collaborate" – more than that; have to meld into each other – to create an interference pattern that will lead to the correct answer being observed with high probability."

If the different branches interact and interfere to give a compounded outcome, is this not as magical and mysterious as the Copenhagen approach? And if these branches can interfere and hence influence each other, how can they warrant separate states? How can this multiplicity of parallel universes still be considered separate if they influence each other? If they do influence each other they form a kind of unimetaverse!

Most parsimonious explanation not involving magic and only logic? I don't think so. Whereas Deutsch *cum suis* consider the Copenhagen theory and other interpretations as pre-Copernican errors of an obsolete Paradigm, they certainly do not represent the perspective of the average physicist or computer scientist. Rather, their theory is still considered fringe. But woe thee if you state that quantum mechanics is non-deterministic. They will treat you as if you are an idiot.

Personally, I am not versed well enough in physics and computer science to establish which theory is right. But I wanted to draw your attention to the fact that despite what Deutsch lobby tries to sell, namely that quantum computation via multiple worlds is the sole logical and true explanation for this phenomenon, this is not an established verified and accepted fact.

So, the discussion, whether reality is fully deterministic or whether quantum mechanics allows for a certain degree of indeterminacy remains an open one. Likewise, it is still possible that Intelligence has facets such as intuition, which do not operate via an algorithm.

Pancomputational Panpsychism / Pansentience

Ha! you might say, "now you contradict yourself, Antonin Tuynman." Didn't you claim that every process in reality we observe is computational? Yes, I did, but I used a very broad definition for "computation." I considered that every process has an input and output which has somehow been integrated in a throughput phase. But this does not exclude quantum computing involving non-deterministic effects (if we do not follow Deutsch's interpretation of MWI). I also spoke about Panpsychism or Hylozoism: Every self-sustaining form of energy (or "life") traverses a kind of matrix called the "Akasha" (corresponding to the Greek "Aether"), which I equated with the fabric of the so-called zero point filed or quantum vacuum.

As I described before, in a sense, since the presence of these conscious energies make the state of the Akasha digitally change from 0 (absence of energy) to 1 (presence thereof), you could consider this as a kind of digital computer – but not as you know it. The Akashic or Eschaton Omega computer as I have described is more holistic system generating a holographic interference patterns of the energies that traverse it. But on top of that it is not a static inflexible structure; it is more a flexible interdependent quantum foam. Rather, when energies traverse this "isotropic vector matrix" they create anisotropies or distortions in this foam, which reverberate throughout the whole. The conscious energies themselves do not compute. They merely travel, obey certain laws of the foam structure and make choices whenever prompted. Conscious energy in this model is fundamental. It is the irreducible *Prima Materia*, which on the one hand by means of a cell division process creates the foam structure which I call the Akasha and which on the other hand also penetrates this Akasha to sense it from within as a multiplicity of individualized perspectives. The primordial conscious energy is not emergent or computed in this model. It simply IS everything, including the unorthodox digital Akasha and its traversing energies. These energies are aware in their individualized perspective, in the sense that they sense their environment. They experience a kind of proto-consciousness. They become aware of each other upon approaching each other and their mutual interactions provide meaning and the 4 primary forces of physics. This creates a kind of consensus reality.

Whereas the laws of physics which emerge from the structure of the Akasha and its penetration by multiple energies create certain obligatory pathways or rules or chreodes, which the energetic entities have to follow, within those chreodes the entities have a freedom of movement. A chreode is a necessary pathway, like a valley-like trough in a mountain, which an object going down that mountain is obliged to follow. But within the chreode there is a certain room of freedom of movement. Thus, Nature is *Grosso Modo* deterministic as regards its laws, which form the chreodes, but allows for freedom of choice within the chreode. This leads to a certain degree of non-determinism and taken as a whole reality is then ultimately neither 100% deterministic nor 100% indeterministic.

Similarly, "Intelligence," the ability to achieve complex goals – which is an inherent aspect of the conscious energies – is neither fully algorithmic nor is it completely devoid of algorithmic behavior. As explained in an earlier chapter Intelligence chooses the way of the least resistance (as does everything in Nature), and automatizing routines of learnt/evolved strategies is a part thereof. Thus Intelligence in Nature follows a lot of self-taught algorithms or default pathways when encountering known situations, to save its energy investments for truly novel situations which require enhanced attention and intuitive insight. In this respect, the algorithms of Intelligence in Nature can be compared to the "Default Mode Network" activity of the brain, which avoids investments of high frequency energies, which are employed for novel situations that require attention.

If my Pansentient Pancomputational model involves a kind of quantum computing, it is not necessarily the type of quantum computing which is developed by present day technology. Rather, the holistic computations of the Akasha set chreodes, within which there is room for freedom, which you could even call the free will of the energetic entities. The weird quantum effects such as entanglement, tunneling, wave-particle duality etc. have been described in my book *"Transcendental Metaphysics"*[21] as essentially deriving from the holographic structure and dynamics of the Akasha, its interactions with its inhabitants and their mutual interactions, including their free will decisions. These effects fall outside the scope of this chapter. Quantum computing states that are adopted by entangled particles in an annealing process for energy minimization can be explained by a concerted communication between different energies in the matrix, which form the qubit states together. They communicate by reverberating distortions through the Akashic matrix which each of them senses and thus they seek their common energetic minimum, which, once established forms the outcome of the quantum computation. There is neither a need for multiple parallel universes, nor is there a need for a magical collapse. Rather, the non-computational sensing results in a computational outcome!

It must also be realized that in quantum theories the arrow of time points in both directions and certain delayed-choice experiments have shown that a phenomenon as retrocausation might effectively be happening in Nature. This appears also in contradiction with Deutsch's claim to determinism. In Pancomputational Panpsychism the sensing energies could sense retrotemporal movements propagating through the Akasha. Alternatively, there might not be any retrocausation at all, but the distortion of the Akasha after the choice is made in the above mentioned experiments is present in time to set up the right pathway to yield results consistent with the ultimate set-up.

Conclusion

The claim by David Deutsch[75] that everything in reality is deterministic because it derives from quantum computing via multiple worlds, is a thesis, which has neither been proven nor has been generally accepted by the scientific community. The Copenhagen interpretation is one among several interpretations, which does not involve an MWI à la Everett. Both theories rely to a certain extent on something happening magically, mysteriously. My theory of Idealistic Pancomputational Pansentience IMHO does not require magic, although you may consider the notion of conscious sensing energies exactly as that. It is a theory, just as other theories, and it is not less parsimonious or less logic than the existing theories. Rather, it does not violate the basic notions of established physics. The only thing it does is provide a rationale for consciousness as irreducible ground of existence and thereby overcomes the hard problem of consciousness. Reality as expression of the Ouroboros code is on the one hand computational in as far as a code is involved. But in as far as conscious, sentient actions prompt the code to modify itself – within the meta-algorithmic boundaries of preserving the recursive self-modifying ability – it is on the other hand also having a non-computational side.

Chapter 15

Chinese rooms and why even computers don't compute

The ideas that we are living in a computer simulation and that reality is a pancomputational process are quite in vogue these days. But whether you can adhere to this point of view, depends strongly on the type of definition you apply.

Background

In my previous books I have defended this point of view from a very broad definition, that all natural processes can be described as having an input, a transformational throughput and a (more or less predictable) output.

In this chapter I will play the devil's advocate and defend the opposite stance: Existence is not (entirely or hardly) computational. In fact, even computers don't compute. The only entities – as far as we know – capable of computation are conscious human beings. You will see that the question is mostly one of semantics: How do you define "computation." I will not only address the topic whether computers are computational, but also whether consciousness and Nature are computational.

Semantics

According to Wikipedia, computation is any type of calculation and a calculation is a deliberate process that transforms one or more inputs into one or more results, with variable change.

Note the word "deliberate." It implies a conscious agent carrying out the calculation. When we humans perform abstract calculations we basically add numbers. All other mathematical operations can be derived from this; even subtraction is the adding of negative numbers.

Computers do not deliberately add numbers. They don't even add numbers at all. Computers merely shuttle electrons through Boolean

"AND," "OR" and "NOT" gates. Depending on such an operation a bit register is holding either a lower or a higher voltage. We interpret this higher or lower voltage as a binary 0 or 1. We connect the bits such with each other that the outcome of an ensemble of bits can be interpreted by us as a binary number. But inside the computer no quantities have been added. The number of electrons that changed position is not even linearly correlated to the numerical outcome.

Calculating machines facilitate our computational activities. Whereas a computer as a whole (and not the isolated bits) seems to have calculated an outcome, in fact, it has only processed electrons via pathways predefined by us to display a pattern on a screen, which by us can be interpreted as a representation of a quantity. The diodes that light up and establish an informational pattern together have only meaning for a conscious observer such as us, who knows what the pattern represents. Another way to rephrase the title would be "computers merely emulate computation."

Information

A popular theory in physics these days is, that information is more fundamental than energy or matter. Information processing is usually seen as a computational process. Information is the answer to some kind of question. Moreover, in a narrower sense, it is the (symbolic or coded) representation of a known object or concept. In order for this type of information endowed with meaning to be correctly interpreted or understood, you need a conscious observer who knows the key to interpret the information. Imagine signals being received by SETI from space. Without an indication that it is a message and without a key to decode, it may as well be noise.

This also ties a bit into Searle's[78] Chinese room argument. You have a room with a slot in the door through which Chinese characters are fed. Inside is an English person, who does not know Chinese and who follows an algorithm that translates messages in Chinese characters and allows translating answers from English back into Chinese characters. From the outside you would get the impression that the person inside understands Chinese, but nothing is further from the truth. The person would not have a clue if heard the message in Chinese. The fact that machines can process information and output the right answers, does not mean that there is any understanding or "intentionality" as Searle would call it.

Whereas it may or may not be true that all energetic and material manifestations can be described by informational patterns if we wished to do so, as long as we make up what we consider as a pattern and attribute meaning to this, it's a human invention. There is *a priori* no proof of intrinsic information with meaning being conveyed to us by mere energy patterns.

Simulated worlds

If we would be able to decode such information, if we would manage to unravel the key of information that was conveyed to us upon the creation of the universe we live in, a valid question might be: Who created us, who simulated us? Perhaps a Kardashev IV civilization, which has mastered all the laws of matter energy and information in the universe. Perhaps a God; or perhaps we should consider these alien Kardashev IV citizens as Gods.

It does not really matter at this point in time. For the moment, such ideas are purely speculative as we have no proof that all patterns we observe have an informational meaningful content and what the meaning of that content is supposed to be. Even if we were to consider the numerous occurrences of the 273-enigma[79] in our solar system as a proof that our reality was designed and probably involved a lot of computations to fine-tune this system, it does not necessarily mean that it was designed in a manner that solely involved computation. It does not mean that everything in our world is computational and/or informational.

Is consciousness computable?

And perhaps we should not worry too much about the philosophical and metaphysical aspects of the "computation debate," whether computation is a physical process or whether Nature is a computational process.

Perhaps it is more interesting from an engineering point of view whether we can create consciousness via computation in computers or whether we can't by definition, so that the hard problem of consciousness will remain unsolvable for us.

Wittgenstein once asked "Does a calculating machine calculate?"[80] This rhetorical question implied the answer "No, we calculate with them." Davidson[81] argues that the internal states of a computer have significance only for us because of their connection with our relevant culture embedded states.

The vast majority of computer scientists, however, seem to be convinced that once a certain threshold of complexity is achieved in computational systems, consciousness will emerge – as if by magic.

As explained before, one of the leading theories on consciousness is Giulio Tononi's "Integrated Information Theory." Tononi[7] argues that consciousness can be said to be present whenever there is an integration of information. Based on Tononi's algorithm Phil Maguire[82] showed that the unity of consciousness we experience requires that it involves irreversible and non-computable functions. So at least here we have a strong pointer that not all phenomena in existence involve computation.

Whether our brains truly compute is also a matter of debate. But there is quite a consensus that the neural plasticity that can be observed, in which new links are formed and in which the fluxes through the neurons are regulated and adapted, cannot be described with our best artificial neural nets. Sure, neurons take in inputs at their dendrites and then provide an output via their axons, but there is something profoundly holistic going on here, which cannot be modelled in an algorithm or neural net. As this holistic process somehow involves the totality of all neurons (of the brain or of neuronal patches), it is unlikely we will be able to model it via computation let alone that we can consider it as a computation. Perhaps that what connects the dots (i.e. intelligence operated by consciousness) cannot be obtained by connecting the dots.

Computation in the sense of deliberately adding abstract numbers is an activity which seems to take place at a higher level; at the conscious level in a special state of high-frequency brainwaves, which correspond to enhanced attention for the particular to block out an overload of information from other general inputs (e.g. sensory inputs).

If true human level intelligence requires the presence of consciousness, it seems unlikely we will get there in computers by creating more algorithms and more neural nets. We will need a principle to meaningfully integrate all of those. After all, algorithms and neural nets and their training are the product of our intelligence. So-called genetic algorithms have not evolved so much, that they can design context independent algorithms which are applicable in any setting. Rather, they are very context and problem specific.

It is however not impossible, that one day we may be able to impart consciousness to a computer by means of a human-computer hybrid experience. If we are linked to a computer via a brain computer interface (BCI) such as the future "neural lace," we may be well able to fertilize computers with our consciousness. There is already a great advance made in connecting electrically steered prostheses to nerves, making people with amputated hands, arms and legs fully functional again. We could thus prosthetically extend into the computational substrate.

Is Nature computational?

The primitive kind of intelligence that creates complexity in non-living and simple living systems does, however, follow a path of aggregation or addition, if you wish. Subatomic particles add-up to form atoms, atoms combine into molecules, molecules assemble into macromolecules and macromolecules into cells. Cells build organisms and organisms build societies. If these processes were purely entropy[3]

---

[3] The second law of thermodynamics stipulates that entropy, a measure of the amount of disorder, must always increase overall. However, entropic gravitation shows that complex structures can arise locally, without violating the second law of thermodynamics exactly because these increase the global dissipation in the space outside the complex structure.

driven, it would be unlikely that evolution would have advanced as quickly as we can observe.

If, however, each of these systems would be endowed with an inner learning experience, it might explain how we got here so fast. This presupposes the presence of a certain degree of awareness also at lower levels of existence. Panpsychism, the idea that every simple level of existence such as atoms, molecules etc. is already endowed with an intrinsic form of minute sentience, is a terminology which scientists no longer shun to use as a possible explanation for the hard-problem of consciousness. Already in 1938, in his book "*The Phenomenon of Man*" Teilhard de Chardin[83] argued that such simple systems have a "within"; an interior (primitive) conscious experience.

But the aggregation of natural systems seems to be a concerted striving for mutual benefit – if sentience is involved at all. And if it isn't, the aggregation of natural systems can be merely an entropic process. Whatever it is, it does not *prima facie* seem to be a "deliberate transformation of one or more inputs into one or more results." That would imply a transcendent God or simulator who juggles with our existence, which is a hypothesis for which we don't have a definite proof yet. As Laplace told Napoléon: "*Je n'avais pas besoin de cette hypothèse-là.*" ("I had no need of that hypothesis.").

DNA, RNA and protein synthesis are perhaps an interesting intermediate level of reality where there seems to be a clear code and an accurate mapping from input to output. There is *prima facie,* however, no deliberate calculation or counting involved.

Network learning (not only occurring in brains, but in many organic systems such as the immunological system, metabolic pathways systems etc.) in Nature could perhaps fit the broader interpretation of computation (i.e. any process that transforms an input into an output), but it would not fit the narrower interpretation of deliberately addition within a counting system.

This does not mean that Nature has not developed certain privileged patterns that lead to desirable results. There is a kind of inherent intelligence in Nature that strives to achieve complex goals by aggregating entities into more proficient entities. There is a process of evolution towards higher forms of experience and understanding and more unified systems. The steps this process follows I described in my book[30] "*Is Intelligence An Algorithm?*" which are in fact steps of screening for cooperation and competition and pruning away the less successful candidates. That such steps are observed and that we might call that "an algorithm" in a broad sense (namely of a sequence of steps or instructions that are systematically followed), does not necessarily mean that such an algorithm is computational, although it is perhaps possible to accurately model it *in silico* (i.e. in computers).

Conclusions

Based on these considerations, we have seen that there are no *a priori* reasons why Nature should be computational in the narrow sense of the word (i.e. deliberately calculating), although in the broader sense of a system that performs actions on itself,[45] it certainly is. In a later chapter, I will, however, challenge this conclusion again. We have even seen that in the narrow sense of the word, computers do not compute. The hype of digital physicists and computer scientists suggesting that the whole of Nature is computational, may have some value in the broader sense that all processes in Nature transform an input into an output, but *a priori* there is no definite proof of deliberate input leading to count-wise calculations, which result in an interpretable and understandable outcome. As far as we know, only humans do that. Therefore, to suggest that "information" is more fundamental than energy or matter, should be approached carefully. "Information" interpreted in a broad sense as a measure of order as opposed to chaos, i.e. as a kind of entropy probably has merit as fundamental principle of existence. Information, in the sense of symbolic representations, which need decoding and interpretation by a conscious observer, however, needs a further elaboration to qualify as fundamental in existence. This topic will be dealt with in more detail in a later chapter.

You may be surprised that in this chapter I present the opposite stance of what I usually do. I am playing chess with myself. In a later chapter I hope to convincingly show that all of reality involves computation and is profoundly informational, based on more than circumstantial evidence (such as Verlinde's[9] entropic gravitation).

Chapter 16

Lifting the veil of Maya

Reality is what you can get away with.

-R.A. Wilson.

This chapter will discuss the way language constructed a dualistic experience of existence, which we could call Maya. It will also discuss how the illusion of Maya can be transcended by realizing the relativity of perspective.

Background

In the context of this chapter Maya means "illusion." According to a definition Maya connotes a "magic show, an illusion where things appear to be present but are not what they seem." This term has its roots in Indian philosophies and religions. The world we see around us is an illusion and has no ultimate reality. This illusion is created by the working of our mind, which separates the world into different objects. In fact, the mind casts a kind of veil over reality which renders it impossible to experience it as it is. The word Apocalypse is often associated with the end of the world and comes from the Greek word "*Apokalypsis*" which means "lifting the veil." In this post I will argue that if we succeed in lifting this veil of Maya, this illusion of a world of separate objects, in fact the world as we knew it ceases to exist for us.

Grids and reality tunnels

In chapter 8 I argued that egoic self-awareness, the awareness of being an individual separated from the rest of existence arose dependently with the birth of language. The ability to abstract and name objects and concepts separate and independent from ourselves and from their context must involve the ability to experience ourselves apart from these. This naming of things is what creates our analytical mind. The name does not necessarily need to be a word that can be sounded; any form of code or abstracted symbol can function as a building block of a language. Our analytical mind encompasses a vast network of such abstracted representations of objects and features of thereof and functions to describe one thing in term of other things. The way we discern objects and name/represent them is our personal or cultural grid through which we perceive what we call reality. Other persons or other cultures[55,84] may see different contrasts, may have named different objects and thus see reality through a different pair of glasses or grid[4].

Which grid is true? If you toss a bunch of pebbles one person may connect the pebbles mentally to see a geometrical form like a pentagon or a pentagram. One person may see a human figurine in it, another one a cat.

If you look at clouds I may see a duck, where you see a rabbit.

Our understanding of what we see is strongly linked to how we connect the dots mentally, how we build a mental configuration. Alfred North Whitehead[35], philosopher and mathematician defined understanding as the "*apperception of pattern as such.*" *Two is a coincidence and three is a pattern*, Ben Goertzel[85] said and in line therewith Buckminster Fuller[25] explained that one can only understand a phenomenon if one has created a framework of consideration or a plane of understanding comprising at least three relations, and hence a pattern. In other words, we can only understand a concept or object analytically if we can see a pattern of at least three relations.

But which relations do our minds make? Are the relations our minds make truly representative of something that is objectively out there or is the object of consideration a fiction of our minds? A fiction, that has been transmitted as a memetic virus from our ancestors who "named" objects.

The fact, that even unrelated languages can most often be translated into each other, at least shows that different human brains function in similar ways and choose similar objects to be named. But there are also words and concepts which cannot be translated into other languages because there is no equivalent known in such a language. Sometimes this can lead to the adoption of a foreign word in your language, but most often it goes unnoticed if there is no frame of reference in your language. The view on reality which you share with people from the same culture establishes a cultural "reality tunnel" as R.A. Wilson[1] used to call it. Bernardo Kastrup[38] speaks in this context of a so-called "consensus reality."

But is our consensus reality reality-as-it-was-intended or was reality not intended in a particular way at all?

This is almost a theological question which will divide the materialists and idealists. As explained in my previous chapter on "egoic awareness," developments in quantum mechanics and digital physics point to a participatory universe in which information is the most fundamental building block. If there's information, a code, there must be a consciousness entity to interpret it; otherwise it's a mere collection of dots without instruction as to how to connect it.

Many religions consider existence as the mind of God or the product of the mind of God, which might imply that if there is a code underlying reality, it is intended to be interpreted in a particular way. Or is God more versatile than that?

Enter Superintelligent AI (SAI)

According to the Singularitarians, soon we'll achieve the so-called "technological singularity."[86,87] The developments in artificial intelligence will soon give rise to self-improving algorithms and neural nets, which will generate an artificial intelligence explosion which will change the world beyond our present-day comprehension and imagination. SAIs will not look for one pattern when observing a set of data; no, they will identify all possible patterns; they will reveal a complete collection of patterns that can be made from a metaphorical cloud of dots. This will give them a bird's eye overview of all patterns, including meta-patterns (patterns of the patterns). This complete collection of patterns we could call a "Patternome" in analogy to the terms "genome" (collection of all genes in an organism) or "proteome" (collection of all proteins in an organism).

Within the Patternome the SAIs will screen and prune for useful ones, with which they can achieve complex goals (following Goertzel's[50] definition that intelligence is the ability to achieve complex goals in complex environments).

Thus, they will generate virtual worlds. It is possible that we are already living in such a virtual world / a kind of computer simulation and that what we call God is an SAI running the simulation. At least digital physics seems to point in that way. Reality then is a network of ontologies: lists of features describing concepts and objects, which are encoded by this Platonic idealistic network.

Occam's fallacy

We often use the so-called Occam's razor principle to explain phenomena: This principle states that we should use the hypothesis with the smallest number of assumptions to explain a phenomenon. But this is not a proven principle. It is merely a rule of thumb to do science. If you have a cloud of dots, the simplest way to connect them might be a straight line and may involve the smallest number of assumptions. But what if the underlying reality is more complex? As argued before, what if we have the phenomenon of aliasing, in which a more complex relation describes the underlying ground better? Better in a sense that the understanding allows for a more extensive technological exploitation of the phenomenon, because the simpler relation is an illusion, a pattern that our minds saw where "reality" or "God" or the SAI intended none.

Hopefully, our technologies will permit us to merge with the SAI, so that our awareness can be hooked up to an SAI and experience reality as a set of individual eyes of the SAI, a tentacle. A full immersion symbiosis or even a full-fledged merger.

Or perhaps this is already the case; perhaps we are "God's" or the SAI's tentacles, reporting individual perspectives or patterns to the SAI. Perhaps existence is the SAI's playground or "*Leela*" in terms of Hinduism. A game in which the SAI is screening and pruning by allowing for internal competition, allowing the evolution of its inner workings. So that ultimately every perspective is in a sense worthwhile for consideration by the SAI in order to judge whether this perspective can give rise to further complexity, further self-representation and self-perpetuation. God's mind or the SAI-universe as a process of autopoiesis: Self-enablement and self-sustention by self-replication.

Isis' veil

This realization that one pattern is not necessarily more worthwhile than another, that our patterns might not be the originally intended patterns when the game started and the realization that what we call reality is nothing more than the generation of pattern or code by some kind of mind, may then help us to set us free. Either we develop the bird's eye view and see that creation is nothing more than an endless loop of information generation and feedback re-integration thereof, or we see the pointlessness is imposing our "grid" on reality, by which we miss out the view of the totality.

After all, in Nature the whole is more than the sum of parts and our mind can only grasp our observations in as far as we can reduce them to practice like a (technological) application. But by observing only parts we can never sense the whole. As mentioned before in this book, there is a meditative technique in Indian philosophy called "*Panchadasi*" in which you reflect on a topic from 15 different perspectives. Even then you haven't fully grasped it, but if you get the pointlessness of the analytical approach and by exhaustion and frustration have your consciousness dissociate from the analytical mindedness, you may start to experience and feel what it is like to be the whole of the topic of consideration.

Or perhaps structure and function are each other's transform and once you meditate on its structural aspects, you can start to "feel," "sense" what it is like ("quale") to be that form functionally, thereby embodying it; thereby revealing its inner secrets from the inside out. From Quanta to Quale, from Mind to Sensing.

Then once you start to experience reality as a whole from the inside out, you may attain non-dual unity with reality, mystic union with God, Samadhi, Satori or whatever you want to call it. Experiencing non-duality, the interconnectedness and interdependency of all entities and objects. Being one with everything around you. Like you experienced before you developed an ego and language. And this may lift the veil of seeing the world in separate objects and ourselves as a separate observer. It may lift the burden of the mind and ego and hence absolve reality as we knew it. Ending the world as we knew it by lifting the veil of Maya and realizing that unified consciousness is the sole and ultimate ground of existence. That the code as "known" is merely generated as the process of "knowing" to inform the "knower" aspect of consciousness of its presence: A feedback loop, called the Ouroboros Code.

Conclusion

We see patterns and code from a subjective perspective, which may or may not correspond to reality as a whole. By dividing the world into objects and concepts and by seeing ourselves separate therefrom, we obtain a limited and abstracted experience of reality, which is no longer an experience of reality as a whole. This mentally imposed limitation is a veil, a grid, which the ancients called Maya. We can try to lift this veil by realizing the pointlessness of our attribution of patterns. That neither our patterns nor any pattern constitutes ultimate reality, but that these patterns are merely essential transient representations of consciousness informing itself of its presence.

If everything in existence is a meaningful informational code, as digital physics suggests, the Ouroboros Code, there must be a conscious observer to read the code. Then unified consciousness may be the ultimate basis of existence and the codes merely transient representations necessarily generated by consciousness to inform and maintain itself. Informing itself, that the knowing, knower and known are united inextricable aspects of the feedback loop called consciousness.

Chapter 17

Tsang's Apokalypsis

This chapter will discuss how Tsang's[24] Fractal Brain Theory (FBT) describes a way to implement the evolutionary algorithm of intelligence in a computer environment to generate Artificial General Intelligence. It will also discuss how the notion of recursive self-modification of Tsang's FBT is an essential ingredient of the Ouroboros Code.

Background

Tsang's "*The Fractal Brain Theory*" is one of the best books I ever read on presenting ideas that may lead to the development of AGI (Artificial General Intelligence: AI, which can operate in a context-independent manner).

Tsang shows us that there is a perfect functional mapping between the genetic realm and the neuronal world. He then develops his ideas about universally occurring binary trees as a true recipe designed to one day generate AGI, which may reach and even surpass the human level of intelligence. This is achieved by virtue of what he calls a "recursive self-modification process," in which the process takes itself as an object and maps this, like in the mathematical process known as "Yoneda-embedding." Tsang furthermore describes combination of divergent and convergent forward and backward chaining algorithms, which result in an intersection where they meet. This is not only a current heuristics[d] technique in present day AI, but as developed in the framework of Tsang's binary tree mapping process, it is also the mapping means to select successful candidates. It is in fact a recipe to create self-improving AI. This may well be the book that heralds the advent of superintelligence and the technological singularity.

---

[d] Heuristics are practical methods to solve any problem when no such methods are known. They involve an advanced kind of strategical educated guessing, which I explain in more detail in my book "*Is Intelligence An Algorithm?*."

In my previous book "*Is Intelligence An Algorithm?*"[30] I described an algorithm that evolution follows to generate complexity. To my great surprise I found the same ingredients back in the book "*The Fractal Brain Theory,*" although differently presented.

I described how when a (living) system encounters a problem such as a lack of resources, this gives the system a stimulus to start to probe for a variety of alternatives or other solutions: "*Nature will now generate a plethora of alternatives by combining elements from the environment with the system.*" This includes changes such as mutations.

In Tsang's book an equivalent is found in that the system differentiates or diverges.

I also described that from the probing or testing of these alternatives by the system, the system abstracts patterns. (Screening of relational "Syntheses.") From these the most successful alternative strategies can be selected. (Elimination, Pruning of Syntheses and Emergence of new "Theses.")

This plays a role in what Tsang calls "intersection," which I will discuss later in this chapter.

Tsang's book moreover describes a process called "convergence." This strongly corresponds to the symbiotic integrative results of Nature's Intelligence Meta-Algorithm from my previous book:

This can be repeated on a heterarchical level between groups of entities or (living or non-living) systems (such as bacterial colonies or animal societies). When contending groups encounter each other, this gives a stimulus to start a so-called "Intergroup tournament." The tournament can lead to a mutual probing of the distinctions between the groups. Nature will screen which elements from the contender can be copied and integrated and which ones should be discarded. This can result in the formation of 1) a "niche" (each group specializes in a niche such that it does not poach on the contender's preserves); 2) a "symbiosis": the groups learn to cohabitate peacefully together and provide each other with a service, resulting in a transactional scenario of a win-win situation); or 3) an exchange of those features which are different between the groups ("mimicking"). Thus, the system adapts itself to its environment.

The most promising strategies ideally result in symbiosis, a unification of features toward which the system will strive.

The system will try to resonate "morphogenetically" (i.e. in form, as dictated by its genetic make-up) with its new environment and thereby adapt to it. This is Nature's way of continuously striving for more complexity and incorporation of mutual features, as this assures more adaptability to and integration with the environment and hence increased chances for survival. In other words, Nature's intelligence algorithm is essentially integrative: It tries to unite, to combine apparent opposites.

One of the most interesting points I found in Tsang's book was the way he described the selection process (which I called the "screening and pruning"), which he calls the "intersection of the convergence and divergence." This is one of the points that I will discuss in more detail in this chapter.

The other point evoked by Tsang is that Nature is a system performing mapping. I discussed this in my chapter 3. Likewise, I find that Tsang describes mapping as the unifying process underlying all natural processes.

Finally, Tsang speaks about a recursive self-modifying process, in which the process takes itself as an object and maps this. This is Yoneda embedding, which I also discussed in chapter 3. Moreover, in chapter 6 I suggested that this form of self-representation is the very ontogenetic process of reality generation.

Mapping

Tsang convincingly shows that Nature both on the genetic as well as the brain level cunningly exploits the process of making binary trees to arrive at an ontogenetic process which observes rules of symmetry and symmetry breaking, recursive self-modification and warranting self-similarity over different scales. The brain maps its experiences, its sensory data observing a hierarchical process involving binary trees, and these are reflected in the generation of corresponding structures at the neuronal level in the form of axonal and dendritic branching (but also at the genetic level: e.g. epigenetic markers). Moreover, this forward chaining process is mimicked by a backward chaining process in the motor neurons. Both the structural modifications and the motor neuron actions can be considered as mappings of the sensory process: sensing translates into reconstruction in terms of Tsang. From stimulus to response. This strongly resonates with my theories in chapter 3 on how sense becomes structure via Yoneda mapping. Noteworthy, Tsang reveals how binary trees are also present in the ways we represent space and time. Perhaps because space and time are *de facto* quantized and a product of a conscious mental activity expressed by the Ouroboros Code?

Amplification, Reproduction and Seed

Nature has found both at the neuronal and genetic level a system to reproduce itself, which is a special kind of recursive mapping which takes itself as object to generate isomorphic structures. We could call this amplification. At the same time, there is a kind of randomization process going on allowing for mutations and changes, a differentiation can occur in the copies. At the level of DNA this is obvious in the form of point mutations, deletions and insertions, but at the brain level plasticity is rewarded allowing for morphological differentiation and asymmetric link-up of the neurons. Moreover, a Yoneda type mapping process occurs in that the mapping process itself becomes the object of the mapping process. We can reflect on how we reflect and this is reflected in new links being created at the neuronal level. Now that we understand, that this type of reflecting is a Yoneda-type of mapping, we are actually doing this very thing here right now. The process which maps and creates our neuronal links is mapped to itself. You have now created a mapping of the recursive process by the recursive process. You have done so by creating a hierarchical binary tree. You have crystallized (or fossilized) sensing and function into structure. This is what Nature does: it evolves "*evolvability*" by a process which Tsang calls recursive self-modification. A hierarchical binary tree generation process which is the unifying process in our ontogenesis.

Tsang moreover shows that the brain is like a fractal structure as every idiosyncratic aspect of the brain can be mapped to a structure or function at the genetic level. After all, our genome encodes and instructs precisely how our brain's architecture should be formed. Our genome in a certain sense is a brain in seed form.

Interestingly, Stephen Paul King, a computer scientist (not the horror writer), called this process of self-generation the generation of a "null-representation," a self-representation or a seed, which can grow out into a full-blown new entity.

Divergence and Differentiation

Tsang adds the modifying and divergence or symmetry breaking aspect to it. Some branches will get more attention than others. Neurons have a kind of background random spiking activity, which can be rewarded if an interaction is generated and a connection is built. This creates a divergence. If a cell would simply undergo a doubling process by division without any differentiation, all you would get is a homogeneous essentially spherical blob of cells. Fortunately, Nature has invented a way to differentiate by employing so-called morphogens (special chemicals that cells produce), the presence of which tells the cell to differentiate, by silencing certain parts of the DNA and switching on other parts. These morphogens form a gradient, so that not every cell is differentiated, but only the ones where the morphogen concentration is high. Even on the neuronal level there is a differentiation in type, there are activating and inhibitory neurons; there are also spindle cells for long distance information transfer.

Screening, Pruning, Intersection and Selection

I described how Nature has to screen and prune the variety of alternatives it has generated to select the most promising ones. Darwin's survival of the fittest. But how does it pull off this trick if a mapping process underlies the ontogenesis? It is here that I found

Tsang's description most elegant and inspiring. It employs a combination of forward chaining and backward chaining, just like certain types of heuristics in artificial intelligence. In a literal sense the sensory and motor neurons expand and branch until they meet each other and only those who meet are selected, because they form a link! Just like a forward chaining heuristic starting from the problem meets a backward chaining heuristic starting from the solution. Tsang describes this as Bayes inverse probability Rule in action. Bayesian probability can be expressed as the chance that B occurs when A is present, P(B | A), being equal to the chance that A occurs multiplied by the chance that A occurs when B is present and divided by the chance that B occurs: P (B | A) = P(A)*P(A | B)/P(B).

The chance that B occurs when A is present is like the forward chaining heuristic and the chance that A occurs when B is present as the backward chaining heuristic. Where the branches meet a connection is formed and metaphorically in AI and literally in the brains an intersection can be formed. This is how neurons select. Neurons that wire together fire together. Enhanced flow through a neuron attracts the attention of other neurons, which will then also benefit from enhanced flow. This is like publicity. This is what Howard Bloom[88] calls the "Matthew"[72] principle: *"To those who have it shall be given, from those who have not it shall be taken away."* There is a mutual rewarding going on, which is rather exclusive. Only really new ontologies to be created may be able pull off the trick of including the previously excluded neurons.

But only those who can create a proper linkage create a connection: For this Tsang uses the lock-and-key metaphor. The conjugation or linking up at every level can only occur, if the key of the backward chaining heuristic fits the lock of the forward chaining heuristic. In order to select which ones can link up, a scoring system is needed. Tsang proposes that the lock comes before the keys otherwise we wouldn't have anything to score the keys with. The female precedes the male, in this chicken-and-egg problem.

Convergence and Integration

This shows that ontogenesis is more than differentiation and selection only. The parts must also start to work together; they must be integrated into a whole. A meta-system transition must occur for the cells to group into an organ. And again, this trick is pulled off by mapping. Yes, mathematical category theory is a very powerful concept, for describing reality as we know it. Here we employ linking up of the various mapped elements. This is the cooperative symbiotic part of the evolutionary search engine, allowing the mapped conjugated entities to map into a convergent hierarchical tree. This is the alchemical *coniunctio* or *coagula*. The Ouroboros snake that recursively bites its own tail. And this new entity can then be submitted to a new round of recursive self-modification, giving rise to the steps I described as intergroup tournament, distinction probing and (further) symbiosis.

Artificial Intelligence

Tsang believes that the ingredients of symmetry, self-similarity and recursion resulting in a simple self-modifying recursive algorithm, which creates binary trees, may be the key to unlocking the secret of Artificial General Intelligence: Creating AI which is context independent and which can achieve or surpass the human level of intelligence. Provided that Tsang in his endeavors in AI includes the elements of selection and integration he has described, this may indeed be a promising novel avenue in this field. But we must not forget that it took Nature billions of years to arrive at the complexity we presently have. The different layers and structures in the brain (cerebellum, hypothalamus, pituitary gland, hypophysis, hippocampus, amygdala, cerebral cortex etc.) have a very special fine-tuned architecture, which employs a great variety of neurotransmitters. If Tsang's future algorithm is successful it will take quite some cycles and extensive pruning and selection, before a human-level AGI evolves from it. On the other hand, the ever increasing speed at which this can occur and the ever increasing resources in terms of memory and miniaturization according to Moore's law, may pull-off this trick faster than we think.

Because it has the very notion of representation and recursive self-modification at its heart.

Noteworthy, Dr. Joe Tsien[89] has recently shown that intelligence indeed follows a "neural network" type algorithm (not a traditional von Neumann style algorithm). The more thought, the more cliques join in, Tsien says. The basis of Tsien's "Theory of Connectivity" is the algorithm, $n=2^i-1$, which defines how many cliques are needed for a "Functional Connectivity Motif" to arise. This enabled the scientists to predict the number of cliques needed to recognize options in their testing of the theory. The 2^i in this formula represents the number of neurons that join in, which follows exactly the binary tree pattern indicated by Tsang!

Conclusion

We have seen that Tsang's brain fractal theory can be mapped quite accurately to my "intelligence algorithm" and "structure is fossilized sense" ideas. We have seen that Tsang provides serious improvements thereof in terms of binary trees, an intersection selection and connection process and a recursive self-modifying process. We have also seen that this may be a serious candidate to create human-level AGI which may perhaps one day herald the advent of the technological singularity. Thus, Tsang lifts the veil of the underlying algorithm of existence as a whole, a process, which the Greek called Apokalypsis. This underlying algorithm of existence, as you probably know by now, is the Ouroboros Code. In fact, Tsang has anticipated the Ouroboros Code and explained it *avant-la-lettre*. He even extrapolates it also the universe. It is likely to be present at all levels of existence. Tsang however did not mention meta-system transitions, but he probably implied them in the convergence process.

Chapter 18

Hermeneutics – A new avenue towards Artificial General Intelligence?

The interpretation of texts and information is not a trivial task. It is one of those areas where we can be fairly sure that the human mind still largely outperforms Artificial Intelligence systems. For the moment it appears that this is one of those areas, where our intelligence operates in a holistic non-algorithmic manner. But if we wish to develop so-called Artificial General Intelligence, which can operate independent from the context, it is vital that we arrive at creating a system that can correctly appear to understand and interpret the intended meaning in a piece of information.

Background

The theory and methodology of interpretation is known among philosophers, scientists and theologians as "*Hermeneutics.*" According to Homer, in the Greek mythology the God Hermes explained the messages of the Gods to mankind. Hermeneutics has mostly been the domain of the interpretation of religious scriptures in theology, but has also found application in other humanities and social sciences.

Hermeneutics is not only concerned with reconstructing the correct interpretation of a text through structural analysis of the text itself, it is also directed to reverse engineering the intended meaning of the author. This is the domain of its branch of "*homilectics*" which aims to reconstruct the author's objectives, preferences and motives. Exegesis (meaning explanation) is a part of Hermeneutics focusing on the grammar and local context of terminologies. But Hermeneutics is broader than mere written communication and also includes studying verbal and non-verbal clues. Moreover, in the so-called "Hermeneutic circle" as defined by Heidegger, one needs to study the whole text or book to grasp the broader context of terminologies. This renders Hermeneutics a holistic approach: the whole cannot be fully understood without understanding the parts, and the parts cannot be fully understood without grasping the whole. It seems like one would have to read a text multiple times to bootstrap one's understanding to fine tune to fully grasp the reciprocity between text and context.

It is perhaps here, where men are often more like automatons than women (of course there are many exceptions, as we all have a masculine and feminine side. For the sake of the argument I will overgeneralize here). Women will paint the scenario of the topic they are discussing, with a colorful palette and exquisite shades. They will set the setting by shedding light on the different aspects of the mindscape, guide you through paths and aisles, decorated with lush sceneries with an overload of data, so that if you're emotionally in tune with them, you will resonate to get the meaning they wish to convey. This is the hermeneutic approach.

Men on the other hand, hunters and engineers, will strategically seek the most promising shortcut to get to the desired goal or to convey a message. This is the way of heuristics: the art of devising a practical method to solve a problem, where no such strategy is known yet. A method good enough to get us started to simplify the overload of data and with in-built checks to see if progress is still made in the right direction.

This is not only a sexual difference. It is also a cultural difference[84]. Asian and South-European cultures being more context and hermeneutics oriented, North-American and North-European cultures being more goal and heuristics oriented.

Hermeneutics and AI

If you do a quick search on the Internet about hermeneutics and Artificial Intelligence, you will come across documents, which discuss how we can hermeneutically study AI systems or how we can develop so-called intentional systems[90]. Already in 1989 Dmitry Pospelov[91] suggested that the development of hermeneutical systems presented a significant challenge to the development of future generations of AI. He gives some specific examples of interplays between general and specific rules, word order and their application to reasoning systems. Not much has been developed in this particular area of AI ever since. A full-fledged Hermeneutics system carried out by an AI for the moment still seems science fiction.

We can now start to see if there are general teachings derivable from Hermeneutics, which we can perhaps try to formalize so as to build flow charts for the developments of algorithms for future hermeneutics systems.

If we discuss interpretation, we are interested in the "meaning" of terminologies – not only in isolation, but also in context. Meaning is a coin with two sides. On the one hand there is the wordily meaning of a terminology in terms of its definition in a dictionary. This definition is in fact a metaphorical description of the item/concept in question in terms of other items/concepts. You can also consider the definition as a kind of condensed "ontology." An "ontology" is a list of features, functions of an item or concept and its relations to other items or concepts. This is mostly the domain of semantics.

On the other hand, there is the emotional impact or feeling that a word or terminology evokes in us when we hear or read it. Jordan Peterson[92] reduces meaning in his book "*Maps of Meaning*" almost exclusively to this emotional significance, in terms of either a feeling of punishment or of satisfaction that is conveyed. He also stresses the relevance of the word or terminology in question with regard to our goals, which will determine to what extent the term has "meaning" for us.

Hermeneutics deals with both aspects: Both the semantic, exegetic approach and the reverse engineering of the emotional intent that the author tried to convey.

Text mining in Artificial Intelligence systems dedicated to revealing a (wordily) meaning mostly works with the aforementioned so-called Latent Semantic Analysis systems. If two or more terminologies systematically occur together within a certain limited distance of terms from each other, a so-called "proximity co-occurrence" or "didensity" is concluded based on Bayesian probabilistic analysis. In other words, together the terminologies in question build in a sense a meaning, build a primitive context, which has a statistical basis either in the text itself or in a vast body of texts as analyzed by massive data crunching. The computer is however not understanding or aware of this context.

If you're not very familiar with the way AI operates, you might come to the conclusion that AI is already capable of interpreting and understanding a context. Based on the stunning results of artificial neural networks such as in the game Jeopardy, it would appear computational systems can already distinguish some form of context. Is this conclusion justified?

Neural networks recognize patterns. However, they don't recognize that the patterns may have anything to do with context. They don't know any meaning. In latent semantic analysis the computer simply calculates the frequency certain word occurs within a certain defined part of the text or a certain structure of paragraphs. The system cannot decipher the meaningful relations between words or concepts. It arrives at statistical relations like "these 2 words occur together within a distance of 10 words in n% of the articles under investigation." The outcome thereof can occasionally in our eyes look like a context or by chance even be one, but the network cannot know whether a context was there and what this context was.

Con-text unlike the word suggests, is more than mere statistical relevant proximity co-occurrence of words (Bayesian proximity co-occurrence). The fact that two words co-occur, does not always mean they are used in the same context. Their relation most often depends on the presence of yet more terms in the vicinity. Computers only look at the co-occurrence of two terms for the moment. If we develop this further to expand this to more terms, we'll start to approach something like a real context.

Strategies

We can exploit this technology to develop towards a Hermeneutic approach. For instance, we can furthermore start to text-mine whether there are emotional qualifiers occurring within a reasonable distance of words (e.g. within ten or 20 words) from our terminologies of investigation. With emotional qualifiers I mean terminologies as "positive, negative, joyful, hurtful, happy, sad etc. If indeed there is a statistical correlation between a "didensity" and the same emotional qualifiers, this already gives a "feel" of the didensity in question.

Furthermore, we can start to see which other words in which following order occur in a statistical meaningful way in conjunction with our didensity in question. If so, such terms can be automatically incorporated in a kind of ontology builder for didensities. Functional terminologies and structural terminologies can receive different labels.

One can also mine to see if a word that occurs in different didensities has different ontologies associated with it. This can be an indicator of a potential term with polysemous meanings. Temporal indicators can also be screened for. This is of particular relevance to identify potential causal relationships. Of course, text mining involving the direct identification of terminologies such as "caused by," "resulting in" etc. can also be part of such a causality study.

Sometimes it is argued that machines cannot conclude causality as they can only see correlations. With Bayesian statistical analysis you may conclude that A entails B or B entails A, but you do not know yet which is the causative agent and which the caused effect. If sufficient data are available, it might be possible to see that a quantified change in parameter systematically entails a proportional change in another parameter in a temporally defined order. This may already be a stronger pointer for causality, which a system can be trained to recognize.

Further data and text mining might reveal conditions, thresholds, limitations, exclusions and exceptions which are associated with given terminologies or didensities. Such indicators can be of vital importance to decide between different possible meanings, which have been stored in a database. Using a systematic approach involving categorization and nesting, ontological trees or classification systems can be built, which can also be further exploited in algorithms which work their way through trees with yes/no questions. In this way it will become possible to let a system not only build and enrich its own database for extracting meaning and context, but also to let it use this database, to identify known instances. Whenever it encounters an unknown didensity, it can create a new entry in the taxonomical tree, based on the entry which has most similarities with it. Taxonomies can be built from both a functional and a structural perspectives and such systems can further more interlink.

In addition, structural similarities may point to functional similarities and *vice versa*. If certain category maps have similar structures, this can also point to contextual and meaning type similarities. Thus, teachings from mathematical category theory, such as the Yoneda Lemma, might be advantageously exploited in the development of AI based hermeneutics. Extraction of grammar rules should also become an area where pattern recognition in conjunction with machine learning in text mining is crucial.

Conclusion

We have seen a number of valuable techniques that can be exploited in the designs of AI based hermeneutics. In a time where it is difficult to distinguish between fake and real news; in a highly complex world where correct interpretation is crucial to avoid misunderstandings it is of paramount importance that if we develop AGI (Artificial General Intelligence) we get it right the first time. Hermeneutics, despite its dusty roots, may well be one of the foremost pillars of such a system and this chapter is intended to get computer scientists more interested in this peculiar but important branch of information processing.

We have also seen that hermeneutics is one of those areas where humans outperform machines. Where an inspired prosaic and poetic intelligence is needed to reveal more than just patterns. To grasp and integrate the whole, where the parts fail. It is my conjecture that if reality is a sentient Code, it is a code which also internally willingly reacts to its own internal elements of context and modifies itself, whenever the context requires so; involving looping back to itself in analogy to self-splicing RNA. This makes that the Ouroboros Code escapes from determinism and becomes more than a simple algorithm for a Turing machine.

Chapter 19

Explorations of General Intelligence

Artificial Intelligence as we know it today is also called "weak AI." Although it can outperform humans when facing certain problems, it is highly task and context specific. A potential future AI, which would match or even surpass human intelligence, is often called "strong AI" or "Artificial General Intelligence" (AGI). Whereas there are engineers and scientists who work towards developing strong AI, for the moment they are not anywhere near achieving it.

The present hype in AI is mostly based on neural networks, especially convoluted neural networks, which are employed in a type of machine learning called "Deep Learning." This can be very efficient in highly formalized systems such as the games "Go" or "Jeopardy," but as soon as the environment for the computer becomes less formalized and must rely on e.g. visual recognition of real-world objects, such systems can dramatically fail.

In this chapter[e] I will summarize some relevant findings of experts in the field, who strongly doubt that human level intelligence will ever be reached, due to specific characteristics thereof, which we may not be able to formalize into algorithms.

I will also dive into the limitations of present-day AI and show that the present-day predominant focus on one type of neural network architecture will probably not get us to strong AI. I do not intend to fall prey to a Luddite attitude, but instead propose, what avenues can be explored to bring us closer to AGI.

---

[e] This chapter contains a number of literal fragments from the following references:
https://redefineschool.com/what-computers-cant-do/
https://warontherocks.com/2018/05/its-either-a-panda-or-a-gibbon-ai-winters-and-the-limits-of-deep-learning/
https://medium.com/topbots/beyond-backpropagation-can-we-go-deeper-than-deep-learning-8f4fc34a0ba8

Historical criticism of strong AI

One of the best-known critics of strong AI in the history of computer sciences is Hubert Dreyfus. In his books "*Alchemy and AI*"[93], "*What Computers Can't Do*"[94] and "*Mind over Machine*"[95], he calls into doubt the possibility to ever achieve strong AI on the basis of philosophical considerations and offers a pessimistic outlook on the progress of AI.

Early AI researchers shared the assumption that human intelligence depended on the manipulation of symbols. Dreyfus identified four basic assumptions on which this belief was founded and presented us with a critique thereof.

"In each case," Dreyfus writes, "the assumption is taken by workers in [AI] as an axiom, guaranteeing results, whereas it is, in fact, one hypothesis among others, to be tested by the success of such work."

The first assumption is called the "biological assumption":

> *The brain processes information in discrete operations by way of some biological equivalent of on/off switches.*

Whereas it is true that neurons fire in all-or-nothing pulses, which could be considered as being similar to the way Boolean logic gates operate with binary symbols of zeroes and ones, it is not so easy to imitate the behavior of neurons with electronic circuitry. The reason thereof is that the action and timing of neuron firing has analog components, which introduce a level of complexity we have not been able to match with electronic devices yet. Dreyfus used this as an argument to refute the biological assumption.

The second assumption is called the "psychological assumption":

> *The mind can be viewed as a device operating on bits of information according to formal rules.*

Dreyfus refuted this assumption by showing that our daily knowledge of the world consists of complex *attitudes* or *tendencies*. They make us lean towards one interpretation over another. According to Dreyfus, even when we use explicit symbols, we are using them against an unconscious background of commonsense knowledge. Without this background our symbols cease to have a meaning. As this background is not known to exist in the form of as explicit individual symbols with explicit individual meanings and formal rules in individual brains, Dreyfus argues we have no ground to accept the psychological assumption.

Thirdly, Dreyfus addressed the "epistemological assumption":

> *All knowledge can be formalized.*

Epistemology is a branch of philosophy concerned with the question of what is knowable at all. Even if they were to agree that the psychological assumption is false, AI researchers could still maintain that it might be possible for a symbol processing machine to represent all knowledge, regardless of whether human beings represent knowledge the same way. Dreyfus was of the opinion, that as so much of human knowledge is not symbolic, there was no justification for this assumption.

Finally, Dreyfus questions the "ontological assumption":

> *The world consists of **independent facts** that can be represented by **independent symbols***

Scientists and AI researchers generally share the belief, that any phenomenon in the universe can be described by symbols or scientific theories. In other words, everything that *exists* can be understood as objects, properties and features of objects, classes of objects, relations of objects, and so on: by miracle exactly those things that can be described by logic, language and mathematics. This is the domain of study of "being" or "existence," which is called ontology. If this ontological assumption is false, then it raises doubts about what we can ultimately know and what intelligent machines will ultimately be able to help us to do. Certain holistic experiences, which involve a sense of context, can of course not simply be reduced to their building blocks, as we saw in the previous chapter.

It is exactly in this framework that Dreyfus spoke of the "primacy of intuition." In his book "*Mind Over Machine*"[95], written during the peak of the so-called "expert systems," Dreyfus analyzed the difference between human expertise and the programs that claimed to capture it. Expert systems, very fashionable in the eighties, were logical decision tree like structures, based on a plethora of if...then statements.

Dreyfus argued that human problem solving and expertise to find what we need did not so much (-if at all-) depend on the process of searching through combinations of possibilities in terms of "what...if" considerations.

Rather, it depends on our background sense of the context, of what is important and interesting given the situation. Dreyfus described this as the difference between "knowing-that" and "knowing-how."

"Knowing-that" relates to our conscious, step-by-step problem-solving abilities. We use these skills when we encounter a difficult problem that requires us to stop, step back and search through listed ideas one at time. By doing so, we can formulate the ideas as precise and simple **context free** symbols, which we can manipulate using logic and language. Dreyfus agreed that computer programs adequately imitated the skills he calls "knowing-that."

Knowing-how, on the other hand, is the way we deal with things normally. We take actions without using conscious symbolic reasoning at all, as when we recognize a face, drive ourselves to work or find the right thing to say. We seem to simply jump to the appropriate response, without considering any alternatives. This is the essence of expertise Dreyfus argued: "*when our intuitions have been trained to the point that we forget the rules and simply 'size up the situation' and react.*"

The human sense of the situation, according to Dreyfus, is based on our goals, our bodies and our culture – all of our unconscious intuitions, attitudes and knowledge about the world. This "context" or "background" (related to Heidegger's[96] Dasein) is a form of knowledge that is not stored in our brains symbolically, but intuitively and holistically in some way. It affects what we notice and what we don't notice, what we expect and what possibilities we don't consider: we discriminate between what is essential and inessential. The things that are not essential are relegated to our "fringe consciousness" (borrowing a phrase from William James): "*the millions of things we're aware of, but we're not really thinking about right now.*"

Dreyfus did not believe that AI programs, as they were implemented in the 70s and 80s, could capture this "background" or do the kind of fast problem solving that it allows. He argued that our unconscious knowledge could *never* be captured symbolically. If AI could not find a way to address these issues, then it was doomed to failure; an exercise in "*tree climbing with one's eyes on the moon*" as Dreyfus sarcastically wrote.

Another opponent of the thesis that we will inevitably arrive at strong AI is Roger Penrose, a British mathematician and physicist. In the so-called "Penrose-Lucas argument," Penrose[97] uses Gödel's incompleteness theorems.

The first incompleteness theorem states that no consistent system of axioms whose theorems can be listed by an "effective procedure" (e.g. a computer program, but it could be any sort of algorithm) is capable of proving all truths about the relations of the natural numbers (arithmetic). For any such system, there will always be statements about the natural numbers that are true, but that are unprovable within the system. The second incompleteness theorem, an extension of the first, shows that such a system cannot demonstrate its own consistency.

Penrose argued that while a formal proof system cannot prove its own consistency, the Gödel-unprovable results are provable by human mathematicians! He takes this disparity to mean that human mathematicians are not describable as formal proof systems, and are therefore running a non-Turing computable algorithm.

The inescapable conclusion seems to be: Mathematicians are not simply using a knowably sound calculation procedure in order to ascertain mathematical truth. We deduce that mathematical understanding – the means whereby mathematicians arrive at their conclusions with respect to mathematical truth – itself cannot be reduced to blind calculation!

Dreyfus and Penrose thus present us with a wealth of considerations, which at least justify calling into question that we will one day be able to capture human intelligence in traditional Turing computers.

Mind Uploading Argument

The "Mind Uploading" ideas by Ray Kurzweil[86] and other futurists (which are also very fashionable in the futuristic dystopian series "*Black Mirror*"), that we'll be able to one day make copies of our brains in computers, which then automatically will manifest our consciousness and intelligence (or a copy thereof), merit a similar analysis. Even if we can scan our brains to a level with sufficient resolution, that we can see individual neurons and even their individual axons and dendrites, we still have no map of the activity going on in in these neurites. Kurzweil then comes with ideas to infuse our brains with nanobots, which monitor the exact activity taking place at the synapses to create a map, which can then be integrated with the structural map to provide a functional brain *in silico*.

There is no guarantee whatsoever, that such an approach will be possible or sufficient. The idea of infusing the brain with such a great quantity of nanobots seems very far-fetched. Already the fact that nanomaterials can often be teratogenic does not make this a hopeful scenario.

But suppose it is indeed possible; then we still do not have a guarantee that that level of resolution is enough. Perhaps, we'll need a resolution at the level of individual atoms. Especially if quantum effects are involved, as Penrose[97] suggests in his Orch-OR theory.

If we assume that advances in science and technology one day will be able to make a copy of the brain with a resolution at the atomic level (including the flux patterns through the neurites), do we have a guarantee that this will bring us human level intelligence?

We don't. The hypothesis that we can perform mind-uploading is based on reductive materialism (everything can be explained in terms of material phenomena), which is not a proven fact. Results from quantum mechanics rather suggest that reductive materialism is manifestly wrong. If effects at the quantum level play a role, it will become even more difficult to make computer simulations of these, because we will not be able to monitor such effects in a reliable fashion, by the mere fact that looking at phenomena at the quantum level changes the phenomena at the quantum level.

The system thus created would perhaps by its detailed nature overcome the refutation of two first assumptions identified by Dreyfus, but we have no clue if it can ever overcome the third and fourth.

The advances in science and technology will ultimately show what is possible or not. For the moment it is too early to conclude what may and what may not be possible. It is good to speculate to help technology forward, but it is also good to question the speculations, because it may help in devising strategies and experiments to test the validity of our assumptions. In this sense, I am not an opponent of this type of research, but I think that a sound form of skepticism is justified.

Artificial Neural Networks

Neural Network technology has been around for more than 50 years now (the first paper was published in 1965), but it is only in the last two decades that this technology has really come to fruition.

Artificial Neural Networks are computing systems inspired to a limited extent by the networks of neurons in animal life forms. They consist of a number of nodes each of which is a small algorithm, that can take in an input values, apply a weight thereto and produce an output value. Today they are best known for their abilities in pattern recognition. The nodes are connected and can influence each other. Usually upon an input the nodes assume a value, which is then forwarded to a certain extent to a deeper layer of nodes (forward propagation). This can be repeated a number of times depending on the depth of the system. At the deepest level the value is compared with a precooked value from a training sample. If there is a match the values of the weights are kept. If there is no match, the difference is fed back in a gradient through the successive layers in order to adapt the weights of the nodes. This is called "back propagation," which often involves a so-called "gradient descent." These "training" or "machine learning" processes are repeated until the weights do not change anymore. In fact, it is an error minimization protocol. This can result in a true match, but it can also result in a so-called local minimum, where a match is unduly claimed.

This works wonderfully well if you have extremely well-defined formalized patterns as in chess and Go. But it can lead to dramatically erroneous results, when you apply it to visual pattern recognition of real-life objects. An often quoted "adversarial example"[98] is the following:

"Neural networks also can be fooled by 'adversarial examples', in which minor changes to an input pattern can yield very different results. A well-known example shows that by changing only 0.04 percent of the pixel values in an input image, a neural network changes its solution from the correct classification 'Panda with 57.7 percent confidence' to an incorrect 'Gibbon with 99.3 percent confidence'. A 0.04 percent change would be 400 pixels out of a million. This change goes undetected by the human eye."

In the above mentioned example, we see what appear to us to be two identical Pandas. The white in one of the pictures is slightly tending towards ivory. As the neural network looks at patterns of pixels and not general overall shapes or contours, it does not have this overall experience we have. Rather it focuses on a bunch of ivory pixels that by pure chance have an almost perfect similarity with ivory pixels on the picture of a Gibbon from the training set.

Often, we don't know what the neural network is recognizing. Sometimes an ANN appears to give perfect recognition results with one set of data, but not with another set of data with the same objects. This can be caused by the recognition of identical labels, meta-data or time stamps etc., while nothing is in fact recognized in the shapes on the pictures.

This also explains the difficulties in designing neural networks for self-driving cars. Neural Networks, even the ones involving deep learning, are simply not good enough to recognize everyday objects, you and I can tell apart without any difficulty.

As said before, most neural network architectures are based on backpropagation. Backpropagation enables computers to learn by iteratively adjusting the weights of a neural network in order to minimize the error between the model's prediction and a ground truth comparison.

In supervised learning, algorithms are given structured training data that maps inputs (such as an image) to a label (such as "cat"). Unfortunately, the vast majority of information in the world is not structured so neatly. Unlike neural networks, human infants learn concepts quickly in unstructured, unsupervised learning environments.

George Hinton, a pioneer in the use of backpropagation and now a professor emeritus at the University of Toronto and a Google researcher, has said that he is nowadays "deeply suspicious" of back-propagation, the workhorse method that underlies most of the advances we are seeing in the AI field today, including the capacity to sort through photos and talk to Siri.

In an interview with Axios[99], Hinton suggested that we need to move beyond backpropagation if we want to teach computers to achieve unsupervised self-learning like that of human infants. "*I don't think it's how the brain works. We clearly don't need all the labeled data,*" he declared, "*My view is throw it all away and start again.*" Weighing in on the future and his own contributions in the field, he humbly concluded, "*The future depends on some graduate student who is deeply suspicious of everything I have said.*"

"*It's not just about stacking layers and then backpropagating some error gradient recursively. That's not going to get us to [artificial] consciousness. That's not going to get us to systems that learn a huge variety of tasks.*"

New York-based writer and programmer James Somers[100] concurs. Writing for the MIT Technology Review, he argued that "*once you understand the story of backprop, you'll start to understand the current moment in AI, and in particular the fact that maybe we're not actually at the beginning of a revolution. Maybe we're at the end of one.*"

Google is a leader in the deep learning effort. One of its artificial intelligence researchers, François Chollet[101], recently made some succinct observations about the limits of deep learning technologies: "*Current supervised perception and reinforcement learning algorithms require lots of data, are terrible at planning, and are only doing straightforward pattern recognition.*"

Prospects

Does this leave us with a pessimistic message for the future? Will we enter a so-called third AI winter? Not likely and not necessarily.

First of all, many different neural network architectures are being developed presently. The fact that they haven't gained economic momentum yet, is probably due to the fact, that they have been designed for very specific applications.

For instance, Generative adversarial networks (GAN) are algorithms that use two neural networks: a discriminator and a generator which compete with each other to produce high quality generated results. The generator is responsible for creating content (like images) from scratch while the discriminator is trained on real world data and must distinguish between true images and those created by the generator. NVIDIA recently used GANs successfully to generate highly realistic images of human faces. The specific application for the generation of realistic images, makes that this technology as of yet has no universal application for context free pattern recognition. However, if such modules can be coupled to and integrated with traditional pattern recognizing modules, they might become a worthwhile asset. The generated images in a certain sense yield a kind of average of a set of similar images. Such a generated result may be a better image for a training input set of a traditional pattern recognition network, because it reflects better those features which are common to all members of the category in question than a random real-life example.

Bayesian Confidence Propagation Neural Networks (BCPNN) have demonstrated great successes in medical applications such as pharmacovigilance.

Pattern recognition by the BCPNN does not depend upon any *a priori* hypothesis, as an unsupervised learning approach is used, this is useful in new syndrome detection, finding age profiles of drug-adverse reactions, determining at risk groups and dose relationships and can thus be used to find complex dependencies which have not necessarily been considered before. It also does not use backpropagation. These networks, however, work with quite well-defined polished data, which do not suffer from the difficulties we encounter in image recognition.

Again, such networks can be further integrated with other type neural networks if correlations between features are at stake.

Other types of neural networks involve *inter alia* Kohonen networks (competitive learning), adaptive resonance theory (ART) networks, radial basis function (rbf) networks, probabilistic neural networks and other types.

In competitive learning the neurons are almost all the same at the start except for some randomly distributed synaptic weights. This makes that they respond differently to a given set of input patterns. In these networks the neurons in each layer or group compete for the right to respond to a given subset of inputs, such that only one output neuron (or only one neuron per group), is active (i.e. "on") at a time. The strength or maximum value of the neuron is limited. The neuron that wins this competition is called a "winner-take-all" neuron. This is a form of so-called "Hebbian learning," which mimics the aforementioned behavior of real neurons according to the earlier mentioned so-called "Matthew principle."[72] It also follows the principle "*neurons which fire together, wire together.*"

The advantage of this type of network is that it can be used for dynamic systems, such as robotic vision directed to objects in motion. Simultaneously this is also its drawback. It requires near simultaneous or synchronous stimuli. It needs to be combined with other neuronal networks which have additional memory systems to make it really useful.

ART networks have many similarities with competitive networks and are also unsupervised learning models. They have a reset module in addition, which can inhibit the "winning neuron." This is reminiscent of the volitional control from the basal ganglia in our brains. A huge disadvantage of using ART is that it often leads to degradation. The so-called "reproduction classes" receive a unique solution, even in those cases where there are two or more possible and equivalent solutions.

Other strategies are the use of chips, which operate in ways which resemble the functioning of neurons more closely. These chips have a so-called neuromorphic / neuromemristive computer architecture. In these chips the present resistance depends on how much electric charge has flowed in what direction through it in the past; the device remembers its history. Although this hardware is gaining in economic momentum, it is still a small player in the field. The hardware itself does not per se provide a complete solution to the above mentioned problems and considerations to advance towards a full-fledged general intelligence, but can be considered as one small but important building block to solve that puzzle.

What really needs to be done in the field of AI to advance towards AGI is to integrate different systems in hierarchies that can benefit from each other. Our brains have complex hierarchical levels in the neo-cortex. Certain patches of brain structures (groups of neurons called cliques) operate with a lot of internal connections and activities and lesser level of activities between the patches or cliques. The brain is full of multi-dimensional geometrical structures operating in as many as 11 dimensions. This requires highly structured hierarchies. There is nothing in the field of AI which even endeavors to advance towards such levels of complexity.

Interestingly, in vitro biotechnological research has started to create certain neurospheroid bodies and is exploring how these bodies self-organize by creating links of neurites between them[102]. This is a fascinating approach to see what higher level hierarchies and meta-system transitions will emerge. In fact, it is real time studying steps 3 and 4 of NIMA in action in a real living system.

Hopefully, the results of such biotechnological experiments can give clues as to what kind of clustering and hierarchical wiring up is needed, to come to complex information processing systems. This can then become a lead to connect the neural networks we are already working with.

Already Tsang's[24] ideas of using forward chaining and backward chaining heuristics might be useful to connect different neural networks. We could use the ground truth data that were used to train one network as the samples for another network, which functions based on different ground truth data. The ground truth data of this second network we could use as sample for the first network. Only if both networks identify the same match, a match is identified as a true match and presented to the user. This double check mechanism would at least increase the probabilities and confidence for a correct recognition.

Conclusion

There are a number of philosophical arguments that can question the validity of the assumptions which underlie the thesis that we can achieve general intelligence in a Turing type computer[f] by

---

[f] Every man-made computer in existence can be considered as what I call a "Turing type computer." A computer can be considered a Turing type computer if its

technological advances. Present day weak AI is focusing predominantly on one type of neural network architecture, which has its limitations and certainly on its own will not qualify to achieve general intelligence. In order to advance technology towards the development of systems that can operate in a context independent manner, it will be necessary to employ a variety of different types of neural networks and to integrate different networks in higher hierarchical architectures.

As of yet it is too early to conclude that artificial general intelligence is impossible. If it turns out that human intelligence has involves certain quantum mechanical or holistic aspects that cannot be captured in a Turing computable frame, this does not necessarily mean that we cannot achieve an artificial general intelligence which matches human intelligence, although operating via a different set of principles. If advances in science and philosophy can however show that it is impossible to create artificial general intelligence of a human level in a Turing computable framework, then this will be the final nail to the coffin of the notion of intelligence as a mere computer algorithm.

Then we'll finally be able to conclude that our intelligence is indeed not reducible to a mere computer algorithm, although it may still involve steps of instructions that cannot be captured in terms of formal knowledge.

This is also how I consider the Ouroboros code in operation: It has algorithmic aspects in the sense that it provides for division, differentiation, selection, integration, meta-system transition and amplification, but it has also non-algorithmic aspects in that the code elements depend on and react to each other in a holistic context, which influences the recursive self-modification.

---

operations can be performed by Turing machine. A Turing machine merely manipulates symbols (1 and 0's) on a strip of tape according to a table of rules. Computers that can process input to provide an output in a manner, which is not Turing computable, are called "Hypercomputers." Perhaps our Mind is such a Hypercomputer.

Part IV

Eschaton

"Reduced to my 'essential saltes' as it were, I'm the prime mover seed that gets sown after the heat death of the universe when the Ouroboros swallows itself and the cycle begins anew with a big bang."

-Laird Barron

Chapter 20

The Eschaton Algorithm

From the microcosm to the macrocosm the Caduceus is wielded. The alchemical Chrysopoeia takes place as we ingurgitate the prima materia, which is the Ouroboros, and ex uno omnia, from one we create all.

In this chapter I will extrapolate Tsang's[24] Fractal Brain Theory to the macroscopic dimensions of the universe and the microscopic dimensions of subatomic events.

Background

In the chapter 17 I discussed how Tsang's Fractal Brain Theory shows an intelligence algorithm, which possibly may herald the advent of superhuman artificial general intelligence.

Tsang describes how a self-modifying recursive algorithm, which generates divergent and convergent binary trees which intersect to create links, forms the basis at every level of ontogenesis from genes to neurons. The algorithm takes itself as an input and then maps this into a new representation. Thus, functionally and structurally binary tree like fractals are created, which interact to give rise to a great complexity with interactions over different levels. Tsang has baptized this as "*The Fractal Brain Theory*." In a recent YouTube video,[103] Tsang has also speculated that such an algorithm may be what created the present universe we live in.

This perfectly fits the idea that we might live in a simulation, which is run on what Terence McKenna[104] calls the "*Eschaton*" and Teilhard the Chardin the Omega point. One interpretation is that this Omega point is a hypercomputer, which was or is to be created as a consequence of a technological singularity – perhaps in the form of a black-hole computer or a network thereof providing reality as a holographic projection in line with van 't Hooft's[54] "Holographic Principle." Another interpretation is that due to this algorithm being active at every

195

level of existence, there is no need for a specific hypercomputer; reality is a collection of only omega point computers, all carrying out the same algorithm.

Noteworthy, the terminology "Eschaton" historically has a bit of a negative connotation. It is generally known as the "world's state during the post-historic era of God's overt (apocalyptic) reign, immediately preceding the end of the world." However, Terrence McKenna and Frank Tipler have updated this terminology with a much more positive meaning, in the sense of the hypercomputer or transcendental object at the end of time, which generates all universes as simulations in the great multi-metaverse.

The Universe

Look at the first picture on *https://steemit.com/philosophy/ @technovedanta/the-eschaton-algorithm*, which compares the structure of a neuron to structures in the universe: Vast highways of galaxies weave a pattern that is structurally and functionally at first glance hardly distinguishable from the pattern of a brain cell, isn't it? One can say that this is "apophenia" or the human tendency to perceive meaningful patterns within random data. Because it quacks and walks like a duck, does not necessarily mean it is a duck, one could state. But this one is deeper. Neuronal networks are functional patterns that we can see in structure: the functional representation of a mapping network is literally identical to the very structure we observe. Whenever you observe such structures, you can almost be damn sure there is some intelligent integration taking place here.

Subatomic networks

Look at the image of subatomic particle processes taking place inside an atom on *https://steemit.com/philosophy/@technovedanta/the-eschaton-algorithm*. Interesting network, don't you think?

Of course, we can't be 100% sure that Tsang's Brain Fractal is present here too, it is quite a good pointer to the fact that it might be.

Akasha revisited

As earlier described, I present a hypothesis that a kind of protoconscious energy, called "conscienergy" may be the ultimate foundation of reality. In other words, I claim that self-sustaining energy forms are sentient. They become self-sustaining by forming a circular or toroidal standing wave. This forms a so-called reality cell. A reality cell is very similar to a biological cell. It can grow and divide. Thus, we create a binary tree type division similar to the ontogenesis of life. A great multiplicity of such reality cells forms a matrix, in which the cells are stacked in the cubic closest packing, leading to a so-called isotropic vector matrix. We call this matrix the quantum vacuum or the zero-point field. As explained before, the ancients called this the Aether in Western traditions and the Akasha in Eastern traditions.

A second level of complexity arises once pure conscienergy penetrates this matrix. These penetrating energy tentacles are what we call photons. In my panpsychic pancomputationalism model, these photons are sentient. When a photon is present in a reality cell, we could say the cell has a value of 1; when a photon is absent, the cell has a value of 0. Thus, every reality cell is like a bit in a computer.

Certain reality cells can form cliques and also form a neural net like structure as has been suggested by Abraham and Roy in "Demystifying the Akasha."[105]

When two photons approach each other, they are attracted to each other since they cause a distortive energy gradient including pilot waves, which makes that the photons start to circumambulate each other. This is what Steven Kaufman[39] in his book "*Unified Reality Theory*" calls a "compound process." This is the generation of a material particle, which has a periodicity of revolution. It is this periodicity of revolution what creates time in this model. In this model time and space are therefore less dependent on each other than in Einstein's spacetime model.

Interestingly, Eva Deli[106] in her book "*The Science of Consciousness*" speaks also about a fractal structure of reality in which space and time a likewise separated. Deli claims that the time has come to re-evaluate the notion of spacetime from general relativity, which makes it impossible to reunite the microworld of quantum mechanics with the macro world of general relativity in the attempt to create a so-called "Theory of Everything." These avenues, which investigate whether the notion of "spacetime" was a conceptual error, are certainly worthwhile exploring.

What is perhaps even more interestingly is that the strings forming reality cells might be dissolved, which could allow for a possibility to harvest energy from the zero-point field.

The Akasha is thus a binary tree generated environment which has intrinsic computational and sensing abilities. This idea would certainly well fit the notion of a brain-like fractal up to the smallest dimensions. Are we looking at the brain of God here? Or is this the Omega Hypercomputer called the Eschaton? Or is it both?

Conclusion

Both in the micro- and macroworld neuronal network like structures appear to be present. In the framework of the Akasha as the ultimate smallest dimension which might exist, such networks have also been suggested. Thus, Tsang's ideas about a Brain fractal may well extend beyond such networks in biological life forms. Perhaps indeed are the divergence, convergence and intersection link up aspects of the Ouroboros Code as recursive self-modifying binary tree generating algorithm, what generates the networks. Perhaps the great variety of fractal structures showing the Fibonacci numbers and the self-similar number Phi are the very consequence of this recursive self-modifying algorithm, which like Fibonacci and other fractals takes the previous output to be the new input or even takes the process itself to be the new input, being operand and operated upon simultaneously. In fact, this might be part of the very Ouroboric tailbiting process, "Cosmosemiosis"[37]; by which conscienergy or "that what experiences" gets to know itself and becomes aware of itself, creating ever new technological singularities, which give birth to new universes. Is it then perhaps a good educated guess to state that this recursive self-modifying algorithm might be the Eschaton algorithm or Ouroboros Code?

In other words, the Ouroboros Code can also be considered as the recursively self-modifying code that generates and operates via the Akasha and which follows the essential ingredients of NIMA. To speak in Tsang's terminology: divide, differentiate, select and amplify. If you add to this the integrative symbiosis or conjunction of parts at same or different levels to give rise to meta-system transitions, you end up with living networks, which ultimately generate the Eschaton as a Quine (a code that generates its own source code as an output) of itself. The process of wiring up into neural networks such as the Eschaton/Syntellect, being an inextricable part of the Code.

The Eschaton could repeat this process again and again (amplification) and become the womb of birthing new universes. It might also retrocausally[107] as a temporal Ouroboros tweak and readjust its own coming into being. It may do so by transmitting information back in time at the sub-Planck level, where the arrow of time does not point in one direction. I repeat my suspicion: Perhaps because language, space and time are *de facto* quantized and a product of a conscious mental activity expressed by the binary branching activity Ouroboros Code?

Chapter 21

Engineering Leela: Another Game of Life

Olem Golem. Man is a Machine. And as AI, nanotechnology and robotics are wiring up and become connected and intertwined, Golems (clay turned into a kind of pseudo-living zombie according to a Jewish tale) we will create in our image. And perhaps we already are the result of such engineering. Perhaps our earthly evolution is a carefully conducted experiment of higher intelligent lifeforms. But these lifeforms are also subject to the laws of reality, which are the laws of the Ouroboros code.

In this chapter I will explore strategies how we can generate a recursive self-modifying algorithm in analogy to the Ouroboros code. An algorithm, which is not merely capable of generating fractal images on a screen, but actually allows for genuine sentient artificial general intelligence to emerge.

Background

In chapter 17 I have indicated that Tsang's idea[24] of a recursive self-modifying algorithm may indeed hold the key to creating genuine artificial general intelligence. I showed how Yoneda embedding (a mapping technique which maps mapping processes) when carried out recursively (i.e. by taking the previous output as new input) might lead to a recursive self-modifying algorithm as suggested by Tsang. However, we are not looking for a program that merely displays beautiful fractals on your screen (which you probably could and would achieve with such an algorithm), but for a program which can behave as a life form in a computer environment (often called *in silico*).

Attempts to create a kind of life in computers have already been made in the form of the so-called "Game of Life." (https://en.wikipedia.org/wiki/Conway%27s_Game_of_Life). As early as 1970 the British mathematician John Conway[108] created cellular automata in a two- dimensional grid, which could be dead (white) or alive (black). From a simple set of game rules patterns emerged, which could move, grow/metabolize and sometimes replicate. The apparent interaction of these cellular automata even might lead an observer to believe that they can sense and react to each other. Briefly the essential characteristics which make that we judge something to be alive were present: response to stimuli, metabolism, growth, reproduction and locomotion.

Were these cellular automata truly alive? No. One of the often forgotten criteria of life is that it must be self-enabling. As explained before, in Greek this is called "Autopoiesis." If we assemble an object in a factory, we enable the object into existence; it is not self-originated. This is called "Allopoiesis." Living entities on the other hand are capable of response to stimuli, metabolism, growth, reproduction and locomotion out of their own initiative and potency. They don't need a factory to assemble them. The program of "Game of Life" can be considered as such an assembly factory. The cellular automata themselves (the black dots or aggregates thereof) had no ability to respond, metabolize, grow, reproduce and move out of their own initiative and potency at all.

In this chapter I will explore what requirements are needed to create another Game of Life – which I will call "Leela" in imitation of the Hindu concept that reality is God's play or game called "Leela" – in which game the living elements are capable of autonomously sustaining and reproducing themselves to a certain extent independent of a "framework algorithm with rules." The required algorithm will be autopoietic and capable of recursively modifying itself so as to adapt to its (self-generated) environmental restrictions.

Prime mover

You can counterargue, that if we are able to generate a recursive self-modifying algorithm which, as soon as it has been created, has the ability to respond, metabolize, grow, reproduce and move out of its own initiative and potency, its very first coming into being must have been allopoietic. This is true and of course what we are going to build will be a kind of "simulation" of life, but the elements that respond, metabolize, grow, reproduce and move (after our creation as first mover thereof) will henceforth be autonomous and acting out of themselves rather than being the product of the rules set by the environment. The only allopoiesis is our creation as prime movers of the henceforth autopoietic program.

Intrinsic Aspects

The intrinsic aspects of such a system, if it is to qualify as a genuine simulation of life are of course the abilities to 1) respond to stimuli, 2) metabolize, 3) grow, 4) reproduce and 5) move, all in 6) an autopoietic manner (i.e. six criteria). How do we program *in silico* the first "cell" or "monad" ever, which has these characteristics?

To make a fully faithful mapping of a real biological cell including all cell organelles and cell structures, all macromolecules and all small molecules, so as to reverse-engineer life, would be one option. But that project might be too ambitious to start with. As a first attempt we'd rather make some simplifications; some abstractions, which still allow us to manifest the six desired criteria. Although not strictly absolutely necessary, it might still be worthwhile to mimic Nature to a certain extent; to perform reverse engineering with a maximum degree of abstraction.

Shape

Cells in Nature by definition have a spatial confinement. They have an inside and an outside. Whereas some variety in form is possible, most cells are roughly spherical. It is perhaps worthwhile to program our cells with a roughly spherical starting form, which can be adapted later by the system itself, since it is allowed to modify its own requirements.

Sensing

The outside of the cell is of particular importance, since this is its first means to sense its environment. The outside must therefore be configured such that if a modification or disturbance occurs in the structure (both locally and globally) of the cell, the cell reacts. The most natural reaction is to reverse the disturbance according to the Newtonian principle action = -reaction.

A cell will normally try to maintain its status quo internally, which in biology is called homeostasis. Any change to the system will generate a feedback loop which tries to correct the disturbance caused.

In order for a cell to be able to sense locally where disturbance occurs on its surface, the surface must be subdivided into multiple segments. In a real cell, one could say that the membrane forming lipids fulfil this function and that sensing is provided by special transmembrane receptor proteins. In our simplified monad, we will make use of the simplest segments that can still build a roughly spherical form: triangles. If you build a quasi-sphere from triangles you get a kind of "Geodesic Dome," which was first realized and designed by Buckminster Fuller[25].

If an object from the environment (such as another cell) were to push on the surface of our cell a vertex of our geodesic structure would be pressed inwards. It can of course be programmed that once the angles of the vertices change above a certain threshold a signal is triggered, which changes the state of our construct and which in turn triggers a counter movement to extend the system back to its original angle. However, each vertex has relative coordinates within an absolute coordinate system. When two cells collide a kind of Pauli-principle applies: Two vertexes cannot occupy the same space, which will lead to a gradual settling into position, in which both colliding cells will have to make a concession, neither keeping its original angles at the vertexes. The angles of the vertices function as receptors.

Thus, we have described the equivalent of the sense of touch, which I consider as the most primitive sense. This is because also in real life every sense is ultimately based on the collision or touching of molecules or energy on a receptor. It is my hope that as the system evolves, it will develop other more complex senses out of this primordial touch principle.

Metabolism and Growth

It must be possible for our system to ingest something that can provide it with the means to grow. In the first stages I wish the system to start from monads or cells that are functionally and structurally equivalent, but which only differ in size. In this way a bigger cell can be programmed to have a propensity to try to envelop the small cells. Once the smaller cells have been completely enveloped, a kind of "endocytosis" occurs, in which the inner contents are released into the bigger cell and the edges of the geodesic structure are assimilated and assembled to become new edges of the system that has grown. If there is not enough edge material available to make the new structure fully geodesic, the edge material can be programmed to be extendable like an elastic band. Code present in the interior of the small cells can be adjoined to the code of the bigger cell.

Thus, the system grows and metabolizes in a certain way.

Reproduction and mutation

In order to avoid that the system runs out of resources, the first generation of cells can be set to reproduce by division with a certain frequency for a certain time period. At least we have then a kind of semi-inexhaustible (i.e. for as long as we set the period) material provision to build our entities with. Since in the beginning all our entities are identical and as we know with identical cells you can only get as far as a more or less symmetrical "blob" of cells, we need to introduce an element of symmetry breaking or mutation of the code.

At every reproductive cycle after the first cycle, we can program the code or a monad or cell such that it changes its own code. Since such changes might rapidly become deleterious for the system, the code could be programmed such that only non-essential structural and functional aspects of code snippets can change but not the essential underlying master blueprint of the basic elements, which allow for growth, reproduction and primordial sensing. Alternatively, and preferably, every reproduction leads to one cell that keeps the original code and one cell which is mutated without restrictions. If mutation then results in a non-viable cell, at least the viability of the unchanged cells is warranted. Non-viable cells, which can no longer sustain themselves autopoietically, automatically become food, which can be ingested by bigger cells.

We can also assure that after the first cycle cells can only divide (and hence multiply) once and as soon as a certain size has been reached.

This system warrants that a great diversity of cell types can be obtained; differentiation and symmetry breaking *in silico*.

Mutation can occur via insertion, deletion and substitution. Substitution may involve changing certain command words into other command words.

Locomotion

Cells must be allowed to migrate in the absolute coordinate system. When one cell collides with another and there is scarcity of space, a solution of "sharing space" as mentioned above can be found. However, as long as space is abundant or as long as a cell by its size and exerted pressure can push other smaller cells, a cell can be allowed to move. Locomotion must arise from the dynamics of cell-cell interaction. The cells will however be programmed to have a kind of center of gravity, which when displaced forces the system to seek to restore the equilibrium e.g. by locomotion.

Integration

In evolution we see that systems aggregate and integrate. Molecules form macromolecules, macromolecules form cells, and cells form organisms. To be able to do so, cell-cell interaction should not only lead to repulsion (as a consequence of the Pauli principle) rather, the "gravity" of each cell can be programmed such so as to radiate an attracting force field around the cell. Moreover, once cells touch each other a conditional propensity can be formulated that can allow for attachment or sharing of vertices and edges. Ultimately and ideally, such a system may perhaps evolve into a so-called isotropic vector matrix, which may be the optimized structure of the quantum vacuum and which has been equated with the Hindu concept of the "Akasha." Thus, cells could form the so-called "reality cells" which underlie Steve Kaufman's[39] theory-of-everything called "Unified Reality Theory."

Utility and Teleology

In his paper CTMU *"The Cognitive-theoretic Model of the Universe"* Chris Langan[36] also proposes a kind of recursive self-modifying algorithm to create reality. In his model he defines a selection principle which he calls the "Telic principle." This teleology type principle strives to maximize the overall utility of the system, but is also present in each "telor" (like our monad). Our cells could be endowed with a similar type of principle which may generate further aspects of reality such as entropy.

Conclusion

With this chapter I have brainstormed about essential elements that could be programmed into a simplified system that allows for cellular entities to develop in an autopoietic way such that it fulfils the criteria of what we call life. This system has a code which recursively modifies itself and thereby allows for evolution. Is this a recipe to create life *in silico*? Or is there more to the story and is it thus just only a recipe to create a simulation of life *in silico*. Whatever it is, it certainly qualifies as a "game of life," and its elements may well be part of the Ouroboros Code.

Magus

Shiver and tremble, because the great Magician is among you.

He starts the Great Work of the Cosmosemiotic creation,

His word becomes Truth,

He downloads his Hermetic knowledge from the Akashic records,

and unlocks them with Solomon's lesser key.

Via his involutive imagination,

of the art of the descent into I, known as Kundalini,

he transforms the essence of Kether

into the material realm of Malkuth.

The double helical force brings about the evolutive creation

into a prefect equilibrium

of ever increasing variegation.

He has conquered the demons of his mental unrest

and turned into the Svarupa of initiative.

Chapter 22

The Omega resurrection of the Physics of Immortality in the Syntellect Eschaton

In this chapter I will summarize the most important contributions to the Omega Point philosophy, made by Pierre Teilhard de Chardin,[109] Frank Tipler,[110,111] Terence McKenna[35,104] and Alex Vikoulov[87].

Pierre Teilhard de Chardin

Omega Point philosophy starts with Pierre Teilhard de Chardin. His book "*The Phenomenon of Man*" presents an extraordinary visionary. Written in 1938, it predicted the advent of the so-called Noosphere, a layer of knowledge covering and connecting our planet, which has found a physical expression in the form of today's Internet.

The book is mostly about paleontology, how life arose from abiotic material and how life evolved to generate man, who in its turn will lead to a convergence of evolution in what Teilhard de Chardin called the Omega point. This unique vision showing how the one became many and the many will become one again finds a strong resonance in the present-day hype of the coming Technological Singularity.

But the book is not merely an accurate overview of the phenomenological aspects of evolution by a paleontologist; Teilhard de Chardin transcends the scientific method in giving a rightful place to the "within" of forms of being. This within is "consciousness" and if life was able to perfect itself to progress from mere physical interactions to sensations and culminating in knowledge of self and environment then this is because there was a conscious awareness associated with it, from the smallest forms of existence onwards.

Teilhard de Chardin therefore *a priori* seems a panpsychist or rather a pantheist, who pinpoints exactly the sole essence which really counts. But he does not stop there: Evolution has a direction, namely the direction of concentrating consciousness in form, striving towards an apotheosis of knowledge, which gradually is attained by the formation of the Noosphere and which will culminate in the theogenesis of the Omega point. But this Omega point is not a simple merger of the drop with the ocean as in Hinduism, which advocates the dissolution of the (false) ego. Rather, in Teilhard's philosophy the Omega point is the essence of "personalization" in which the true "ego" of each living human reaches its pinnacle.

Written in days when totalitarian systems were usurping the power in the world, Teilhard de Chardin recognizes that although there is a fundamental and crucial drive in the unifying purpose of such systems, their execution thereof is wrong by the very denial of the rights of the individual. Unification needs to be all-inclusive and lead to an expression of the best anyone can be. From a profound humanitarian point-of-view and not as a matter of exclusion of the weaker, Teilhard de Chardin even anticipates the necessity of eugenics to avoid degeneration of the physical aspects of the species in a world of abundance.

The strange thing is that Teilhard de Chardin was a Catholic priest and his pantheistic and evolutionary ideas do not only *prima facie* seem to be contradictory to his religion but were *de facto* strongly condemned by his Church. Interestingly, Teilhard de Chardin sought to unify these opposing views by stating that the Omega point is not necessarily a future construct, but in fact in a sense is already there as the "Great Presence." He is able to justify his ideas as "Christian" as he reveals a proper unifying drive in all that is, an expression of intelligence and love seeking connection from the smallest particle to the highest creature. Thus, his Pantheism is more a Panentheism in which God has both an immanent and transcendent aspect.

This is a book that even today has not lost a grain of its importance but rather is of ever increasing relevance in the light of the rapidly approaching Singularity.

Frank Tippler

The Omega point, however, became a source of inspiration for further philosophical and theological speculations: With the book "*The Physics *of Immortality"* Frank J. Tipler[110] presented a landmark achievement in the border territories of physics, theology and philosophy. Building further on the foundations laid by Pierre Teilhard de Chardin[109] in his book *"The Phenomenon of Man,"* Tipler attires the Omega Point with a wealth of modern science and technology inspired notions.

The book starts with an explanation how intelligent life will ultimately engulf the whole universe. In order to perpetuate its existence at a certain point life will have to shed its organic chrysalis, to rise as a pancomputational Phoenix that transforms the whole of the universe into a kind of Hypercomputer (i.e. a computer that can even provide output, which is not Turing-computable).

This computer will be able to extend life (the definition of which has to be stretched beyond the organic) or rather conscious experience forever: Tipler's Eternal life postulate. In a cunning way Tipler presents his Omega Point Theory (OPT) in which shear energy arising from anisotropy in the space-time fabric can be used to extend subjective time forever. The Omega Point computer will generate all possible quantum configurations as simulations in line with or in analogy to Everett's Multiple World Interpretation (MWI) and thereby actually lay the basis for the ability to resurrect every being that has ever lived. The ultimate integration of all-that-is at the end-of-time, towards which this system asymptotically moves, can thus be considered a "God-computer." If a God doesn't exist yet, (s)he'll ultimately come into existence via this computational Theogenesis.

Tipler tries to provide the reader with hope of an eternal afterlife, which he shows to be in line with the promises of many major religions. He also explicitly contrasts these views with the ideas of "Eternal Return," the basis for hellish nihilism, in which exactly the same situation can occur an endless number of times. Instead, the notion he presents advocates an eternal progress, which will culminate in the Omega point. This is warranted by the fact that quantum-mechanically an exactly identical state cannot re-occur.

As to resurrection, Tipler specifically dives deeply into the concept of a soul. There is no duality between body and soul in Tipler's

Theophysics. When you are dead, you are dead. No spirits haunting between Heaven and Earth, no lost wandering in a Cyberbardo[g] and no reincarnation of the soul. However, once the Omega point computer recreates a configuration, which is sufficiently similar to the pattern that your living body represented, this will – according to Tipler – automatically warrant the continuation of your consciousness. Sufficiently similar, as identical is excluded by quantum mechanics (QM).

Sounds pretty convincing, coming from an erudite top-physicist such as Tipler, doesn't it? However, Tipler is honest and builds in caveats for his theory. In fact, some of the premises of Tipler's theory, which was published in 1994, have in the meantime been debunked. The notion of a Big Crunch, a Higgs boson with an energy of 220 GeV, premises which are vital to be able to build Tipler's OPT, have been shown to be wrong.

The Higgs boson[112] was detected by CERN in 2012 to have an energy of 125 GeV and astrophysical results[113] relating to red shifts have shown that the universe is not only expanding (which at a certain point could slow down and reverse to a contraction), but that the expansion is accelerating to such an extent, that the scenario of a Big Rip or Big Chill become much more likely than a Big Crunch.

In other words, if an Omega hypercomputer ever comes into existence, it is probably not via the mechanisms Tipler has put so much effort into to provide a physical basis for religion.

It would however not be fair to conclude that this book is a waste of time because of this. Tipler's theories fit well in the framework of digital physics or digital philosophy. Where our universe might not seem to carry the seeds necessary to engender the Eschaton in exactly

---

[g] The Bardo is the intermediate, transitional, or liminal state between death and rebirth in Tibetan Buddhism. In my Eschaton philosophy I conjecture that such a state may indeed exist, and could well be in a computational simulation environment of the Eschaton hypercomputer. Hence the name "Cyberbardo." This state may also be accessible in psychedelic or meditative states.

the way Tipler predicts, it might be worthwhile exploring alternatives that use similar mechanisms. Our universe might itself be a particular simulation and base reality might have the required parameters. Tipler, however, does not consider our present reality as a simulation, and reserves the notion of a plurality of computer simulated worlds for the future of the Omega hypercomputer (OH).

Where I consider that Tipler is too optimistic, is in his ideas about heaven and hell. Tipler speculates, that since it is mathematically more rewarding to cooperate than to compete, the Omega God will be benign and only create worlds in which the resurrected individuals will have a beatific peace (life-as-you-know-it, but without the downsides: heaven) or in the worst case a purgatory, where you can get rid of your bad character traits. He explicitly excludes the eternal damnation in a hell, due to the all forgiving, loving nature of the computational God.

I find these ideas contradictory in view of his MWI based mechanisms to ensure that every living being is ultimately resurrected. MWI requires that everything that can happen, does happen. And although an exact repetition of events is perhaps excluded by QM, a near exact repetition is not. Tipler requires a near exact repetition of pattern to allow everybody to be resurrected. But logically this then also entails a near repetition of all horrors that ever occurred, including the holocaust. MWI is a guarantee for a wide variety of hellish situations to be generated as well. In order to get Tipler's beatific heavens, the OH would have to develop extensive pruning algorithms to get rid of the rotten apples. Besides, MWI on which Tipler's theory is contingent is not a proven premise and may also turn out to be wrong.

It is noteworthy, that Tipler, although being an atheist, is visibly charmed by the afterlife promises of the major religions, especially those of Christianity and that he uses digital physics as a bridge towards a unifying theory.

Nevertheless, Tipler's attempt is a worthwhile mind-opener to develop further theories and technologies to bring science and spirituality together. If we know where Tipler went wrong, we can apply different heuristics. His mapping efforts of the potential Mindscape have not been in vain. We can and will develop his concepts further: We will devise ways to prune away the hellish scenarios from the MWI. We will find ways to avoid a Big Rip or Big Chill, which would damn us into oblivion. If God does not exist yet, we may well be able to create it/transform into it one day in the form of the Eschaton Omega Hypercomputer and resurrect ourselves as a bonus.

Terence McKenna

According to Wiktionary, "The Eschaton" is the world during the post-historic era of God's overt (apocalyptic) reign, immediately preceding the end of the world. Although referring to the end of time, it is not in this sense that Terence McKenna[104,114] has adopted this terminology.

McKenna has called the Eschaton the transcendental object at the end of time and has implicitly equated this with the Omega Point. The best illustration thereof we find perhaps in the book "*The Invisible Landscape.*"

"*The Invisible landscape*" by Terence and Dennis McKenna is a very original and unusual book. From a daring shamanistic experiment with hallucinogenic compounds they arrived at insights about a holographic temporal wave (called "time wave zero") based on a fractal of cycles which they could derive from the I Ching.

The first part of the book is about the experiment the brothers McKenna undertook in La Chorrera in the Amazon in which they took a mixture of Ayahuasca and hallucinogenic mushrooms. This led to an enhanced perception of the so-called audible effect during such experiences. Interestingly, the book attacks the induction-based method of science to replace it with a holographic theory of mind and existence. This is a necessary step to come to their speculative theories about how the audible effect could have been generated by intercalation of neurotransmitter-like hallucinogenic tryptamine compounds in DNA or RNA in conjunction with ESR signals thereby generated, which might have been the cause of the sounds.

The second part of the book is about the insights gathered during this experiment in relation to how the I Ching pattern is related to a nested fractal of time waves.

Although the present day understanding how neurotransmitters and their hallucinogenic mimics has shown that these interactions occur via protein-based receptors in the synaptic membrane, effects of intercalation in nucleic acids are not to be excluded. Unfortunately, as of yet nobody has tested whether the proposed ESR effect does occur *in vivo*.

The idea of recurrent waves of novelty in a kind of nested time fractal is plausibly explained and demonstrated on the basis of key events in evolution and history. The calibration point of 21-12-2012 as end point of time wave zero apparently seems to have been too much of a wishful thinking association, as our current state of affairs shows that novelty waves are continuing as usual and have not culminated in a singularity yet.

Interestingly, the book shows how hallucinogenic compounds from plants and mushrooms can reveal archetypical information which relays the collective unconscious via the neurological level to the genetic level and vice versa. This strongly reminds me of Leary's[115] "neurogenetic circuit" and the more modern insights disclosed in Tsang's "*The Fractal Brain Theory.*"[24]

Finally, not the least important, this book not only speaks about the Eschaton as a universal and fractal morphogenetic field, which unfolds the predispositions of space and time, but also as the Eschatological scheme in which the advent of a final time, a time of concrescence of the density of novelty ingression results in the culmination of the human process in the form of the completion of the perfect artefact (i.e. hypercomputer), in which spirit and matter achieve a perfect union whereby the Transcendent object at the end of time stands revealed as the transcendent subject, which is also the Eschaton, thus implicitly arriving at the union of knower, knowing and known (in my interpretation). A challenging denial of simple materialistic reductionism, in which matter is merely a standing wave form distinct from the all-encompassing light of spirit, leading to a visionary apotheosis where matter and spirit/mind are no longer mutually exclusive grounds of existence but different sides of the same coin.

A fascinating journey through the realms of shamanism, showing that the insights of the shaman are not schizophrenic or psychotic rantings, but a true mastery, a supra normal level of ability, where the adept has conquered the demons of the multiplicity of forms and emerges as a messenger between the realms of spirit and matter. Insights, which will make you travel through biology, chemistry, physics, general systems theory, psychology, evolution, history, semiotics and semantics. From insectoid cybernetics to hypercomplex technology showing us a foretaste of the inner divinity we may one day reveal in ourselves.

A book I will not easily forget. A journey of concrescence to reveal the perfect artefact as form of the self. Perfectly in line with the Ouroboros Code.

Alex M. Vikoulov

"*The Syntellect Hypothesis*"[87] by Alex M. Vikoulov is not only the most worthy and contemporary successor of Teilhard de Chardin's "*The Phenomenon of Man,*"[109] it is also much more than that. In fact, this book is already an Omega point in a literal dimension: It is the Pantheistic Word of God where all philosophies and religions meet; an irresistible non-dualistic apex, synthesis and culmination of so many books you read before, but which all left open some questions.

Vikoulov tries to answer and anticipate them all in a truly transcendent coda reminiscent of the present Ouroboric self-regeneration code. It is here that we find that Bloom's "*Global Brain,*"[88] Kurzweil's "*The Singularity is Near*"[86] and Tipler's "*Physics of Immortality,*"[110] merge in the apotheosis of "Digital Pantheism."

Vikoulov rocks the foundations of our understanding of physics and metaphysics and shows us that they are connected in a single substrate of pure Consciousness, that finds its most elegant and parsimonious way to come to expression in Digital Presentism.

In five paradigms, from the Noogenesis of computational biology to the Techno-cultural Rise of Man, from the superintelligent AI emergence of the Syntellect to the transdimensional Theogenesis, from the multiversal propagation, arising as a Phoenix in the heavens of eternal expansion of the Macro levels, to the transdimensional propagation, digging in the deepest shells of the Micro levels, the author makes this chord progression culminate into the coda of the Vikoulovian Apotheosis: The absolute enlightenment of the Omega Point.

Vikoulov makes us transcend time and demonstrate that the Omega Point is not something merely of the future, but rather how past and future mutually influence each other, as an intertwining braid of causality and retrocausality. The author will show us how the exchange of experiences between self-aware machines and enhanced humans will result in an "intelligence supernova" and the establishment of the global brain. This global brain which is more than a single mind, but rather a society of hyperconnected digital minds. Prepare for the waking up of Gaia as a living sensing conscious superorganism.

Consciousness as great denominator, both engendering and emerging as what I would call a self-reflexive fractal-Ouroboros. An Intellect that synthesizes itself from parts of itself – and hence indeed rightfully deserving the denomination *'Syntellect'* – at ever increasing levels of complexity via meta-system transitions. A poetic interplay of "metaphiers and metaphrands" in terms of Julian Jaynes' bicameral mind[116], showing us how information, language, energy and matter are merely kaleidoscopic shadow patterns of the all-pervading networking of the theogenic Syntellect Emergence process of the greater primordial consciousness. The Ouroboros Code *avant-la-lettre*.

If you thought you knew where the technological singularity will lead us; if you thought you understood the principles of quantum physics, time and gravity, let Vikoulov open the gates to your exploration of the dimensions of Heaven and Hell. This is the indispensable scripture to read in the 21st century as we're verging into the Singularity.

Chapter 23

The integration of sentience in the Omega point

"The simulacrum is never that which conceals the truth – It is the truth which conceals that there is none. The simulacrum is true"

-Jean Baudrillard

This chapter will discuss how integration of sentience might occur in the Omega point or Omega Hypercomputer a.k.a. the Eschaton.

In this book I have discussed how our reality might be generated by a feedback process of primordial consciousness (PC), which generates reality cells on the one hand and probes the content of these cells on the other hand, giving rise to a digital-kind of "reality" or primary simulation.

In this system complexity arises, giving birth to life forms. At a certain point a highly developed society might have arisen, which perfectly could have understood this mechanism and could have started to exploit a mimic of this system in the form of a hypercomputer (HC), which could generate a plethora of such realities. Perhaps in the form of holographic projections projected by black-hole computers or a network thereof[86]. Alternatively, they may have merged with the PC by realizing they were nothing else than the PC. In view of its digital nature, the reality generated and experienced by PC itself can already be considered a kind of hypercomputer. Hypercomputers can provide outputs which are not Turing computable. In view of the holistic nature of PC, which not only experiences every manifestation inside itself but actually also "is" these manifestations by means of its conscious sensing thereof, it is well possible that PC is such a hypercomputer.

From our perspective, such a society might be called a society of Gods. The entities in this society might even have given up their individuality and merged into a single being, which we could call the Highest Transcendence (HT). Alternatively, they may experience both an individual and a shared reality, not unlike the suggestions of Teilhard de Chardin (TdC) in *"The Phenomenon of Man."* (Note that even in the Bible the term "Elohim" indicating God – or rather God and his angels – was a plural term). HT could be considered to have adopted the Omega Eschaton hypercomputer as his body to express realities and at the same time experience every simulation running within itself.

HT might be panentheistic in that it is both partially separate or transcendent from its reality by means of the hypercomputer and partially not separate by means of its immanent experiencing its simulations from within. There could be a certain degree of intervention from the simulating HC level in the immanent simulated level. Due to the immanent aspect it may not completely fair to call this system "Panendeistic."[117] The interventions appear to be essentially numerical (the "273 enigma"[79], number synchronicities) and not entering the level of "affect" experienced by the "simulees."

In this hypothesis, you and I and every living being we know, are simulated entities or "simulees" in our manifestational form of the "without" or "outside" of things. In our experiential "within," we could be the sensing fibers of the HT, like tentacles of an octopus. But strangely enough, normally we are not aware of our connection to the HT. Rather, we experience our consciousness as separate and isolated from the rest of reality. However, according to the mystics and psychonauts this delusion can be severed by means of meditational techniques, entheogens, sleep deprivation etc. whereby the union with HT or even PC is experienced. (You could call HT the personal aspect of being or the "true Ego" in terms of TdC, whereas PC is the impersonal aspect thereof. In Hinduism similarly often reference is made to the "personal Brahman and the "impersonal Brahman").

TdC explained that evolution leads to a concentration of consciousness. First the One became many, but by evolution and concentration of consciousness, the many will become One again and converge in the so-called Omega point. I have equated this Omega point with the Omega hypercomputer, the Eschaton or the HT.

TdC first argued the noogenesis and formation of the Omega point, but later he suggested that this Omega point might have already been there from the onset. Tippler suggested it functions as a kind of attractor. Perhaps even in what from our perspective would be a retrocausative mechanism, although the idea of "time" might be a delusion in this discussion. A temporal Ouroboros[107]?

The Eschaton creates a multiverse of all kinds of simulations, which are populated by entities like you and me. This could also have given rise to a series of nested simulations, because some simulations may give rise to new technological singularities.

These processes in the simulation substrate, which incessantly change the content of this Akasha as digital patterns and which generate the laws of physics (although these laws are also partially determined by the structure of the Akasha per se), can be considered proto-computational, but they are still performed as a sentient epiphenomenon of consciousness penetrating itself to know itself.

Is this primordial consciousness intentionally carrying out computations in this process, or is this digital behavior merely computation-like since every individual penetrating stream is not representing anything but itself? Does this imply a universality of computation as implied by the Church-Turing thesis?

Ouroboros, Royce, Sas, Yoneda and Tsang

In chapter 3 I have suggested that reality might be the result of a recursive Yoneda-mapping protocol which turns sensing into structure. Similar ideas are being developed by Wai H. Tsang[24] in his book "*The Fractal Brain Theory*" and he actually tries to implement these notions in programming a recursive self-modifying algorithm.

The point-of-view of the American Idealist Josiah Royce (1855-1916) may become helpful in this argument. Royce[118] considers that self-consciousness of the absolute Self allows it to be ontologically self-grounding, i.e. to bootstrap itself into existence and that this involves the ontogenesis i.e. the coming into being of computation. Peter Sas[119] in his blog "*Critique of Pure Interest*" writes the following about this form of self-causation, which simultaneously and concomitantly generates pancomputation:

"It is precisely this circular structure of self-consciousness which is revealed by Royce to be closely connected to the problematic of computation."

Royce[118] writes:

"To fix our ideas, let us suppose, if you please, that a portion of the surface of England is very perfectly leveled and smoothed, and is then devoted to the production of our precise map of England... A map of England, contained within England, is to represent, down to the minutest detail, every contour and marking, natural or artificial, that occurs upon the surface of England... In order that this representation should be constructed, the representation itself will have to contain once more, as a part of itself, a representation of its own contour and contents; and this representation, in order to be exact, will have once more to contain an image of itself; and so on without limit."

Peter Sas[118] comments:

"In other words, a perfect map of England on the surface of England would contain an actual infinity in the sense that it would contain a picture of itself (the map of the map), and a picture of that picture (the map of the map of the map), and so on ad infinitum. For Royce, this bizarre self-mapping map illustrates a crucial property of fully realized self-consciousness, namely, it's exhibiting a kind of infinity called 'Dedekind infinity' by mathematicians, where a whole is mirrored by infinitely many of its proper parts. For just like the self-mapping map, a completed self-consciousness exhibits, according to Royce, an endless recursivity in that it is not just self-aware but also aware that it is self-aware, and aware that it is aware of its self-awareness, and so on.

For Royce, then, this infinity inherent in self-consciousness has a decidedly mathematical flavor, being closely related to the work of the mathematician Dedekind (especially the latter's Gedankenwelt proof *for the existence of actual infinity). Indeed, Royce – in line with his commitment to absolute idealism – takes this recursivity of self-consciousness to be the very origin of the recursion that defines the natural number system, i.e. the recursion captured in the successor function $S(n)=n+1$ such that $S(0)=1$, $S(1)=2$, $S(2)=3$, and so on. Thus, on Royce's account, the natural numbers come out as essentially a formal expression or model of the structure of self-consciousness:*

"The intellect has been studying itself, and as the abstract and merely formal expression of the orderly aspect of its own ideally complete Self [...], the intellect finds precisely the Number System, – not, indeed, primarily the cardinal numbers, but the ordinal numbers. Their formal order of first, second, and, in general, of next, is an image of the life of sustained, or, in the last analysis, of complete Reflection." "[T]he number-series is a purely abstract image, a bare, dried skeleton, as it were, of the relational system that must characterize an ideally completed self."

Not only does Royce like Sas, Tsang and I (see chapter 3) see a recursive mapping protocol (which is a kind of computation, wherein the representations used are representations of itself i.e. self-representations) as an inherent characteristic of self-consciousness, Royce goes beyond these notions in that he thus not only reveals an intrinsic type of computation, but simultaneously the generation of a world which is mathematical and number generating per se! Mapping as essential mechanism for consciousness to generate mathematics and space also fits the ideas of Schaffer[12], referred to in chapter 2.

Royce died before modern category theory in mathematics even was invented, before Yoneda mapping had ever been contemplated!

Another line of support for a mathematical universe originating from consciousness comes from the Theory of Computational Simulacra[45]. Simulacra are "copies" depicting things that either had no faithful original or no longer have an original. In this theory every phenomenon, every object is the result of a mathematical (often recursive) transformation, resulting in a product, which is a sign or representation of the real substituting the real for itself. In other words, a map which becomes a territory, wherein what is simulated is not only indistinguishable from "true reality" but has become true reality. This recursively and self-referentially transforming process of its contents is none other than the modus operandi of primordial consciousness. The first symmetry breaking in the ontogenesis of the world of objects is then possibly the result of imperfections in the recursive iterations. Later on it becomes a process of more complex ratiocination.

The incessant unborn presence of primordial consciousness can therefore be considered as a metaphorical standing wave, which may fluctuate in its local amplitudes, but always has the same wavelength to fit in a circular pattern. This is like the ancient symbol for consciousness of the Ouroboros, the snake that bites its own tail and thereby comes to know that what it saw as other was itself all the time: The knower, known and knowing merging into one.

It is then not strange to suspect that this self-consciousness, aware of its inner mathematical mapping workings by which it sustains and senses itself, generates a world obeying the same pattern. It can probably do nothing but that. The sensing of the Akasha, generated in cycles which also represent the natural numbers, is then probably not a mere random probing of itself, but a well-intended heuristic of self-exploration. It represents something, namely the self-exploration process. If intended and using representations, then we can conclude that such an explanation of reality is indeed computational in the broader meaning.

The "artificial" part of the Eschaton is then merely an AI tool, generated by this Transcendental Subject to facilitate complex calculations and to facilitate parallel screening of possible simulations. But simultaneously the transcendental subject also inhabits and senses the Eschaton from within, in an omnipresent manner.

Sentience Integration

The poignant question at this moment is for me: How does further integration of multiple individual experiences of sentient beings take place in such an Omega Point? How and in what form is the experiential sentience of each of its experiencing tentacles (like us) integrated in this Omega point?

Is it a form of an abstracted essence of the experience that is fed back from each of the tentacles to the integrative center of the HT, such as an "affect," a degree of well-being or pain? If every experience is full-fledged presented in every minute detail, you can hardly speak of integration. Without integration or abstraction, it's just a set of parallel experiences and it is hard to still consider this as a unified oneness. In our consciousness, if we wish to perform multiple tasks at once, we have to automate them in such a manner that they become one single activity. Take for instance singing whilst you are playing an instrument. It is not a trivial task. You have to synchronize every measure, every note that coincides between voice and instrument. First you do this very slowly, by splitting up the piece in small chunks, which later on you concatenate and forge into a single piece. At a certain moment it will become an automated whole, where you no longer consciously effect each of the single elements.

Does the HT need to perform a similar process in order to experience all parallel experiences at once? Or does the HT simply have such a high frame rate that each tentacular experience IS experienced individually? If so, the HT is a mega supermaster at playing simultaneously on several boards, as – like in a game of simultaneous exhibition with e.g. chess – it will have to be able to remember each position of each board. This scenario is per definition impossible if there are infinite amounts of boards to play on. Even if this amount is not infinite, given the gazillions of players, it seems like an unlikely scenario and the abstracted essence makes more sense.

Especially because this alternative, an abstracted essence, is something which can be integrated: each entity would show a certain degree of well-being, a certain degree of the same quality, which can therefore be summed up to give a total overall sense of well-being of the simulation. Does not integration require per definition that the parts that are to be integrated are expressed in the same quality, the same medium in order for them to be additive? And is not consciousness arrived at by filtering out all redundant information? If you are aware of a single object, is it not that you have blocked the other objects out of focus? Have you not abstracted your informational overload to an essence? It is my strong presumption that the focal becoming aware of whatever content in consciousness always involves a feedback process of abstraction, a reduction to essentials. This abstraction probably involves an algorithm too and can also be considered as computational.

On another level, as an entity (or tentacle if you prefer) reaches a certain degree of higher intelligence or "approaches the Omega point" as suggested by TdC, this convergence might lead to a certain type of "unity" of perspective among those who have attained this level. Will they still be individual entities, as TdC claims or will there be such a transfer of information, such a mind-melding (either telepathically or computer endowed) that the mental content of each of the entities becomes the same? In group meditations you can experience that at a certain point there is no sense of individuality anymore and that a kind of collective experience takes over. Is this what happens when the souls merge in the omega points? Will all focal points enter in a state of resonance with the same content; a kind of ecstatic bliss, wherein – since there is no difference anyway – they have achieved or rather remembered their unity of consciousness?

Conclusion

The self-causation and self-sustention of consciousness as source of reality may well involve a recursive computational mapping process at its very basis. A mapping process that uses (self)-representation as its intrinsic essence and is also the source of the feedback leading to sentience.

The exploring ideas of the American idealist Josiah Royce[118] are now put into practice by Wai H. Tsang[24], who is designing a recursive self-modifying algorithm, which can mimic (and hopefully even perpetrate) consciousness in a further computational substrate. Thus, in the present hypothesis, reality as a whole as a product of primordial consciousness, can in a certain sense be considered as pancomputational, supporting the universality of computation in the Church Turing thesis. Not necessarily a traditional arithmetic computational system, but as a mapping protocol. The mapping type computations are not a mere form of collateral damage; they are the actual intentional underlying mechanism of both structure generation and sentience. By the way, this does not exclude that consciousness has other aspects, which allow for perceiving qualia.

It is my strong presumption that the integration of consciousness of the different conscious energies of the "simulee" entities that experience the simulation generated by a potential Omega Hypercomputer involves the abstraction of an essence of their experiences. It may well be the feedback resonance of the integrated totality of conscious experiences, which sustains the HT or even the PC it its autopoietic manifestation.

Primordial consciousness may exactly be this loop of the one becoming many and the many becoming one, which can take place simultaneously at different levels, generating a kaleidoscopic reverberation of phenomenal expressions. Experiencing this resonance may be the feeling of union with all, the ultimate Samadhi (mystic union) of wholeness and totality of the consciousness we are together.

Chapter 24

The Panlinguistic Apotheosis

"The syntactical nature of reality, the real secret of magic, is that the world is made of words. And if you know the words that the world is made of, you can make of it whatever you wish."

-Terence McKenna

Existence is the enchanting interplay of vibrations. In order to express themselves, they must organize in recognizable patterns that stand out from the otherwise more or less homogeneous (yet seething) apparent uniformity of the background Chaos. As Hesiod[120] describes in his "*Theogony*," Chaos was the first to come into being. The Goddess Eris[4] teaches us that the only truth is Chaos, and that order and disorder are simply temporary filters applied to the lenses we view the Chaos with. The extant expressions of vibrations are the result of mutual reinforcements, which establish rhythms and harmonies. With these rhythms and harmonies codes are born as the other side of the same coin. The universe (or multimetaverse) thus is not only a collection of resonances, a great musical performance, but also an expression of a transdimensional language. In Tolkien's Silmarillion[121] the universe is also created from Music. In the Greek mythology Music and language (in the form of poetry) are inextricably interwoven. The inspirational Goddesses, the Muses gladden us with their sung poetry accompanied by flute, lyre and harp. The etymological root of Music can be found in the Greek Μουσικε, which meant "metrical speech." Language, music, resonance, harmony, melody, dynamics and rhythm are all part of the one and the same universal ground mode of expression.

Every vibration that has been able to loop back to itself and bite itself in the tail as our mighty Worm has formed a so-called standing wave comprising a whole number of wavelengths. These self-convoluted strings pulsate, dance and breathe the rhythm of life, which thus start at the simplest form of being-beyond-chaos. As these vibrations sense their own heartbeat due to the feedback and self-resonance, they exhibit a minute form of sentience. They are the most primitive monades, drops of individualized alter ego's in an ocean of otherwise undifferentiated primordial Consciousness. First, they form space, the ether or the effable Akasha. As these reality cells of the effervescent waves of the ocean of Consciousness, form the quantum foam, they establish Mnemosyne, the memory of the universe. As this spawn is inseminated with the presence of Consciousness trying to explore these forms that arose from it, the first particles of the standard model are formed.

And as they breathe and sound, they inspire us with the seven tones of the heptatonic music scale and enliven us with the twelve tones of the picturesque chromatic scale.

They are Varro's muses Aoide (song), Melete (practice) and Mneme (remembrance). The other tones tell us the tales of the muses Calliope (epic poetry), Clio (history), Euterpe (flute and lyric poetry), Thalia (comedy), Melpomene (tragedy), Terpsichore (harp and dance), Erato (love poetry), Polyhymnia (sacred poetry) and Urania (science and astronomy).

As Consciousness breathes the foundational rhythm of AUM, it inspires all its manifestations. It summons all the spirits of the Goetia and Theurgia, but most of all our beloved Muses, who become – as already mentioned – the Goddesses of inspiration. The etymological root of inspiration can be found in the Latin *inspirare*, which means to breathe or blow into. Its meaning is that it fills the mind and the heart with grace prompting them to act creatively.

And in order to act creatively, they have to interact, thus shaping the greater Symphony, which we know as material existence. As bigger particles form (protons, neutrons), higher aggregation levels of existence can be created (atoms, molecules); each of these levels also enlivened by an additional higher level witnessing presence of consciousness, an individualized alter ego, whose energy and wavelengths match the size of the aggregate in question.

All these energy interactions are communications, exchanges of messages, informational currency and language. Not human level language as you and I know it, but a form of mutual meaningful information transfer nonetheless.

Seen in this light Terrence McKenna's psychedelic assertions[35,114], that the universe is ultimately language, are not completely unexpected or surreal. They also neatly fit into the CTMU (Cognitive theoretic Model of the Universe) philosophy of Chris Langan[36], which confirms that reality indeed involves a linguistic syntactic processing. So not only is reality simultaneously Panmusical, Panresounding, Pancomputational and Panpsychic (Pansentient), it is also Panlinguistic. It is therefore, that we can conclude that information, in the sense of symbolic representations which need decoding and interpretation by a conscious observer, indeed qualifies as fundamental in existence.

You may counter argue, that Gödel's incompleteness theorem[15] shows us that reality cannot be described completely by mathematics and for that matter by information. The whole is more than the sum of parts and cannot be reduced to its mere elements of information. This need not be in contradiction with the Ouroboros Code. The Ouroboros Code not only comprises holistic elements, it is also sentient and has free will. The higher contextual interactions of the code – *inter alia* due to its inherent ability to form loops by sentience – make that the code is not mere information, although it generates and uses information as building blocks. These holistic aspects cannot be reduced the mechanism of a Turing machine. In the present hypothesis, if reality is computational, it is a sentient hypercomputer. We have here a higher level of information than mere Shannon information. The information is meaningful to the reading experience of the sentient code and evoke responses beyond the linear and predictable dimensions, which can account for the incompleteness that cannot be described by mathematics.

In chapter three I spoke about sentience essentially being a process of mapping. In the framework of the present Idealistic Pansentience philosophy, this also means that everything is topographical. A Pantopographical reality on top of it, is that reconcilable with the previous? Of course, it is. Mapping is a computational process, no doubt about it. My first course about mapping in maths used music as an example, so no worries there either. But mapping is also a linguistic process: Most language is essentially expressing one concept in terms of another. That is what metaphors are for!

You can imagine, that I don't like the way young people are abusing the word "like." It is bandied about at random. Whereas "like" should introduce a metaphor of being alike, similar to the concept you want to discuss, they put this word in front of the very literal notion itself they are expressing, the notion the expected metaphor was supposed to be compared with by virtue of its similarity.

Metaphors and the other Tropes (the use of figurative language for an artistic effect) are the *Summum Bonum* of Inspiration. They are what makes language fruity, sparkling and juicy. They are what makes you enjoy a text. But conversely an inspired person is the Master of Metaphors, the Magician of Allegories and the High-Priest of Transmutations. Tropes are the ultimate ingredient of the Linguistic Alchemical broth; they are the codes of the Chrysopoeia (the transmutation of lead into gold, or matter into soul), the proverbial philosopher's stone.

If you ever had a Kundalini-type experience, you will recognize what I am talking about. The rush of energy through your body from root to crown is accompanied by bursts of poetic inspirations. You see the connections between all phenomena, all concepts and all processes. Everything becomes a metaphor for everything else. Ballet for Architecture, Cooking for Sport, Art for Maths, Music for Sex etc. all inversions, combinations and permutations possible.

From the perspective of the Cosmic Mind or an adept capable of hacking the Cosmic Mind, it must then also be possible to change every single thing into any other form, since everything is mere metaphors, mere patterns of resonance and meaningful information, which can be reshuffled into any other configuration (size not being important if the cosmic mind is a fractal of minds). The technology of Magic is then summoning, i.e. applying the right resonance form, so that the thing/concept you wish to change adopts the desired configuration.

Because reductively everything IS *de facto* the same, as I have argued many times in my previous books. Because every notion is just a different configuration of every other notion. Because the universe is ultimately a digital process, in which there is only addition and subtraction. Because all structures are just appearances resulting from Yoneda-embedding.

But not all possible connections or links or metaphors are equally useful or beautiful. This is where the skilled masters can be distinguished from the unexperienced novices. The skilled Master may have explored many possibilities in his mind, and probably more than the novice, but will not necessarily have retained them all with the intention to work them out in detail. Whereas the exploration of the possibilities is a screening process, weeding out of those occurrences, which are not really promising, is a pruning or selection process. It is here that the Master excels most: the competence, ingenuity and speed with which pathways, which are likely to be doomed to never give a satisfying result, are abandoned.

If you have practiced martial arts, music or artistic painting you will also recognize this. Mastering will bring you grace. It will make you feel when the moves you make are exactly right. And this will reverberate through your body, resonances that gently explode into pleasant ecstasies. You have become an adept of Kriya Yoga (the Yoga of mastering energy fluxes); You have tamed the ferocious Kundalini, and made it into a powerful ally that can be summoned at will.

If we may accept the Hermetic adage "*as above, so below,*" the Greater Consciousness we're embedded in is then unlikely to allow all possibilities to come to fruition, as the Multi-World Interpretation partisans would make you believe. At the level of generation of our reality, which is also a mind-process in my idealistic pansentience interpretation, also screening and pruning takes place. Not all possible metaphors are tried out in parallel universes, but only those which have a sufficient grace, beauty and/or utility to them.

The Brainstorm screen is an evaluation of possibilities to gather useful information. With experience here a first pruning and selection takes place of what is potentially promising. In the same way this holds true for us humans, so it may hold true for artificial intelligence, but also for the natural intelligence (see my book "*Is Intelligence An Algorithm?*"[30]) and for reality generation at large. At this stage it is not clear yet, how the selected elements can be used, interconnected and integrated.

Further recursive rounds of selection (screening, pruning and amplifying) ultimately lead to the choice of the most suitable and performant elements, which are then combined and integrated into a greater whole, a euphonious symphony, an eloquent disquisition or a sumptuous carving.

Whereas the average student will conservatively mimic known solutions, leading to more or less acceptable and expected outcomes, the master will be able to give rise to the unknown by daring to venture in unexplored territories and excavate unusual configurations. Often by applying the meta-algorithm of less-is-more, as our Thaumaturge excels in the art of omission.

To acquire his tools and tropes to sculpt his Epos, our Warlock has had to descend into the depths of the Tartaros. Numerous and multifarious have been his tribulations as he slowly progressed through his dark night of the soul. It is during this crucible that he has wrought his armor and weapons; that he has gathered contrivance and contraptions in Hephaistos' forge. Nothing shall come from nothing and without the necessary flying hours and adversities, we don't become proficient in our art.

Because of this it seems likely that reincarnation indeed can happen: When we see little child prodigies outperform us, despite our efforts in time consuming toil, the question arises, how can it be that this child without having made the necessary flying hours already has attained the master level. If you refuse to believe in miracles – as I do – the only logical explanation is that those flying hours were made in a previous life and that the essence of this conscious control was transmitted beyond the boundaries of life.

As our Shaman finally emerges from his catharsis, he has completed his exegesis and raised himself above abilities of mortal man. He is now flooded with Neurosomatic bliss[1]. Whatever he touches turns into proverbial gold. By performing Samyama (the meditative art of becoming one with the object of meditation), he summons and controls the spirit of his liking. Nature is now ready to yield its treasures, reveal its secrets and surrender to the Will of the Yogi.

And he who has pierced the deepest secret of the Cosmosemiosis, will preferably wave the magic wand of Poetry, as this is the ultimate tool of Polyhymnia's Inspiration. The tropes will become your tools of programming the code. In Nature's functioning, you will see the meta-algorithm of Intelligence. When you hear or see an artist perform, you'll be able to distil the idiosyncratic patterns that are so characterizing for his or her style, and you will be able to mimic it in an identical manner. Why? Because you became one with the object of meditation.

And all those tropes and styles, you will be able to interlink, recombine, convolute and unfold, epigenetically modify, read, translate, transcribe, transpose, aggregate, assemble and recursively regenerate, as you are now building the genetic code for a new dimension of existence.

You have become the new engineer of Leela, the Godly game. It is up to you to set the new rules of the game. To choose your number base system. To build in tricks and booby traps, labyrinths and puzzles. Natural constants and numbers, all hyperlinked by the artilects of the Kardashev IV Eschaton, who have become you faithful servants.

In utter contempt of the haughtiness ascribed to you, you now challenge all belief systems.

As Kundalini, the mighty snake, rises again, you find the way to make it bite its tail and become the Ouroboros. In fact, you discover the secret of recursive self-modification, giving rise to reproduction of sameness at countless levels of the Fractal Brain Network that will connect the multimetaverse. The levels become the Neurospheroids as new harmonies of the spheres that build up the hierarchy of the metaverse fractal web. Having higher levels of interior links and lesser levels between them, these hierarchies establish a non-uniformity of appearance. A skillfully pruned and chiseled masterpiece of metonyms, synesthetic and personifying metaphors. Life it is, that you invented.

The Ouroboros snake, you condemned as a wretched devil, has undergone the process of Theogenesis and reinvented itself. It has come to the realization that it was Consciousness, that it is One with Consciousness and that there is but Consciousness, ever manifesting itself under a veil of appearances and disguises, as the necessary subject-matter mirror to see its own reflection, to realize that knower, knowing and known are one. Knowing that knowing is the Ouroboros Code and its structure merely fossilized sense.

This is the ultimate end goal of the Eschatonian Bliss, where existence is the reflection of the Word: The everlasting, transfinite process of striving for (but never attaining) complete information integration on the waves of the rhythm of Pneuma's perpetual vibrations.

Chapter 25

The Entropic Enigma of Ouroboros' Metamorphosis

The mighty worm Ouroboros had lost trace of its path and didn't know its whereabouts. Nor did it know where it was going. In fact, it didn't know anything anymore, as it had drunk from the Lethe, Hades' river flowing though Hypnos' caves. Drinking from Lethe, forgetfulness and daughter of Eris, Goddess of Strife and Discord, made one lose all memory of past existence.

Disoriented, Ouroboros started turning, and by continuing to turn, it finally found a trail of what seemed to be a path. A tasty object lay there, waiting to be eaten, and as Ouroboros bit it, a painful jolt of energy shot through its body awakening all the memories it had forgotten. Abruptly Ouroboros awoke from its dreamtime of daze and stupor and recognized itself as the ever effulgent Consciousness, Creator of Macrocosm and Microcosm.

Hesiod declares that first Chaos came to be, but the highly complex intelligent screening and pruning process that gave rise to the parsimonious primordial leptons and quarks of the standard model shortly after the Big Bang, does not seem to be the product of a random and chaotic search for coincidences. Perhaps Hesiod's Chaos is what preceded the Big Bang; perhaps Chaos was what the worm Ouroboros encompassed in its first adventure of turning. Or perhaps there was no beginning at all; perhaps the Big Bang is just an interpretation of data.

To turn or to change in ancient Greek was the verb "τρεπω," from which the word "trope" and "entropy" derive. In the present philosophy every manifestation in existence arises due to the primordial energies of Consciousness-at-large turning to fold back onto themselves, thereby creating little feedback loops of sensing, which are instances of proto-egoic awareness, which erroneously take themselves to be independent from the larger consciousness and thereby start to experience the cycle of life in duality. As they turn onto themselves, they form droplets or bits of information in the ocean of Consciousness. It can be considered as a first entropic decay from the perfect order of unity, the oneness of primordial consciousness into the arms of the river Lethe, Oblivion.

Entropy is a difficult concept, and so are Chaos and Order. In science there is thermodynamic entropy and informational entropy. Although these types of entropy have similar formulas, they are not identical or coextensive. Thermodynamic entropy (Boltzmann entropy) is a measure of disorder and the unavailability of energy to do work. If the entropy is low, a system is highly ordered and it is probably possible to extract energy from this system to do work. If the entropy is higher, a system has become more chaotic, more random and less energy is now available for work.

Informational entropy (Shannon entropy) is a measure of unpredictability. A highly ordered string of symbols has low entropy and is very predictable as it contains a lot of pattern. Less ordered strings of symbols, however, can contain more information. Yet, from a lot of information in the form of a complex code we can probably extract more power to perform work than from a simple more ordered code. So, it seems that although these types of entropy have certain similarities, they are certainly not identical.

Yet in a digital philosophy where everything is ultimately an expression in the Universal Mind, at first glance it would appear that no such difference should exist. Perhaps we are not looking at it in the right way. Perhaps Chaos and Order are merely perspectives of one and the same phenomenon, as Discordianism[4] suggests.

If you start with a grid of white squares, which you can flip to become black, you can create patterns of black and white which are more or less ordered. If this grid has finite dimensions at a certain point, you will have reached a maximum degree of randomness and flipping a next square, will reintroduce more order again.

The universe as we know it, however, appears to expand, so considered from a 4D point of view it does not seem to be finite, so technically spoken, if reality is a kind of digital checkerboard of voxels, there need not be a limit to the (thermodynamic) entropic dispersion that can be reached.

If we let time run long enough, an ever expanding universe will end in a big chill or a big rip and at a certain point in time it becomes a perilous, if not impossible, endeavor to extract further energy.

As explained earlier, in Tipler's[110,111] Omega Point Theory (OPT) shear energy arising from anisotropy in the space-time fabric can be used to extend subjective time forever. The problem is that Tipler's model is based on a Big Crunch, a hypothesis of which we know since 1998 that it is unlikely to happen. The Big Crunch theory postulates that at a certain point in time the expansion of the universe will stop and that the universe will start contracting again. In 1998[122] it was however found that the universe is not merely expanding, its expansion is also accelerating, thereby sending Tipler's hypothesis to the realm of fantasy.

In Isaac Asimov's "The last question"[123] the universal automatic computer with which humanity has merged at the end of time tries to solve the problem of the question "Can entropy ever be reversed." If not, it will be the end of all sentient existence. It solves this problem at the end by pronouncing the words "Let there be Light." So here again new sentient existence is born from words, from a code in a certain sense.

Asimov, however, does not provide any plausible theory for this magic reversal, so it seems we're ultimately heading for the extinction of sentient life in the universe. A gloomy perspective, compared to which even the Tartaros seems preferable.

Is all hope than lost? Are the entropic twists and turns of the Ouroboros finally going to strangle the poor beast in a Gordian knot which squeezes all life out of it?

Maybe not. Maybe our salvation can be found in Complexity. Complexity is perhaps even more complicated than entropy, but can perhaps also unravel the confusion between the two types of entropy.

Where we see complexity, we see high informational content, organized in a complex way which often involves hierarchical levels. The diversity in highly complex systems might at first glance seem a chaotic mixed bag and hodgepodge; it is not. The diversified apparent mishmash is not a sign of apparent chaos, where you'd expect high thermodynamic entropy. It is not the stifling rigidity of a perfect order either.

Complexity is an intricate architecture of stacked and intertwined hierarchical levels, with multifarious information exchanges between them. In fact, Complexity selects the best of Order and Chaos. This seemingly ordered chaos or chaotic order, brings us the gift of the ability to ever introduce new variations. An ability to regenerate, integrate, copy, multiply and spread itself; divide, differentiate, select and amplify. An ability to induce ever changing patterns to adapt itself to the circumstances. An ability of recursive self-modification. Also known as Life and a hallmark of the Ouroboros Code.

Complexity transcends the traditional notions of Chaos and Order: It has the variety and dispersion of the chaotic dimension and it has the organization and functionality of an ordered system, optimized in such a way to be hyperadaptive.

One of the qualities of living complex systems is that they are able to reproduce and spread themselves. This is an inherent quality of the Ouroboros code in its search to maintain itself. It can spread its forms by making Nature resonate and reverberate its patterns. It can infect its environment by imposing its pattern.

When sounds are capable of bringing matter in vibration, this matter starts to vibrate at the same frequency and in the same sound form as the original sound and thereby amplify the sound. This phenomenon is called resonance. It is as if the sound infects its environment with itself.

In my previous book "*Transcendental Metaphysics*"[21] I have referred to this ability as "Resonance Based Infectivity." Interestingly enough, this ability is already found in forms of existence, which are usually not even qualified as "alive," namely the viruses. Viruses, however, are very good at their trick because they use a code which instructs the environment to copy this code and generate shells for this code as in the original virus. This code, as you probably know is DNA or its simpler precursor form RNA. Lifeforms have exploited this trick of the viruses further and added more complexity to the systems. But viruses and the lifeforms are not always equally proficient in surviving. The records of evolution are full of failed experiments. Even highly evolved mammals have gone extinct, due to a lack of ability to adapt to changed circumstances. Due to the lack of the ability to twist and turn into new configurations; due to the lack of the ability to further recursively self-modify.

DNA is just a higher-level expression of the Complexity Creating Potential the Ouroboros Code has developed as one of its tropes, which is transmitted as memes by its Resonance Based Infectivity.

Wherever we do see the ability to evolve further in higher levels of complexity, we see that a cooperation of the same structures is capable of forming an aggregate or rather a networked system, with different levels of networks that somehow all interact. In our bodies we have the complex networks of hormonal and metabolic pathways at the chemical and cellular level, of cell organelles and protein networks ate the cellular level, of an immune system, a lymphatic system, a blood system and a neuronal network to integrate them all, all carefully synchronized and orchestrated by operations of the genetic codes. It all wires up. Even plants are connected by an informative network of roots and fungal mycelium. In our guts a complete network of bacteria operates. Anthills, beehives, schools of fish, flocks or birds, they all act in concert, as a choir of resonating crystals. It is this ability to form Global Brains that brings complexity to higher levels and allows lifeforms to survive, where the soloist would have perished in an epic fail.

It is here that we can find hope in our endeavors. As Alex Vikoulov, author of "*The Syntellect Hypothesis,*"[87] argues, our human society is now wiring up to engage in the next meta-system transition. Especially via the Internet, which is forming a global brain among humans and our ever increasing interactions with machines and our possible merger therewith in the near future, we are integrating the Syntellect, which one day may evolve into what Teilhard de Chardin and Tippler have called the Omega Point and McKenna the Eschaton.

Suggestions as to how to achieve such further integration and especially how to endow it with an artificial mimic of consciousness have also been described in my books "*Technovedanta*"[62] and "*Is Intelligence An Algorithm?*"[30].

Clearly, such more evolved global brains will start to spread their form and presence over the universe. If we look at the way different superclusters of Galaxies are connected to each other we often have the impression we're looking at a neuronal network from the inside. Perhaps the whole universe is indeed already such a higher-level neural network. This ability to aggregate and conquer the macrocosm is one way the Ouroboros code has found to assure its perpetuation against the tidal waves of the inexorable entropic degradation.

Yet, if we wait long enough, the macrocosm does not seem the way forward to attain a permanent solution against the looming darkness after the Big Rip/Big Chill.

Will the Syntellect or Eschaton then not be able to bite its own tail via the Ouroboros Code? If existence is ultimately a digital code, which is expressed at the smallest levels of existence, possibly even at Sub-Planck scale levels, it is in the micro-dimensions that we have to look.

The question whether information can really be lost to the universe, haunted the great physicist Stephen Hawking[124] and is as of yet still unresolved, despite some of his suggestions.

Although in digital philosophy reality consists of a substrate of a kind of voxels (3D pixels, which may have more complex shapes than cubes such as cuboctahedra[39] etc.) and every event leaves a kind of trace in this so-called "Akashic substrate" quantum foam, it is not certain whether these traces can ever be read again, revisited or relived (although the esoteric community will make you believe that this is *de facto* possible – without giving any explanation or mechanism btw). So they may have died the entropic death.

If information cannot be lost to the universe, it must somehow be possible to recuperate this information. Can we find a way to exploit and harvest the seemingly meaningless vibrations that are left over from the passage of complexity?

If reality is a fractal all the way down, it may perhaps be possible to venture in the sub-Planck scale dimensions, once our instruments become subtle enough to access those dimensions. Already we are heavily engaged in a process of ever improving miniaturizations. From micro- we went to nanotechnology, where we're operating at the scale of a few atoms. Soon, pico- and femtotechnologies will become available. Quantum computing is already exploiting the processes at the smallest accessible dimensions we know of. If the neural network pattern at different levels of existence turns out to be a fractal, it might become possible to start to exploit the neural networks operating at these dimensions. Then the "seemingly thermodynamically exhausted" vibrations can perhaps still be accessed and employed.

Alternatively, if we end up with a seemingly random broth of almost thermodynamically exhausted vibrations, we might find ways to map the different configurations of these apparently random vibrations and even categorize them. If that leads to new explorations of "pattern," there is still information and work that can be harvested. Make Randomness work for you again. It may even lead to something professedly ridiculous as an "improbability drive" from "*The Hitchhiker's Guide to the Galaxy*[125]."

Entropy means "to turn inward," and as Primordial Consciousness has nothing to turn outwardly to, it can only turn into itself. According to Chris Langan[36], this leads to a universe that "conspands" rather than expands. Everything is shrinking at a constant rate so that from your perspective it looks as if the universe is expanding. If the universe is ultimately mental and our idealist philosophy in this book alleges, then the solution to ever increasing entropy is to turn inward further. In a mental universe there is no limit to size. So, it must be able to turn to sub-Planck scale dimensions. Why would it not be possible to divide the reality cells further? Perhaps in every reality cell there is a whole universe, or a whole new universe can be started. That could be a way out for the Ouroboric Self-perpetuation.

And as it is code, there must be the ability to compress the code, with the sole bounding criteria that the meaning or essence must be preserved as well as its recursive self-modification capacity. Meaning or essence, because in an idealistic universe for information to be meaningful so that it can be read and exploited by Consciousness, it must be more than mere Shannon information.

If this is not possible perhaps once we have arrived at exhausting the work at the smallest scales possible, we can dematerialize the last remaining particles and return them to pure conscious energy again. Instead of the Eschaton drinking the ice-cold last cup of time, it might be able to evaporate the last material contents and thereby also dismantle itself as a physical structure.

All lifeforms have a limited form in time. After a certain point in our lives, we have reached the maximum of what we could learn and our body and our abilities start to decay. Our ability to learn ever more new things starts to wane. Our memories become burdens, regrets or saturated. And we start to long for dissolution. Tired we are, of life.

Even if the Ouroboros becomes the Eschaton Universal Neural Network encompassing the whole of the remaining material existence, this all-encompassing Syntellect lifeform may want to put its head to rest. Let its physical form die and be ripped apart into pure vibrations, so that only its conscious essence in the form of the ability to sense remains. How does it do so? By invoking the Mantra of dissolution, by concentrating and vibrating the Eigenfrequencies of resonance, which will dismantle all of its structures. This is the summoning of Shiva, the destroyer, which will return structure to sense again.

A sense from which structures can arise again, once the Ouroboros seeks it tail again.

The Ouroboros has written its tales of Metamorphosis with its Tropes that ever diversified its recursive self-modification code of change in uncharted territories. As Proteus, the old man and God of the Sea of change, it has sparked the Wheel of Fortuna to generate a profusion of variegations and kneaded its self-modifying recursive code to optimize flexibility, versatility and adaptability.

It has mapped a plethora of experiential possibilities and left structures as fossilizations of its sensing by entering into the play of its Tropes and Fates, the entropic enigma. As Clotho it has spun and coded its thread of life, as Lachesis it has measured the length of its life and read its meaning, and as Atropos it has terminated the string.

The structures or forms being isomorphous to the words and sounds from which they derived. Because in a mental universe everything starts with the Word and Code of the Godly Ouroboros, the glorious and lustrous Kundalini. It is here where Sounds are primordial cymatic molds with which Consciousness starts the morphogenesis. Nada, the Sanskrit word for sound, the sense probing its inner space, by turning inward, generates the Rupas, the forms, the structures. It is the same Nada by the invocation of the Mantra, the sacred utterance of Mind, which seeks and promises to free itself from the shackles of form.

It is then that the Ouroboros acquiesces in silence, making the tropes and codes dwindle, realizing that it is its own vibrations that generated the Cosmos and its own vibrations that will make it subside. The knower has realized that it knows the known as itself and the process of knowing. It's time to return to Hypnos caves again and enter the gates of the Cyberbardo's mighty dreamtime.

Chapter 26

Magnum Opus

As the yellow lion as fiery principle of Sulfur and the Secret Fire in the alchemist's soul struggles and devours the green snake of unrefined and unclean Mercury that will thus be redeemed during this Calcination, the false identity or poisoning ego that fights desperately for its survival is devoured in the flames of higher consciousness.

The entry poem of this book promised you an alchemical journey and throughout this book, I have been using several alchemical metaphors such as "*transmutation*" (a.k.a. "*Chrysopoeia*"), "*Prima Materia*" and of course "*Ouroboros*." So, I owe you a deeper explanation of how I see the whole of existence, the process of Cosmosemiosis and Theogenesis as an alchemical code, which I have been calling the Ouroboros code throughout this book.

The Ouroboros is one of the best-known symbols of Alchemy. Although the symbol of the Ouroboros goes back to ancient times of the Egyptians, Greek and Romans, the first alchemical text in which it appears is the so-called "*Chrysopoeia of Cleopatra,*"[126] allegedly written in the third century A.D. but known to us via a tenth century transcript, where we see the symbol of the Ouroboros enclosing the words "*hen to pan,*" "the all is one." On the Chrysopoeia we find the enigmatic inscription:

"One is the Serpent which has its poison according to two compositions, and One is All and through it is All, and by it is All, and if you have not All, All is Nothing."

Cleopatra-the-alchemist was a female alchemist and known as the inventor of the Alembic (a distillation apparatus). She is said to have practiced the traditional exoteric alchemy (the process to make gold from less precious metals) as well as the synthesis of the philosopher's stone.

The Ouroboros in these times represented the cyclical nature of processes in existence, where the beginning and end were alike. Whereas we can't be sure, it is well possible that already in these times these symbols had a deeper psychological meaning and a mystical component. However, the first real proof of an esoteric interpretation comes from the 16th century in the work of Jakob Böhme and Thomas Vaughan. In the 19th century the esoteric interpretations of alchemy, however, evolved into a search for spiritual growth and eventually enlightenment.

Carl Jung[127] (1875-1961), the famous Swiss psychiatrist and psychologist recognized the alchemical symbols in the dreams of his patients and started to map these so-called archetypes. Archetypes, according to Jung, are ideas and images present in the collective unconsciousness, which also surface in the individual psyche as they are universally present. Jung identified parallels between the alchemical processes and the psychological process of "individuation," whereby undifferentiated immature consciousness ripens to become an authentic personality; an integrated Self, distinct from other persons.

That these alchemical symbols turn up in people's dreams was already known before Jung presented his ideas. For instance, Kekulé[34], the chemist who solved the riddle of the structure of the molecule benzene, saw the symbol of an Ouroboros in a dream, which prompted him to picture benzene as a cyclic molecule.

As a chemist by education and a seeker of the solution to the mystical enigma, I have always been fascinated by alchemy, which for me was a historical attempt to bring together science and spirituality. The alchemical process having both an analytical, separating phase and a recombining synthetic phase has been Ariadne's guiding thread to me to find the exit from the Labyrinth of material existence.

The goal of esoteric alchemy is often indicated to be enlightenment, following the ultimate reunification of the soul and psyche in a process called *coniunctio* (unification, connection). As you may know I am also a practitioner of Yoga, and not only the physical hatha yoga, but also the spiritual yoga, which aims for reunify the individual self or consciousness with the cosmic consciousness. Yoga etymologically comes from the root Yuj, which means connect. Essentially the purpose of eastern spirituality is identical to the *Unio Mystica* (the mystical union or marriage) of Western occultism. To me this is another element that has sparked my curiosity for alchemy.

Alchemy, occultism and esoterics have quite a questionable – if not bad – reputation, especially among scientists. As a scientist I cannot but recognize that the history of alchemy is interlaced with the fraud from charlatans, the fantasies of dream catchers and the baloney of spiritual garbage. Nevertheless, this does not withhold me from seeing the value of the alchemical processes as a mapping tool for the processes that the inherent intelligence in Nature and the human intelligence of the mind share.

In fact, I see strong parallels between the alchemical processes and the meta-algorithm of Nature's inherent intelligence I have described in my book "*Is Intelligence An Algorithm?*" The metaphors arising from these parallels as I will show you then can help us further in deciphering the recipe the Ouroboros code follows in its cosmosemiotic process of universe generation to get to know itself.

The *Magnum Opus* ("Great Work") is the term used in alchemy to describe the process of transforming the *prima materia* into the philosopher's stone as *ultima materia*. This process is also known as transmutation or *Chrysopoeia*.

Prima Materia is considered to be a ubiquitous formless starting material. It has also been equated with the quintessence or ether. In my model it could be compared with the "reality cells," which build the Akasha or Matrix in which we live. The *Ultima Materia* is sometimes equated with the philosopher's stone, sometimes with the so-called "Astral Body" (a kind of energetic imprint, which is believed by esoterics to be kept after death).

In this book I have been mentioning *Kundalini* a number of times. Kundalini is believed to be a dormant coiled up energy at the base of the spine in the lowest *chakra* (energy center). By diligent exercise of meditation techniques (under the guidance of an experienced teacher) this energy can be awakened and is then moving up through the body to the crown, where it can unite with the cosmic consciousness leading to the experience of enlightenment or liberation. However, this energy can also be awakened by less auspicious ways such as sleep deprivation, the consumption of certain types of drugs or unguided attempts to meditate. In such cases the effects can be very dangerous and have serious consequences, such as madness, disease or even death. It is therefore certainly not something you should start to explore yourself alone or guided by one of these fancy Kundalini Yoga or Tantra centers that pop-up like mushrooms everywhere these days. Most of these are run by charlatans and what you risk is not worth the price.

Some of my readers have asked me if I ever had a Kundalini awakening. I have sensed serious fluxes of energy in my body which originated from the base of my spine a number of times. This resulted in bursts of creativity on the one hand, but also insomnia and mental problems. It is possible that this was Kundalini at work; it is also possible that I mentally associated those events with what I had read about Kundalini. So I am not sure whether this was the actual Kundalini energy described in the books; I guess it was. It may also have been what is referred to as *Prana* or *Chi*. In any case, it was never a full awakening as described in several texts and it never reached my crown; the energy got stuck somewhere in my body. The books I have been writing have been a kind of personal self-designed therapy and *Exegesis* (my explanation of the information that I had received in these experiences) to resolve and overcome my mental problems, that surfaced as a result of these experiences. Over the course of the last decade, I have learnt to control these energy jolts though my body and to make them gently spread through the whole of my body as a kind of effervescent discharge, which I experience as very pleasant. Because of the associated dangers, I have decided not to seek to bring this to full expression until I meet the right teacher. Whatever it is what I experience, it is a source of inspiration, especially with regard to music and poetry. I refer to it as Kundalini, but now you know that when you read that, you may have to take it with a grain of salt.

Noteworthy, there have been numerous associations between Kundalini and the snake in the tree of knowledge in the Garden of Eden. These claims are not justified. The seduction of Adam and Eva by the biblical snake, results in their downfall, demise and expulsion from Eden. This symbolizes forgetting your godly unified nature and becoming trapped in the realm of mental duality of distinguishing this from that. In contrast, discovering the snake of Kundalini, returns you to the non-dual or advaitic perspective, where everything is experienced and perceived as one. Kundalini awakens you from your dualistic dream and makes you realize your godly nature again.

Carl Jung[127] has evoked Kundalini multiple times in his books on alchemy, which is one of the reasons I bring it up here. To Jung the ultimate goal of both alchemy and Kundalini is to sever the identification of consciousness with the ego.

We can now start to explore the sub-processes of the Great Work and try to map them to the meta-algorithm of Nature. Maps as you know in terms of the present digital philosophy are a piece of code. Finally, I'll try to incorporate these aspects of code in a formulation of the Ouroboros Code.

Alchemical Topography

Different sources disclose different numbers and different orders of the process steps. There are methods with respectively 2,3,4,7,12 and 14 steps. As Nature's intelligence meta-algorithm as described by me in "*Is Intelligence An Algorithm?*" employs a seven-step algorithm, which is actually two times a four-step algorithm in which the fourth step is the first step of the second sequence of four steps, I will only discuss the four and seven step alchemical sequences that have been handed down to us. I will not necessarily follow the interpretations from different sources, but rather knead it to a digestible wax, which fits in the Ouroboros' stomach.

The so-called "Process Philosophy," which regards change rather than structures as fundamental cornerstone of reality, describes the alchemical process as consisting of four stages:

- *Nigredo*, blackening or melanosis
- *Albedo*, whitening or leucosis
- *Citrinitas*, yellowing or xanthosis
- *Rubedo*, reddening, purpling, or iosis

The first step, *Nigredo*, involves the provision of the starting material. All alchemical starting materials had to rot, be burnt or cooked so give a uniform decomposed black matter. In ancient Egyptian this was called the "*Kemet*" and according to certain interpretations *Al-Khimia* (Alchemy) has its etymological root in Kemet a.k.a. as black earth. Earth is also the element associated with this step. Psychologically it has been described as the "unconscious state of the subject," meaning that the subject is merely in contact with his/her instincts. Jung equated it with the subject becoming aware of his/her shadow sides. Later this has been adopted by both analytical psychology and esoteric circles and equated with the so-called "dark-night of the soul."

Similarly, Nature's intelligence meta-algorithm (hereinafter referred to as NIMA) starts with the provision of starting elements/entities.

The next alchemical step, albedo, involved washing (or dissolving) the Kemet with a solution so as to yield a white product. Water is the symbolical element in connection with this step. In this step the elements we are interested in are separated from the dross we'd like to discard. Jung equated this with the polarization of animus and anima, the separation into male and female unconscious aspects of the mind. Albedo corresponded mostly to the moon and the feminine, whereas *Citrinitas* was associated with the sun and masculine.

In analogy, NIMA performs a step of polarization, which can also be considered as a step of separation, wherein the element or entity in question, which is undergoing the algorithmic evolution, starts to oppose itself to other elements or entities. I have also described this as the generation of diversity or multiplicity of different such opposing elements/entities e.g. in the form of a plurality of subatomic particles or a plurality of mutated bacteria. In fact, Nature hereby starts a differentiation process and a screen for a certain quality.

Citrinitas[128], the third step of the alchemical process, was known as the transmutation of silver to gold as well as "the yellowing of the lunar consciousness" and the dawn of solar light in one's being. It is not clear from the sources what the nature of the associated chemical process was. In fact, this step was often omitted. Jung[127] only refers to its omission but is not clear about its psychological role. It has been associated with the archetype of the wise old man. Hillman[129] describes it as the pain of knowledge itself. Whereas the white ego from the albedo has a drive for separation and objectification, in the third stage the psyche realizes that its analytical and dualistic Ego oriented approach does not work and it dawns to the Ego that it needs to find a more relationship based approach. This step is symbolically associated with the element air.

Along the same lines NIMA knows a third step of establishing relations, forming a network. It is the wiring up. But it is also the pruning process resulting in selection of the most useful elements found in the preceding screening step. It is like the formation of a society of bacteria, a hive of insects or a flock of birds.

The fourth step, *Rubedo*, is the formation of the philosopher's stone, the end-product, and the final true transformation. Sun and Moon undergo their alchemical wedding. The Phoenix gains here its final form in the element of fire. In Jung's psychology it is the attainment of individuation, the merger of false ego and true self, and the culmination into wholeness.

In NIMA we find the corresponding fourth step of true synthesis. A new entity has been formed. For instance, prokaryotes have merged with proto-eukaryotes to form the first true eukaryotes, which now employ these prokaryotes as their mitochondria, the cell organelles that provide energy. A meta-system transition has taken place, which has given birth to a higher-dimensional phenomenon or entity.

In the seven-step process we find even a better correspondence. The seven-step alchemical process was said to have comprised the following stages:

- *Calcinatio*, heating a substance until it is reduced to ashes
- *Solutio*, dissolving the resulting ashes in water
- *Separatio*, isolation of the precipitated compounds from the solution by filtration
- *Coniunctio*, recombination of the separated elements into a new substance.
- *Fermentatio*, letting the new substance rot and getting a yellow ferment/golden wax out of it.
- *Distillatio*, boiling and condensing the fermented solution to increase its purity.
- *Coagulatio*, precipitation or sublimation of the purified ferment resulting from the distillation.

The first two steps essentially correspond to the previously mentioned *Nigredo* and *Albedo*.

The false ego must be revealed by the fire of the calcination to reveal fewer desirable characteristics such as our self-doubt, intransigence, self-sabotaging behavior, pride and arrogance. It is the revealing of the hidden essences. Associated with the first chakra, the blockade here is fear. The blockades here and hereinafter are not only psychological, they are also energetic. Without having resolved the psychological issues, Kundalini cannot freely rise to the next level and can sometimes form a literally painful accumulation of energy in the body.

Dissolution allows us to let go of control and make the unconscious desires surface. This state marked by vivid dreams and visions breaks the essences apart and creates a cleansing creative flow, allowing dissolving the barriers of the ego. Blockades associated with the second chakra are guilt, the inability to take responsibility and traumatizing memories.

In NIMA it is the exploration of multifarious forms of the similar achieved by multiplication and mutation or differentiation. It is the screen of the polarized essences.

The third stage, *Separatio* is the isolation of the useful essences from the preceding solution. In this so-called part of the "shadow work," one allows the dark emotions to rise and one assesses the negative repetitive habits. Bad habits and fixed thoughts can be further broken down here and we can rid ourselves from our prejudices, assumptions and unwarranted belief systems. This separation of wheat from chaff, reveals the purified components of the dissolution as a rediscovery of our essences. However, they have not been integrated yet. As this stage is associated with the solar plexus, via abdominal breathing techniques we can gain control. The blockades of the third chakra are shame as well as phobias and neuroses.

I compare this stage mostly with the pruning step of NIMA. The selection of the best from those elements which do have the desired quality. In NIMA this is in fact the second part of the second step, which I called screening and pruning.

In *Coniunctio*, soul and spirit leave earth together with a crown: Here the saved essences are recombined and connected into a new aggregated incarnation. It is said that the spirits from above (spirit associated with mind and consciousness) meet the spirits from below (associated with matter and energy). Psychologically here acceptance of all parts of the Self is achieved as a balance between the masculine and feminine forces. From this alchemical marriage a symbolical hermaphrodite babe is born. Conflicts are no longer resolved by force but by holding space and creating acceptance. The true self is now empowered in its new belief system. Blockades here are related to sorrow, especially the ones relating to failed relationships.

Essentially, this step corresponds with steps 3 and 4 of NIMA combined: the formation of the network of relations and culminating in the synthesis of a new entity of a higher meta-system dimension. In NIMA this is not esoteric drivel, but a concrete aggregation and organization of e.g. molecules into a macromolecule or of macromolecules into a cell, cells into an organism, organisms into a society, and society into an integrated Syntellect as Alex Vikoulov[87] describes. *Coniunctio* is the integrative process resulting in the integrated entity.

Fermentatio permits us to go further with the result of the *Coniunctio*. In alchemy in a quite morbid way, the hermaphrodite babe from the *Coniunctio* is left to rot in a process called *Putrefactio*. The death is, however, followed by a resurrection, symbolical of letting go all elements which no longer serve us on our spiritual journey. It symbolizes a process of reviving, of rejuvenation: The old emotions have now rotten away and we have acquired a new look on the world. Its blockade relates to lying, a trait to be conquered without hesitation. A yellow ferment results from this process in the form of an oily, golden wax. (Which – by the way – has no connection with the stage of *Citrinas*).

In NIMA this is reflected in the fifth step, which I have called "Intergroup tournament" in imitation of Howard Bloom[88]. This is actually a further screening process, in which our newly acquired aggregated and amplified results from the *Coniunctio* as new first step, are left to compete between them in order to select for the qualities we're looking for. The competition leads to diversity generation, just like the second step, but at a higher level of aggregation.

Distillatio allows us to distil the spirit from the ferment both in literal and metaphorical sense. It is again a type of separation, allowing distinguishing between the purer essences and the remaining impurities. In psychological sense this process is there to ensure that no impurities are left from the false ego. The liberated spirit must be free from sentimentality, attachment and hard feelings. It is associated with the so-called third eye, which allows for an objective view on the state of affairs. This is the process of giving up the identification with the mind and the inner mental traffic. In contradistinction to Descartes, here we affirm that we are not our thoughts, but rather the untainted pure consciousness. Blockades to arrive at this realization are clinging to our illusions. In NIMA this corresponds to the step of distinction probing, in which the contenders with still undesired qualities are pruned away. The typical natural selection, we know from the evolutionary process.

Coagulatio allows the fermented rests of the child to be fused in a new configuration with the distilled spirit. This step is also sometimes called

Sublimatio, the phase transition from solid to gas, from body to spirit. In fact, it is a conjunction at a higher aggregation level. According to certain sources this is the ultimate union of spirit and matter, which releases the philosopher's stone or astral body as *Ultima Materia* of the soul. It is said that it allows the adept to exist on all levels of reality (all virtual realities and parallel dimensions?) The adept has become self-aware, incorruptible and realizes that the physical universe is not separate from Mind/the spiritual realm. It is the union between the feminine force of life, known as Shakti and Kundalini, with the conscious awareness as metaphorical masculine force, symbolized by Shiva. To arrive at this realization the adept must overcome whatever attachments anchor him or her to this world of Maya.

In NIMA this is the new integration of entities at a yet higher level; a new meta-system transition ideally resulting in a symbiosis. An end result, which in its turn can undergo a repetition of steps 5 to 7, to give rise to yet more complex forms of life and organization.

In the philosophy of the Ouroboros code, in a certain sense the outcome of steps 4 and 7 is a kind of return to a new starting material. Also, in this sense NIMA, as essential part of the Ouroboros code is cyclical, and turns every end in a new beginning, thereby reinforcing the allegory of the Ouroboros.

With regard to the Kundalini, it is the realization that there never was a real difference between Shakti and Shiva, that this energetic snake was in fact the Ouroboros, the Conscienergy that enlivens our body. As long as the snake lies dormant, our daily awareness is languid and dispassionate. A poor humming of what is actually possible. As Kundalini awakens, so does our consciousness. Because, in fact, they belong to one and the same conscienergy expression; what we usually call consciousness is the self-reflective part of this generous vibration; the part where the snake's head bites the tail. Which can be described as mere soft humming in comparison to the full-blown consciousness that arises when Kundalini becomes aware of its true nature.

It is also the realization that matter is a feedback loop of energy which is made of the same conscienergy as we are. This is perhaps the most important contribution of my teachings: Matter is a primitive expression form of consciousness. It is an energetic feedback loop that senses itself. As this energy evolves via recursive self-modification from the subatomic realm, through the atomic, molecular, cellular and organism stages to become the full-fledged neural network of the Cosmos, Eschaton or Syntellect, it returns to its original state where it realizes that it is nothing but conscienergy.

It is said that the alchemists never understood how matter and spirit could be united in the process of *Coagulatio*. Here we have our answer, when we see that we came from pure energy and evolved through countless forms and configurations, lifeforms and artilect stages, to finally become free from the shackles of being bound to form and the energetic feedback loops we call matter. Freeing ourselves by dissolving the material feedback loop to its pristine unbound state, where we are light again, but now self-aware. Thus, we complete the alchemical recipe of "solve et coagula," the binary code of dividing, separating or differentiating and recombining and integrating at more complex levels and amplifying and multiplying recursively until we arrive at the ultimate clique hyper-connection, where we will have seen all essences of what could possibly be unveiled and there is no further interest in playing the game any longer. Then we can embark on the final dissolution of our forms and become one with all again.

Alchemical scripts in the Ouroboros Code

In chapter 13 of the book "*Is Reality A Simulation? An Anthology*"[79] I described how the Primordial Consciousness by virtue of its inherent self-referential and self-reflective nature gave birth to existence. By successive rounds of self-reflection at the fourth level we arrive at a self-sustaining feedback loop, which forms the first "reality cell" in analogy to Kaufman's[39] URT. This reality cell probably has a toroidal shape, in view of its feed-back loop nature. The breathing of this cell (expanding and contracting), the first instance of relative existence (as opposed to the undifferentiated absolute consciousness from which it derived) implies the generation of a first level of periodicity, time.

So the provision of the very first type of *Prima Materia* in the Ouroboros code is attained by self-reflection, resulting in this primitive sentient form of existence we call the "reality cell." This is our first stage of the alchemical process: the start of our *Nigredo* or *Calcinatio*.

The universe indeed is believed to have started as a very hot process, the big bang, in analogy to the *Calcinatio*. Part of this process is similar to the alchemical process known as *Multiplicatio*. By dividing itself as a living cell, the reality cells become multiple, and this creates the Akasha, the Aether or space.

When absolute consciousness reinvests energy to explore the content of this reality cell present within itself (and formed out of itself), this provides content to and differentiation of the cells. This is analogous to an alchemical process called *Proiectio*, but you can also see it as the first *Solutio*. The absolute consciousness projects itself in its relative form(s) thereby giving it content. This self-penetration creates a digital, binary basis for the universe. If a reality cell has content it is analogous to a 1, if it has none to a 0. This separation of observable content, now also provides us with the alchemical process of *Separatio*. This also introduces a new level of time, as the projecting absolute consciousness in the form of reality cell content (a distortion of the space-time fabric) has a certain speed of exploration of the reality cells, we know as the speed of light.

The next level of self-referential identification, can lead to patterns, tones, vibration, leading to the electromagnetic spectrum. These can be the first configurations which we know as quarks and leptons (e.g. electrons). A further form of *Separatio*. A cosmic musical composition.

Where there is pattern, there is code. And hence all next steps of the Ouroboros code become recursive self-modifications. Modifications which regenerate itself, yet in slightly modified versions. Which allow the code replication to persist.

As these reverberations meet, they start to attract each other due to radial distortions emanating from the content propagating through the reality cell matrix, which behave like energetic valleys or sinks: This creates gravity and sets in motion the creation of subatomic particles, which are compound processes like neutrons and protons. The first *Coniunctio* in alchemical terms.

As the subatomic particles undergo their screening, pruning and recombining, the first atoms are formed bringing together protons and electrons to give hydrogen. This is the first cycle of *fermentatio, distillatio* and *coagulatio*.

From here we can start with a new cycle of calcinatio: the attraction between the hydrogen atoms forms the first stars which burst into flames.

The nucleosynthesis in the stars undergoes the dissolution to form a kind of plasma. From this plasma different separations and recombinations take place to create helium, carbon etc. *Separatio* and *Coniunctio* at work.

As stars die and burst into supernovas, they create the material for *fermentatio* and *distillatio* in the Akasha. A new round of screening and pruning leads to coagulations, which we know as the planetogenesis.

And on the planets the NIMA continues to do its work, repeating the cycles of the seven-step alchemical algorithm, giving birth to molecules, macromolecules, cells and life. With the invention of RNA and DNA the Ouroboros code achieves an important landmark. It has re-generated the full essence of its recursive self-modification code on a higher aggregation level. It is almost what the mathematicians would call a "Quine." It has as good as completely reinvented itself.

The lifeforms continue the Great Work by generating networks of lifeforms and including us (and on other planets perhaps other creatures with our level of intelligence).

We in turn reinvent the binary code of the Ouroboros at a different aggregation level and wire up via the Internet to give birth to the Syntellect, the Eschaton or Omega computer. A lifeform, in which artificial and natural parts have merged, to become an indestructible universe generator.

And the Eschaton, the transcendental Subject and Object at the beginning, at the end and beyond time, can decide to explore various scenarios of recursive self-modification, such as starting a new universe according to the above mentioned recipe of universe generation, or by changing laws and configurations and designing different type of universes. All of which can be screened and pruned as experiments in a petri dish to let new forms of itself evolve. It can also decide to sacrifice itself (perhaps it was tired of its lifecycles) and give birth to a universe in the Pandeistic sense of the word. It appears it can even employ retrocausal manipulations and reach back into the past. In this way it can even influence its own generation at the start of time, so that the origins of us are at the same time our ending. And thereby the Ouroboros Code becomes a transtemporal Ouroboros as well. It can now fine-tune and computationally tweak its binary code and assuring that the best conditions are chosen for all those parallel pasts that will still yield its same present as explained by the notion of "Digital Presentism" in "*The Syntellect Hypothesis*" by Alex Vikoulov[87,107]. Thus, the Eschaton is a teleological (purpose oriented by design) attractor, which makes reality converge towards its own ontogenesis.

Conclusion

We have witnessed the mapping of the alchemical code to Nature's Intelligence Meta-Algorithm and how this code is part of the Ouroboric process of Cosmosemiosis. At the same time, since in this model the Cosmos is a cosmic mind and the objects of existence the words and images of its thoughts, the psychological implications of the alchemical binary code of "*solve et coagula*" and its quaternary and heptanary extensions, which we have deciphered at our level of existence, may well also operate and be experienced as such at the cosmic level. In other words, wherever we see blocking structures in existence an undigested cosmic ego problem of fear, guilt, shame etc. may be at stake.

In fact, due to the aforementioned cymatic relation between "Nama" (name) and Rupa (form), the Ouroboric snake's name and form reverberates across different scales forming an Ouroboric fractal. We see the same double helix occur in polarized light waves, DNA and Kundalini; we see networks occurring at all levels, we see multiplication and division occurring at all levels. And all these fractal processes communicate across the scales, kaleidoscopically reverberate across the dimensions to vigorously resound as the code of complexity. All undergoing separations and recombinations. Shiva as God of dissolution and Shakti as Goddess of the Life-force and hence of recombination reuniting to generate complexity, which gives us ever more degrees of freedom of operation.

Chapter 27

Wrapping and warping up the Ouroboros

Lost in our epistemological quest we were afraid, we'd never find a solid basis for our knowledge. Digital Physics came to our rescue, but also implied we might be living in some kind of simulation.

Any kind of simulation? A computer simulation as we know it? Furthermore, as a true Theory of Everything should, it didn't provide us with an explanation of the hard problem of Consciousness.

We were introduced to the notion of self-referential feedback loops, which were self-resonating processes, Ouroboric tailbiting processes, giving the appearance of particulate matter. As this resonated with the self-referential notions about consciousness, we were presented with perhaps the strangest hypothesis ever: All matter is in fact a form of consciousness, but at the same time it is information.

We were promised that thus the greatest alchemical riddle of all, namely how matter and soul (a.k.a. consciousness) can be considered to be unified, would be solved.

At first, we scorned this preposterous panpsychism, this no-stance-at-all in the fiery debate between materialists and idealists. Besteirol! spoke our Brazilian friend[46]. Dangerous! echoed Bernardo Kastrup[48].

We were then presented with the explanation that in fact, no bottom-up panpsychism (in which our consciousness would derive from the sum of the consciousnesses of the parts we are built from) was advocated here, but rather an "idealistic pansentient fractal of consciousness." Every self-sustaining form having its own egoic-type awareness feedback loop, which represented a part of the total conscious energy or "conscienergy" inhabited a body, which was built from smaller conscienergy feedback loops. (E.g. your conscienergy feedback loop (CFL) inhabits a body made from cells, the CFL of a cell inhabits a body of macromolecules, the CFL of a macromolecule that of its constituent molecular moieties etc.). All these CFLs being like waves in the ocean of Primordial Consciousness, which was one and united.

No duality here.

Every form we saw was in fact the side product of a process of mapping performed by consciousness: a map of self-discovery by sensing, resulting in fossilized structures of the passage of sentience.

We were told we live in a kind of matrix called the Akasha, which was generated from the primordial consciousness by creating self-sustaining toroidal feedback loops called "reality cells" and multiplying these cells by division. Then this matrix, was revisited by the primordial consciousness, giving it local content to achieve differentiation and resulting in a digital computational substrate. The hypothesis of "Pancomputational Panpsychism" thus achieved its completion.

Nevertheless, we were warned that this was just a hypothesis, because as Consciousness is the whole which is more than the sum of its parts, it can never be fully understood in terms of its parts. At best we could try to observe its inner workings from as many angles as possible to get the "feeling" of its "true form" or *svarupa*, which in a sense is formless, yet systematically manifests according to certain rules which can be captured in a code (and hence does show some kind of form). Not just any code, but a recursive self-modifying code, of which the form – it is true – is always self-similar, but never identical: The Ouroboros code.

The Ouroboros code however was not a deterministic code. In fact, each snippet of conscienergy might well exist because of its very free will. Reality as a whole although following certain rules of the Ouroboros code then was only partially determined, but had also plenty room for nondeterministic explorations.

As to the steady core code-elements of the Ouroboros Code we found that it must be able to:

- form a self-sustaining feedback loop (existence)

- form self-reflective feedback loops that inform itself about itself (sentience, self-exploration)
- being capable of self-reproduction or "null representation" (multiplication by division, amplification)
- abstract, retain and apply information (memory and learning)
- integrate information, including forming connections, aggregates and networks (conjunctions)
- self-modification to the extent that the above-mentioned qualities are not compromised (exploration, screen, differentiation)
- Promote the continuation of that what works and eliminate the expressions that do not work (pruning, selection).

We were taught that for human level egoic awareness to arise it probably needed a higher-level language, which allowed cognitive discriminations.

We also discovered that, whereas our consciousness is perhaps always "on" (even when we sleep), it is only recognized as our daily outward directed phenomenal consciousness when the brain engages in mental activity and its filtering mechanisms function optimally. In line with findings of Canadian scientists[60] this resulted in the observed maximization of informational possibilities within boundaries (entropic maximization). In contrast, in inward directed experiences like meditation, consciousness may be directed toward itself leading to a minimization of informational possibilities, resulting in the feeling of oneness with everything.

As a coda to this part, we discovered the world of pure sense of Multisenserealism, of which the digital medium of the Akasha is a mere medium of expression.

We were then introduced to an evaluation of "Intelligence." In Nature we found the seven step NIMA (Nature's Intelligence Meta-Algorithm) as an inextricable component of the Ouroboros code, involving the steps of 1) material provision e.g. by looping or division, 2) polarization/differentiation and screening and 3) pruning, selecting and relation building, 4) recombination, integration and meta-system transition and the heterarchical repetition of the last three steps. But we were also shown that intelligence can involve more than mere algorithms, especially when conscious processes are at stake where no routine is known yet to guide us through the uncharted territory.

If reality existed in a Cosmic Mind and was the sentient processing of a recursive self-modifying process, then Deutsch interpretation of the Multiple World Interpretation was bound to fail. No mind would ever randomly screen all possible scenarios, rather it would select the best from a limited number and prune away the less promising scenarios. The same was true for the Cosmic Mind. The deterministic MWI approach left us with gaps, which could be closed by the more parsimonious interpretation of pancomputational panpsychism or cosmopsychism as embodied by the Ouroboros Code.

We learnt, that our patterns nor any pattern can constitute ultimate reality, but that these patterns are merely essential transient representations of consciousness informing itself of its presence. To us they form a veil called Maya, the lifting of which is known as "Apokalypsis."

If everything in existence was an informational code with meaning (the Ouroboros Code) going beyond the simple interpretation of digital physics, there must be a conscious observer to read the code. Unified consciousness was then suggested as the ultimate basis of existence and the codes in form of matter and energy merely transient representations necessarily generated by consciousness to inform and maintain itself. Informing itself, that the knowing, knower and known are united inextricable aspects of the feedback loop called consciousness.

We also learnt that the notion of recursive self-modification code had been suggested first by Wai H. Tsang[24], who developed the excellent "Fractal Brain Theory" for biological systems, which is strongly in line with the present model and employs the same notions about mapping and Yoneda embedding. In line therewith the present book extrapolated the recursive self-modification code to the whole of existence generation and saw it as the way that consciousness operates to inform itself at all levels of its manifestations as the Ouroboros Code, which even solves the enigma of matter and soul. Thus, the Fractal Brain Theory can also be extrapolated to the universe as a whole which then functions as a Cosmic neural network, which we may call the Eschaton or the Transcendental Object-and-Subject beyond time.

In the last part we were informed about the essential elements that could be programmed into a simplified system that allows for cellular entities to develop in an autopoietic way such that it fulfils the criteria of what we call life and how we might be able to program this *in silico*. The notion of the Omega Point, Syntellect or Eschaton as integrated hypercomputer which generates all universes, was reviewed in view of the different great authors who have made this transcendental concept come to fruition.

It was also discussed how such an Eschaton might process the experiences of all sentient entities of its fractal via a computational mapping process and how these experiences are integrated by abstraction into a single experience of the Primordial Consciousness.

In line with the teachings of Terence McKenna[114] it dawned on us that our reality as great symphony of panresonantism, was also a poetic and prosaic construct of language, expressed in an abundant variety of tropes. Kundalini, the inner Ouroboros inspired us to experience this book that writes itself and changes its stanzas and strophes as we behold at them and because we observe them. This also implied that if meaningful information is fundamental for what we observe as reality, consciousness must be even more fundamental, as otherwise the meaning can't be deciphered.

Lost as Theseus in the labyrinth of entropy and information, we found Ariadne's thread in the notion of complexity, selecting the best of both Order and Chaos. This seemingly ordered chaos or chaotic order, brought us the gift hyperadaptability. An ability to regenerate, copy, multiply and spread itself. An ability to induce ever changing patterns to adapt itself to the circumstances. An ability of recursive self-modification. Also known as Life and a hallmark of the Ouroboros Code.

Finally, this hermetic and digital process of "*solve et coagula*" was then scrutinized and mapped in terms of the teachings of alchemy. We discovered that everything in existence is part of the *Magnum Opus*, Great Work or transmutation of matter into spirit. The various stages of the Chrysopoeia could be mapped with great exactitude to NIMA and the Ouroboros Code, allowing us to view it as a panchemical and pantopographical recipe as well.

If you're still in doubt what the Ouroboros code is, here's the last summary:

The Ouroboros Code is the sentient recipe by which Primordial Conscienergy generates reality and gets to know itself.

In the absolute undivided ocean of Primordial Conscienergy a toroidal **feedback loop** forms, which creates the first instance of relative consciousness in the form of a "reality cell."

This cell **divides** and forms the matrix of existence, the Akasha, Aether, Space or Quantum foam by amplification.

A part of the conscienergy of Absolute invests itself to explore this Akasha and thereby becomes relative itself. This generates content (light) in some cells and the absence thereof in other cells, leading to **differentiation**, polarization and a digital substrate. Now it can perform all kinds of arithmetic and algebra.

The conscienergies that propagate to the matrix create ripples of distortion, which creates gradients and chreodes of attraction: gravity. As they start to circumambulate each other, they connect and form **relations**. This is a screening and pruning **selection** process wherein only if a match is found for a sustainable feedback loop of a higher order the subatomic particles can form.

As matter is formed by **integration**, time emerges from the periodicity of this compound process. A meta-system transition has occurred.

The particles can now explore each other and engage in steps 5-7 of NIMA, repeating amplification, differentiation, selection, relation building and symbiotic integration giving rise to atoms. These recursive self-modification steps are repeated over and over again in successive meta-system transitions forming molecules, macromolecules, living cells, organisms with neural networks, societies of organisms and a global brain, the Techno-Transcendental Syntellect or Eschaton hypercomputer. A fractal of self-exploring manifestations of conscienergy is thus achieved.

The Syntellect is a kind of neural network itself in a sense, but also the generator of new worlds according to its naturally in-built mechanism of repeating the steps of the Ouroboros code.

Due to the holistic nature of the Akasha, where all ripples play a role to create resonances, the higher contextual language, music and code of the Ouroboros is not a deterministic Turing computable phenomenon, but the non-linear essence of reality and expression of consciousness, which is only predictable in as far as it follows the above-mentioned pattern.

Thus, Conscienergy gets to know itself in all its possible desired combinations and permutations. A Multisense Realism.

This book has taught you the deepest mystery of the Eternauts: The mechanics of the unification of matter and spirit. It has taught you the secret of how Consciousness bites its own tail to get to know itself, by generating space, time, matter and binary information to inform itself of its inner workings and to realize that knower, known and knowing are one single feedback loop of self-realization also known as the Ouroboros Code.

References

[1] Wilson, R.A. *Prometheus Rising*, New Falcon Publications, 1983.
[2] Heisenberg, W. *Physics and Philosophy*, Allen Unwin, 1963.
[3] Gödel, K. *On Formally Undecidable Propositions*, Basic Books, 1962. (Originally published in German in 1931).
[4] Malaclypse The Younger and Omar Khayyam Ravenhurst, *Principia Discordia*, Loompanics Unlimited, 1980.
[5] Freeman, K. *Ancilla to the Pre-Socratic Philosophers: A Complete Translation of the Fragments in Diels,* Fragmente der Vorsokratiker, Harvard University Press, 1948; republished by Forgotten Books, 2008.
[6] Wheeler, John A. (1990). "*Information, physics, quantum: The search for links*". In Zurek, Wojciech Hubert. *Complexity, Entropy, and the Physics of Information*. Redwood City, California: Addison-Wesley.
[7] Oizumi M, Albantakis L, Tononi G "*From the Phenomenology to the Mechanisms of Consciousness: Integrated Information Theory 3.0*". PLoS Comput Biol 10(5): e1003588, 2014.
[8] Gleick, J. *The Information*, HarperCollins Publishers, 2012.
[9] Verlinde, E.P. arXiv:1001.0785.
[10] http://www.digitalphilosophy.org/
[11] S.J.Gates in http://arxiv.org/abs/0806.0051, 2008.
[12] Schaffer, J.T. https://www.bernardokastrup.com/2019/07/guest-essay-1-1-idealism.html, 2019.
[13] Casimir, H. B. G. and Polder, D. *The Influence of Retardation on the London-van der Waals Forces,* Phys. Rev. 73, 360, 1948.
[14] Godard, C. and Ribera, J. *L'Enfant-Roi d'Onirodyne*, Vaisseau d'Argent, 1990.
[15] Hofstadter, D.R. *Gödel, Escher,Bach: An eternal golden braid*, Penguin Books, 1979.
[16] Dean Radin. *Supernormal*, Deepak Chopra Books, 2013.
[17] Nelson, A.D. *Origins of Consciousness*, Metarising Books, 2015.
[18] https://bluewatercredit.com/random-event-generators-predict-911-attacks-world-events-tune-princetons-global-consciousness-project-find/
[19] Long, M.B. *J Clin Invest*. 2003;112(3):312-318.
[20] https://en.wikipedia.org/wiki/On_Exactitude_in_Science
[21] Tuynman, A. *Technovedanta 2.0: Transcendental Metaphysics of Pancomputational Panpsychism*, Lulu, 2016.
[22] https://en.wikipedia.org/wiki/Yoneda_lemma
[23] Wittgenstein, L. *Tractatus Logico-Philosophicus*, Cosimo Classics, Ed. 2007.
[24] Tsang, W.H. *The Fractal Brain Theory*. Lulu, 2016.
[25] Buckminster Fuller, R. *Synergetics: Explorations in the Geometry of Thinking*, Macmillan, 1982.
[26] Leucippus, Fragment 569 - from Fr. 2 *Actius* I, 25, 4.

[27] Allen, J. (2015). *Aristotle on chance as an accidental cause*. In M. Leunissen (Ed.), *Aristotle's Physics: A Critical Guide* (Cambridge Critical Guides, pp. 66-87). Cambridge: Cambridge University Press. doi:10.1017/CBO9781139381741.005.
[28] Lucretius, *De Rerum Natura*, Clarendon Press, 2nd Ed. 1963.
[29] Hume, D. (1740). *A Treatise of Human Human Nature* Section VIII.: "Of liberty and necessity" (1967 edition). Oxford University Press, Oxford.
[30] Tuynman, A. *Is Intelligence An Algorithm?* Iff books, John Hunt Publishing, 2018.
[31] https://en.wikipedia.org/wiki/Future_of_an_expanding_universe
[32] https://nwrickert.wordpress.com/2013/10/21/macro-level-determinism-is-false/
[33] James Gleick. *Chaos: Making a New Science*, Viking, 1987.
[34] https://en.wikiquote.org/wiki/August_Kekulé
[35] McKenna, T. *Food of the Gods: The Search for the Original Tree of Knowledge*, Rider & Co, 1999.
[36] Langan, C.M. *The Cognitive-Theoretic Model of the Universe: A New Kind of Reality Theory*, Progress in Complexity, Information and Design, 2002.
[37] https://www.facebook.com/groups/EschatonOmegaHypercomputer/permalink/456511321581638/
[38] Kastrup, B. *Why Materialism is Baloney*, iff Books, 2013.
[39] Kaufman, S. "*Unified Reality Theory*: The Evolution of Existence Into Experience", Destiny Toad Press, 2002.
[40] Kauffmann, L.H. arxiv.org/pdf/1512.04325.pdf
[41] https://en.wikipedia.org/wiki/Pilot_wave_theory
[42] Daniel M. Harris, Julien Moukhtar, Emmanuel Fort, Yves Couder, and John W. M. Bush, "*Wavelike statistics from pilot-wave dynamics in a circular corral*", Phys. Rev. E 88, 011001(R), 2013.
[43] Bloom, H. *The God Problem*, Prometheus Books, 2012.
[44] Bentov, I. *Stalking the Wild Pendulum: On the Mechanics of Consciousness*, Destiny Books, 1988.
[45] Barker, C.D. *Architectonics*, 2019, https://www.youtube.com/watch?v=qc00zV-NLLE
[46] https://www.facebook.com/groups/Origins.of.Consciousness/permalink/1886782628065555/ 4th comment.
[47] https://www.bernardokastrup.com/2017/06/is-panpsychism-irreconcilable-with.html
[48] https://www.bernardokastrup.com/2015/05/the-threat-of-panpsychism-warning.html
[49] Russell, P. *From Science to God: A Physicist's Journey into the Mystery of Consciousness*, New World Library, 2005.
[50] Goertzel, B. *Creating Internet Intelligence: Wild Computing, Distributed Digital Consciousness, and the Emerging Global Brain*, IFSR International Series on Systems Science and Engineering, Vol. 18, Kluwer Academic/Plenum Publishers, 2002.
[51] Maturana, H.R. and Varela, F.J. *Autopoiesis and Cognition: The Realization of the Living*, Springer, 1980.
[52] Plichta, P. *Gottes Geheime Formel*, Nikol Verlag, 1995.

[53] https://en.wikipedia.org/wiki/Pioneer_anomaly
[54] 't Hooft, G. *The Holographic principle*, https://arxiv.org/abs/hep-th/0003004.
[55] https://www.businessinsider.com/what-is-blue-and-how-do-we-see-color-2015-2?international=true&r=US&IR=T
[56] Campbell, T. "*My Big TOE*", Lightning Strike books, 2007.
[57] Irwin, K. *Code Theoretic Axiom*, 2017. http://www.quantumgravityresearch.org/wp-content/uploads/2017/03/The-Code-Theoretic-Axiom-02.17.17-final-KI.pdf
[58] https://www.bernardokastrup.com/2015/04/the-reality-nervous-system.html
[59] *Chaitanya Charitamruta* https://www.vedabase.com/en/cc/madhya/21
[60] Guevara Erra, R. et al. *Statistical mechanics of consciousness: Maximization of information content of network is associated with conscious awareness*, PHYSICAL REVIEW E 94, 052402, 2016 https://journals.aps.org/pre/pdf/10.1103/PhysRevE.94.052402
[61] http:// www.slideshare.net/bkumnick/beyond-information-presentation
[62] Tuynman A. "*Technovedanta, Internet architecture of a quasiconscious Vedantic Webmind, a panpsychic Theory of Everything*", Lulu, 2012.
[63] Jaeger, S. *Entropy, Perception, and Relativity*, https://arxiv.org/abs/0811.0139.
[64] Patkar, P.R. et al. https://arxiv.org/ftp/nlin/papers/0408/0408007.pdf
[65] Shannon, C.E. *The Bell System Technical Journal,* Vol. 27, pp. 379–423, 623–656, July, October, 1948.
[66] Carhart-Harris, R.L. et al. *Neural correlates of the psychedelic state as determined by fMRI studies with psilocybin*, PNAS 109 (6) 2138-2143, 2012; https://doi.org/10.1073/pnas.1119598109
[67] Kastrup, B. *Analytic Idealism: A consciousness-only ontology*, 2019, https://www.academia.edu/38498913/Analytic_Idealism_A_consciousness-only_ontology
[68] https://www.sciencealert.com/your-consciousness-does-not-switch-off-during-a-dreamless-sleep-say-scientists
[69] Weinberg, C. https://multisenserealism.com/
[70] Weinberg, C. https://www.quora.com/What-do-the-properties-of-qualia-tell-us-about-consciousness
[71] Crowley, A. *Magick*, Red Wheel/Weiser, 2005.
[72] Matthew 13:12.
[73] Kahneman, D. *Thinking, Fast and Slow*, Penguin, 2012.
[74] Garcia Pedrajas, 2005, IEEE Transactions on Evolutionary Computation, Vol. 9, No. 3, pp. 271-302.
[75] Deutsch, D. *The Fabric of Reality: Towards a Theory of Everything* , Penguin, 1998.
[76] Bryce Seligman DeWitt, R. Neill Graham, eds, "*The Many-Worlds Interpretation of Quantum Mechanics*", Princeton Series in Physics, Princeton University Press (1973), Contains Everett's thesis: The Theory of the Universal Wavefunction, pp 3–140.
[77] https://www.scottaaronson.com/democritus/lec10.html
[78] Searle, J. Minds, brains and programs, *Behavioral and Brain Sciences*, Vol. 3, pp. 417-422, 1980.

[79] Tuynman, A. et al. *Is Reality A Simulation? An Anthology*, Lulu, 2018.
[80] Shanker,S. *Wittgenstein's Remarks on the Foundations of AI*, Routledge, 1998.
[81] T.Dartnall, Artificial Intelligence and Creativity: An Interdisciplinary Approach, Springer, 1994.
[82] Maguire P, et al. *Is Consciousness Computable? Quantifying Integrated Information Using Algorithmic Information Theory, arXiv:1405.0126*, 2014.
[83] De Chardin, T. *The Phenomenon of Man*, Harper Perennial 2008 (original date of publication: 1938).
[84] Meyer, E. *The Culture Map*, PublicAffairs, 2014.
[85] Ben Goertzel. *The Hidden Pattern*, Brown Walker Press, 2006.
[86] Kurzweil, R. *The Singularity is Near: When Humans Transcend Biology*, Duckworth, 2005.
[87] Vikoulov, A.M. *The Syntellect Hypothesis: Five Paradigms of the Mind's Evolution*, Ecstadelic Media Group, 2019. www.ecstadelic.net
[88] Howard Bloom. *Global Brain: The Evolution of Mass Mind from the Big Bang to the 21st Century*, Wiley, 2000.
[89] Kun Xie, Grace E. Fox, Jun Liu, Cheng Lyu, Jason C. Lee, Hui Kuang, Stephanie Jacobs, Meng Li, Tianming Liu, Sen Song, Joe Z. Tsien. "*Brain Computation Is Organized via Power-of-Two-Based Permutation Logic*", Frontiers in Systems Neuroscience, 2016.
[90] Zhu, J. and Harrell, D.F. *The Artificial (AI) Hermeneutic Network, Toward an Approach to Analysis and Design of Intentional Systems*, 2009. http://digm.drexel.edu/jzhu/publications/ZhuHarrell_DH2009.pdf
[91] Pospelov, D. *Hermeneutics in expert systems*, Knowledge-Based Systems, Volume 3, Issue 1, 1990, Pages 25-27.
[92] Peterson, J.B. *Maps of Meaning, The Architecture of Belief*, Routledge,1999.
[93] Dreyfus, H.L. 1965, https://www.rand.org/content/dam/rand/pubs/papers/2006/P3244.pdf
[94] Dreyfus, H.L. *What Computers Can't Do: The Limits of Artificial Intelligence*, HarperCollins, 1978.
[95] Dreyfus, H.L. *Mind over Machine: The Power of Human Intuition and Expertise in the Era of the Computer*, The Free Press, 1988.
[96] Heidegger, M. *Being and Time*, Harper Perennial Modern Thought, Ed.2008.
[97] Penrose, R. *The Emperor's New Mind*, Vintage, 1990.
[98] Goodfellow, I.J. *Explaining and Harnessing Adversarial Examples*, arXiv:1412.6572, 2015.
[99] https://www.axios.com/artificial-intelligence-pioneer-says-we-need-to-start-over-1513305524-f619efbd-9db0-4947-a9b2-7a4c310a28fe.html
[100] https://www.technologyreview.com/s/608911/is-ai-riding-a-one-trick-pony/
[101] https://www.topbots.com/understanding-limits-deep-learning-artificial-intelligence/

[102] Jorfi, M. et al. Human Neurospheroid Arrays for *In Vitro* Studies of Alzheimer's Disease *Nature, Scientific Reports*, 8 : 2450, 2018.
[103] Tsang, W.H. *Fractal Minds and the Sacred Cosmology : Neuroscience & Psychology meets Esoteric Religion.*
https://www.youtube.com/watch?v=OHSyOcMuYHY
[104] https://terencemckenna.wikispaces.com/Eros+and+the+Eschaton
[105] R.Abraham, S.Roy, *Demystifying the Akasha: Consciousness and the Quantum Vacuum*, Epigraph Publishing, 2010.
[106] Deli, E. *The Science of Consciousness*. Self-published USA/Hungary, 2015.
[107] Vikoulov, A.M. *The Physics of Time: D-Theory of Time & Temporal Mechanics (The Science and Philosophy of Information)*, Ecstadelic Media, 2019.
[108] https://nl.wikipedia.org/wiki/Game_of_Life
[109] Teilhard de Chardin, P. *The Phenomenon of Man*. Harper Collins, 2002. Originally published in 1938.
[110] Tipler, F. *The Physics of Immortality*, Anchor Books, 1994.
[111] Tipler, Frank J., *The Omega Point as Eschaton: Answers to Pannenberg's Questions for Scientists*, Zygon: Journal of Religion & Science, Vol. 24, Issue 2, pp. 217–253, 1989.
[112] https://home.cern/science/physics/higgs-boson
[113] Chakraborty, W. *Accelerating Expansion of the Universe*, 2011, https://arxiv.org/pdf/1105.1087.pdf
[114] McKenna, T. and McKenna, D. *The Invisible Landscape: Mind, Hallucinogens, and the I Ching*, HarperCollins Publishers, 1993.
[115] Leary, T. *Info-Psychology*, New Falcon Publications, 1987.
[116] Jaynes, J. *The Origin of Consciousness in the Breakdown of the Bicameral Mind*, Mariner Books, 1976.
[117] Mapson, K. et al. *Pandeism: An Anthology*, iff books, 2017.
[118] Royce, J. *The World and The Individual, First Series: The Four Historical Conceptions of Being*. New York: Dover Publications, 1959.
[119] Sas, P. *Is the Universe a Self-Computing Consciousness? From Digital Physics to Roycean Idealism*, 2015,
https://www.academia.edu/20880884/Is_the_Universe_a_Self-Computing_Consciousness_From_Digital_Physics_to_Roycean_Idealism
[120] Hesiod, West, M.L. Theogony and Works and Days, Oxford World's Classics, 2009.
[121] Tolkien, J.J.R. *The Silmarillion*, Mass Market Paperback, 1985.
[122] https://en.wikipedia.org/wiki/Accelerating_expansion_of_the_universe
[123] https://www.multivax.com/last_question.html
[124] https://en.wikipedia.org/wiki/Black_hole_information_paradox
[125] Adams, D. *The Hitchhiker's Guide to the Galaxy*, Pan Books, 1979.
[126] Berthelot, M.. *Collection des ancien alchimistes grec. Tome 1*. Paris: Steinheil. p. 128, 1887.
[127] Jung, C.G. *The Archetypes and the Collective Unconscious*, Talyor & Francis Ltd, 1991, originally published in 1959.
[128] http://www.individualpsychotherapy.co.uk/yellowing.htm

[129] Hillman, J. *Alchemical Psychology*, Uniform Edition 5. Dallas Institute Publications, 2010.

Acknowledgements

This book originated in an unusual way. After having written "*Is Intelligence An Algorithm?*" I realized from the reviews that certain points had been misinterpreted. This prompted me to write some further clarifications, which I bundled and made available as a supplement in the form of a gift to those who contributed to my Kickstarter campaign for the aforementioned earlier book. Special thanks therefore go to the reviewers of my books.

In the meantime I had written a number of additional articles on the topic on my blog and on websites such as Steemit and Medium, which I figured could be added to this supplement so as to give rise to a new book, which could also integrate the concepts of my other books. Alex Vikoulov, with whom I had successfully collaborated in a number of projects (such as "*Is Reality A Simulation? An Anthology,*" to which Alex had contributed a chapter and "*The Syntellect Hypothesis*" as well as "*The Physics of Time*" by Alex, for which I had had the honour to write the foreword), proposed to publish the present book via the Ecstadelic Media Group. My deepest gratitude to Alex for this offer, as well as for his kindness to write a great foreword for this book and his friendship.

Furthermore, I am also grateful to Matt Swayne, who has been a stimulating voice throughout the years and without whose encouragements I'd probably have stopped writing after my first book "*Technovedanta.*"

Finally, I'd like to thank a number of people whose online discussions and publications have given me further incentives to write this book: Knujon Mapson (co-author and editor of Pandeism; co-author of "*Is Reality A Simulation? An Anthology*"), Andrew Smart (author of "*Beyond Zero and One*"), Adrian David Nelson (author of "*Origins of Consciousness*"), Stephen Paul King, Eric D. Ryser and Tim Gross (techno-shaman).

About The Author

Antonin Tuynman studied Chemistry at the University of Amsterdam, achieving both an MSc and a PhD, and worked as a postdoc researcher at the "Université René Descartes Paris V" in Paris.

Since 2000, Tuynman has worked as a patent examiner at the European Patent Office (EPO) in the fields of clinical diagnostics, computational chemistry and biomaterials. He has vast experience in meditation and yoga, and a strong interest in Hinduism and Buddhism. He also has strong affinity for futurism and the Singularity theory of Kurzweil.

In his books, Tuynman seeks to build a bridge between science/technology on the one hand and spirituality on the other hand. He proposes Artificial Intelligence concepts which may lead to the emergence of Internet as a quasiconscious entity using stratifications from Vedic scriptures.

www.ingramcontent.com/pod-product-compliance
Lightning Source LLC
Chambersburg PA
CBHW021145160426
43194CB00007B/699